"Cuts through the hype and makes all others look like nerdy textbooks"
The Australian

"In the tradition of the best guidebooks, you'll want to take it with you wherever you go"
The Australian Way

"Essential reading"
BBC Education

"Best little guide to the Internet I've ever seen"
British Computer Society Bulletin

"A boon. Simply written, painless practical advice"
Business Traveller

"A model of brevity and clarity"
Courier Mail

"Clear, comprehensible and suited to nervous starters"
Daily Telegraph, London

"Pocket-sized bargain that will prove its worth many times over"
Database

"This has it over all the bigger Internet guides.
Highly recommended"
Evening Post (NZ)

"A rare, if not unique, instance of a Net guide I can
recommend without embarrassment to the unwired"
The Independent, London

"The only Internet book we recommend to friends"
Internet Magazine

"Written in the plain English that made the Rough
Guides indispensable for travelers"
MacWorld

"Written by a clever man – he even manages to keep
complete novices like us interested without wanting
to ram the book back down his throat"
Men's Health

"Even old Web hands will find this concise shortcut to
all the interesting stuff on the Net extremely useful"
Sydney Morning Herald

"Amazing range and depth of topics. Both enlightening
and pleasantly surprising. Like Dr Who's Tardis, it
appears bigger on the inside than the outside"
Sys Admin

The Internet

THE ROUGH GUIDE

There are more than 150 Rough Guide travel,
phrasebook, and music titles, covering
destinations from Amsterdam to Zimbabwe,
languages from Czech to Thai, and musics
from World to Opera and Jazz.

To find out more about Rough Guides, and to
check out our coverage of more than 10,000
destinations, get connected to the Internet
with this guide and find us on the Web at:

www.roughguides.com/

Rough Guide to the Internet Credits

Text editors: Mark Ellingham, Vanessa Dowell
Design and layout: Henry Iles
Production: Susanne Hillen, Julia Bovis, Katie Pringle
Proofread by Carole Mansur

This fifth edition published Oct 1999 by Rough Guides Ltd
          62–70, Shorts Gardens, London WC2H 9AB
          375 Hudson Street, New York 10014
          Web site: http://www.roughguides.com
          Email: mail@roughguides.co.uk

Distributed by The Penguin Group
Penguin Books Ltd, 27 Wrights Lane, London W8 5TZ
Penguin Books USA Inc., 375 Hudson Street, New York 10014
Penguin Books Canada Ltd, 10 Alcorn Avenue, Toronto, Ontario MV4 1E4
Penguin Books Australia Ltd, PO Box 257, Ringwood, Victoria 3134
Penguin Books (NZ) Ltd, 182–190 Wairau Road, Auckland 10

Printed in the United States by R.R. Donnelley

© Angus J. Kennedy, 1999
512 pages; includes index
A catalogue record for this book is available from the British Library
ISBN 1-85828-442-2

The Internet

THE ROUGH GUIDE

by

Angus J. Kennedy

This book is dedicated
to my mother

Contents

Help us update

Trying to keep up with the ever-changing Internet is a near impossible task. So don't be alarmed if you find a few addresses that don't work, or dubious recommendations. It was all correct at time of press. Honest. But it's sure to change. So, if something's not right, or you think we could have explained it better, please let me know via email at: angus@easynet.co.uk and I'll attend to it in the next edition.

In the meantime, keep an eye on:
http://www.roughguides.com/net/

Read Me

There's nothing worse than feeling left behind – when everyone is talking about something, but for you, it just doesn't gel. The Internet's had this effect over the last few years. Everywhere you look. Virtual this, cyber that. But, unless you've been connected, you're probably still in the dark. Getting to grips with the Net can be daunting, but it's a short (though steep) learning curve, and the basics don't take long to master. This guide might look small, but it's jam packed with practical advice, trouble-shooting tips, step-by-step tuition, and the addresses of everywhere you'll need to go. We'll make you a Net guru in the shortest possible time. Guaranteed!

Internet books fall mostly into two categories: the hefty bricks that tell you far more than you want or need to know; and the patronizing simplistic ones that make it look easy in the bookstore with cute icons and corny titles, but don't help with solutions once you start having problems. And being such a fast-moving subject, if they're written before mid-1999, they might as well be filed under ancient history. The truth is you don't need a fat expensive book to get started on the Internet. It's too much work. Not to mention boring.

In contrast, this guide gives it to you straight, in plain English. We won't waste your time, or your money. If something's no good, we'll tell you so. As long as you follow our instructions, getting on the Net should be a pushover. That's not to say you won't have a few teething problems. You will. That, unfortunately, is just a fact of online life. But don't worry, we'll show you how to solve them and where to go for help. Rather than compile everything there is to know about the Net, we'll give you the basics and show you how to use the Net itself to join the dots. Since the Net and its associated technology changes almost daily, it's wiser to get your information from where it's always freshest.

Along the way, we'll show you how to: get the best deal on Internet access, set up your connection, choose the right software for your machine, and become an instant expert in searching the Net. You'll soon be able to send messages across the world instantly for the price of a local call; locate information on just about anything; manage your finances online; create a personal Web page; tune into live music broadcasts; go online bargain hunting; play games; and loads more. All without having to learn any difficult commands. Or, if you're really impatient, you can wing it and go straight to our listings chapters to explore the weird, wild, wonderful World Wide Web; or just get those nagging questions off your mind in one of the special-interest discussion groups. Who knows, you might even make a few friends along the way.

Well, what are you waiting for?

PART ONE

Basics

Frequently Asked Questions

Before we get into the nitty-gritty of what you can do on the Internet – and what it can do for you – let's answer a few of the most Frequently Asked Questions (or FAQs, as acronym-loving Netizens call them).

Big-picture questions

Okay, what's this Internet good for?

The Internet, or the **Net** as it's more often called, is a real bag of tricks. Some say it's like having 150 million consultants on tap – practically free of charge. You can seek, and usually find, answers to every question you've ever had, send messages or documents across the world in a flash, shop in another continent, sample new music, dabble in the stock market, visit art galleries, read books, play games, chat, catch the latest news from back home, make new friends with similar interests, grab free software, manage your bank account or just fritter hours away surfing across waves of visual bubble-gum.

That's not to say the Internet is merely something to

play on when you get home from work. Far from it. The Net is also a serious business communications tool for everyday correspondence, marketing products, financial transactions, customer support, publishing, and much more. In fact, it's become as indispensable as the fax and telephone.

Sounds like fun, but what is it exactly?

Strictly speaking, the Internet is an **international network of computers** linked up to exchange information. The word Internet is a contraction of **inter**national and **net**work.

The core of this international network consists of computers permanently joined through high-speed connections. To get on the Net, you simply connect your computer to any of these networked computers via an Internet **Service** (or Access) **Provider**. Once you're **online** (connected to the Net) your computer can talk to any other computer on the Internet whether it's down the street or on the other side of the world.

That's plain enough, but if you want a more picky definition you have to consider what it's used for as well. Mostly, that's the transfer of **electronic mail** (**email**) and digital publishing on the **World Wide Web**. So when people say they found something on the "Internet", they didn't find it by randomly zipping around the wires hooking up the computers, they either retrieved it from where it was stored on a computer connected to this international network, or someone sent it to them by electronic mail.

Most importantly, the Net is not about computers or the fancy phone lines that string them together. **It's about people, communication, and sharing knowledge**. It's about overcoming physical boundaries so like minds can meet. And that's why you want it.

So, is this "the Information Superhighway"?

The Information Superhighway is a term that's so out of fashion, indeed almost cringe-worthy, that it's almost due to come back in. Whatever you want to call it, US Vice-President Al Gore's vision, as talked up by software magnate Bill Gates and pals, is still some way beyond the horizon. The Net has huge capabilities for cheap, global, and immediate communication; it may grow to dominate areas of **publishing**, **news**, and **education**; it is already providing an alternative **shopping mall**; and it will almost certainly make major inroads into **banking** and **customer support**. But, to get big-screen fingertip action, like video on demand, we'll need a much faster network than today's Internet.

The Net's main arteries are already straining under the pressure of new users, and some fear it may suffer a seizure before it gets better. Until the **Internet backbone** can withstand the added demands from **high-speed alternatives** such as ADSL, cable, and direct satellite feeds, the real digital "revolution" is still on hold.

Is it another state of the USA?

If you're reading this from the relative comfort of one of the 50 United States of America, you've every reason to feel smug. The Net is about as chock-full of US content as your average bottle of diet cherry soda. If not, you might find it a touch frustrating at times that you can, say, get everything down to the local traffic conditions and grasshopper counts in some Midwest burb, but next to nothing about your bustling tropical metropolis. You needn't worry too much as the rest of the world's rapidly catching up – though the US will probably continue to lead the way in many

Note:
Alaska & Hawaii
Not to scale
www.50states.com

areas. Of course, if you feel entrepreneurial you can always plagiarize a few smart ideas from abroad and apply them locally. Or better, start a world first on your home turf!

What is "new media"?

Advertising suits and recruitment agencies use the term **new media** mainly to differentiate between the **old** media world of print, radio, and television and the **new** media world of audio, video, print, and software publishing on the Internet and other digital formats such as CD-ROM.

Can I shop online?

It won't be long before you can buy almost anything you want via the Internet. Hundreds of new **online stores** are popping up every day and many exist only online. Yet online commerce has been slow to take off in a big way especially outside the US, largely due to the cost barriers involved in getting online and the hype surrounding credit card fraud. Of course you can be conned on the Net, as much as anywhere else, but your card details are actually a lot more secure on the Internet than when you make a purchase in a shop. For more, see "Shopping" in our Web guide (p.245).

Can I make money out of the Internet?

Yes, no, maybe – perhaps it's better to ask, "Can I continue to make money without the Internet?" The last few years have seen a gold rush in the computer hardware, software, training, and publishing industries. Some who got in early, made a killing getting businesses on the Web – the Net's "commercial zone". Today, it's settled down somewhat. Web page designers are commonplace, and can no longer charge extortionate rates unless they're tied in with a major agency. However, those with

serious technical and programming skills are always in big demand.

If you're wondering whether to throw a Web site into your existing **marketing mix** to help boost sales, the answer's probably yes. But rather than use it to try to attract customers, it's better to think of the Net as a place to post in-depth product literature, provide customer support, and canvass feedback. Not too many companies are making big money from **direct sales** – though that's improving, particularly for hard-to-get products, or deep-catalog items such as CDs, books, and computer parts.

Another way to profit is to charge others to **advertise on your Web page**. You'll either need to run a very popular site or attract a certain type of customer, and you are usually paid according to the number of times visitors pursue links from your site to your sponsor's. Alternatively, if your site generates heavy traffic and looks promising, someone may want to buy you outright.

Advertising on the World Wide Web is perfectly acceptable but emailing protocols are more delicate. **Never, ever, ever, send bulk email** other than to people you know or who've requested information. And never post an advertisement in Usenet or to a mailing list. **Junk email is called "spam", and those who send it (spammers) are universally detested.** Try it and you'll be flooded with hate mail, and potentially kicked offline. On the other hand, email is by far the most efficient direct response device you'll find. For instance, you could set up an **autoresponder** to send out product details upon receipt of a blank message. No dictating over the phone, no data entry from a coupon, it's instant and informal. Plus, you'll have their email address on record to follow up later. Next time you put your telephone number on an advertisement, put on your email address, too, and compare response rates.

Is there a lot of really weird stuff on the Net?

Yes, lots. Just like in real life, except it's easier to find.
See our Web guide, "Weird" (p.391).

Which is better: the Net or an encyclopedia?

They don't really compare. You can look something up
in an encyclopedia and get a concise answer instantly.
Encyclopedias are generally well researched and reliable, and the answer is probably correct. They're also
expensive, bulky, date quickly, parochial, conservative,
and might not provide enough, or any, information. The
Net, on the other hand, isn't edited by a single publisher,

so you can find a diverse range of factoids and opinions on even the most obscure subjects. That means you're more likely to get a rounded view, but the process might take longer. Of course, the Net has the best of both worlds as most of the major encyclopedias have their very latest editions online.

So who's in charge?

Well, technically no-one, though a number of powerful commercial players such as **CompuServe**, **AOL**, **Microsoft**, **Cisco**, **MCI**, **Worldcom**, and **Netscape** have played major roles in putting the framework in place, and there are various bodies concerned with the Net's administration. Foremost among the latter are the Internet Network Information Center (**InterNIC**), which registers domain names, the **Internet Society** which, amongst other things, acts as a clearing house for technical standards, and the World Wide Web Consortium (**W3C**), which discusses the future of the Web's programming language.

No-one, however, actually "runs" the Internet. As the Internet is, in effect, a network of networks, most responsibilities are contained within each local network. Say you have connection problems, you would call your connection supplier. If you object to material located on a server in another country, you'd have to complain to the administrator of that local server.

While it certainly promotes freedom of speech, **the Internet is not so anarchic** as some sections of the media would have you believe. If you break the laws of your country while using the Net, and you're caught, you're liable to prosecution. For example, suppose you publish a document in the US outlining the shortcomings of a military dictator in "Slobivia". It might not worry the US authorities, but it could be curtains for any "Slobivian" caught downloading the document. The same applies to other contentious material such as pornography, terrorist handbooks, drug literature, and religious satire. **The Internet is not an entirely new planet.**

But isn't it run by the Pentagon and the CIA?

When the Internet was first conceived thirty-odd years ago, as a network for the American Defense Department, its purpose was to act as a nuclear-attack-resistant method of exchanging scientific information and intelligence. But that was then. In the 1970s and 1980s several other networks, such as the **National Science Foundation Network** (NSFNET), joined, linking the Internet to research agencies and universities. It was probably no coincidence that as the Cold War petered out, the Internet became more publicly accessible and the nature of the beast changed totally and irreversibly. **Intelligence agencies** have the same access to the Internet as everyone else, but whether they use it to monitor insurgence and crime is simply a matter for speculation.

So is the Net basically a geek hangout?

It's about as geek as you want it to be, which can vary between twin hip-slung multimeters with a matching pocket protector, to not in the slightest. They say if you're bored with the Net, you're bored with life itself.

But isn't it yet another male-dominated bastion?

No, those days are well behind us. Recent studies reckon the online population to be about 42 percent female, while at AOL, **women actually outnumber men.**

Will I make friends on the Internet?

It's easy to meet people with common interests by joining in **Usenet (newsgroup) or mailing list discussions**. And being able to discuss sensitive issues with strangers while retaining a comfortable degree of anonymity often makes for startlingly intimate communication.

Translating email pen pals into the real world of human contact, or even romance, is another thing. You won't be able to tell your new e-pal Alex's age, sex, appearance, or motives at first glance. And there's nothing stopping anyone from assuming the name of their pet, town, fantasy, or idol as an email user name or IRC nickname. Or from re-inventing themselves. So if you find yourself in private counsel with a "Prince", don't swoon too soon. After all, on the Internet no-one can tell if you're a dog.

More technical questions

What's electronic mail, again?

Electronic mail or **email** is a way of sending text files from one computer to another. Using Internet mail, you can send messages across the world in seconds.

What's the difference between the Internet, the Web, AOL, CompuServe, and the Microsoft Network?

The **World Wide Web** (or Web) is a user-friendly point-and-click way of navigating data stored on the Internet. It's a bit like flicking through a huge magazine by clicking on links with your mouse. CompuServe, AOL, and the Microsoft Network are called **Online Services**. They plug in to the Internet, and thus form part of the Internet, but each also has exclusive services and content available only to their members and not to the general Internet public. You'll find more about them in "Online Services" (p.41), and more on the Web in "Surfing the World Wide Web" (see p.71).

What's an Intranet?

The mechanism that passes information between computers on the Internet can be used in exactly the same way over a local network such as in an office. When this is not publicly accessible, it's called an **Intranet**. Many companies use Intranets to distribute internal documents – in effect publishing Web pages for their own private use.

What are newsgroups, mailing lists, and chat?

Usenet – the Net's prime discussion area – comprises over 60,000 **newsgroups**, each dedicated to a specific topic. So if you have a question, this is the place to raise it. Usenet messages are stored on the Internet for a matter of days or weeks, a bit like an online notice board.

Mailing lists perform a similar function, though the messages aren't kept on the Internet. The discussions are carried out by email. Each list has a central email address. Everything sent to that address goes to everyone on the list.

Chat, on the other hand, is instant, like a conversation. It's typically more of a social medium than an information tool. For more on Usenet, see (p.127); Mailing lists, see (p.122); and Chat, see (p.186).

How can I get my own Web page?

Putting a page on the Web is a two-step process. First, you have to prepare it in **HTML**, the Web's mark-up language. Even a word processor, such as Word 97 (or later) can do a basic job by saving a document as HTML – the same goes for 98 on Mac and soon to be 2000 on the PC. To prepare something more elaborate, you need to use a dedicated HTML editing tool, or to learn HTML code – which isn't too hard for a computer language. Once you have an HTML document ready to go, you need to transfer it to your own special reserved **Web space**. For more on this, flip to "Creating Your Own Web Page" (p.208).

Can I rely on email?

In general Internet **email** is considerably more reliable than the postal service. If a message doesn't get through, it should bounce back to you telling you what went wrong. Occasionally, though, mail does go astray. During 1997, AOL and Microsoft Network – to name just the big players – had severe mail outages resulting in the delay, and in some cases loss, of email. And many corporate mail servers have had growing pains, experiencing holdups and the odd deletion, especially over weekends. But on the whole you can confidently assume that email will arrive. If you don't get a reply within a few days, of course, you can always send your message again. At worst, it will act as a reminder. If you find your mail regularly takes more than a few minutes to arrive, you should seriously consider switching providers.

Who pays for the international calls?

The Internet is barely affected by political boundaries and distance. For example, suppose you're in Boston, and you want to buzz someone in Bangkok. Provided you both have Net access, it's as quick, easy, and cheap as sending a message across the street. You compose your message, connect to your local Internet Service Provider, upload your mail and then disconnect.

Your **mail server** examines the message's address to determine where it has to go, and then passes it on to its appropriate neighbor, which will do the same. This usually entails routing it toward the **backbone** – the chain of high-speed links that carry the bulk of the Net's long-haul traffic. Each subsequent link will ensure that the message heads towards Bangkok rather than Bogotá or Brisbane. The whole process should take no more than a few seconds.

Apart from your Internet access subscription, **you pay only for the local phone call**. Your data will scuttle through many different networks, each with its own methods of recouping the communication costs – but adding to your phone bill isn't one of them.

Then how does the pricing model work?

Once you're on the Net, most of what's there is free. But unless you have free access through work or study, you'll probably need to pay for the privilege of being connected. That means paying an **Internet Service Provider** (ISP) to allow you to hook into its network. Depending on where you live, that could be a set price per month or year, or an hourly rate. Then on top of that, you'll have some sort of **telephone, ISDN, or cable charge**. It's possible – indeed probable – that none of this money will ever go to the people who supply the content you'll be viewing. It simply goes toward maintaining the network. This imbalance is unlikely to continue. In the future it's likely that many publications (or sites) will charge a subscription for entry. As yet, that's still rare, other than for technical and financial publications, so enjoy it while it lasts.

What about free Internet access – is it really free?

Internet access is a costly business to run, so revenue has to come from somewhere. In the UK, where free ISPs have been flourishing to the point of becoming the norm, they survive by getting a slice of your phone bill, both while you're online and through premium rate support lines. This situation exists only because of the UK's extortionate timed local call charges. Still, if you don't use support, a free ISP is cheaper than one that charges. There's no guarantee that either would provide better service.

Elsewhere, where local calls are untimed or free, such as the US and Australia, access can be subsidized by bombarding customers with advertising. As yet, this hasn't proved very successful.

What are hosts, servers, and clients?

In Net-speak, any computer that's open to external online access is known as a **server** or **host**. The software you use to perform online operations such as transfer files, read mail, surf the Web, or post articles to Usenet, is called a **client**.

A Web client is more commonly called a **Web browser** – a field dominated by **Netscape** and **Microsoft (Internet Explorer)**. A **Web server** is a machine where Web pages are stored and made available for outside access.

How do I read an email address?

Internet email addresses might look odd at first glance but they're really quite logical. They all take the form someone@somewhere. As soon as you read that aloud, it should begin to make sense. For example, take the email address angus@roughguides.com The "@" sign says it's an email address and means "at", so the address reads "angus at Rough Guides dot com". From that alone you could deduce that the sender's name is "Angus" and he's somehow associated with "Rough Guides". It's not always that obvious but the format never changes.

The somewhere part is the **domain name** of the Internet **host** that handles someone's mail – often their Access Provider or workplace. Anyone who uses someone's provider or works with them could also share the same **domain name** in their email address, but they wouldn't be called someone. That's because the someone part identifies who, or what, they are at that host address. It's usually a name or nickname they choose themselves, or, with companies, a function like "help" or "info".

What's a domain name?

A **domain name** identifies and locates a host computer or service on the Internet. It often relates to the name of a business, organization, or service and must be registered in much the same way as a company name. It breaks down further into the subdomain, domain type, and country code. Look at: sophie@thehub.com.au The subdomain is **thehub** (an Internet Service Provider), its domain type **com** suggests it's a company or commercial site, and the country code **au** indicates it's in Australia.

Every country has its own distinct code, even if it's not always used. These include:

au	Australia
ca	Canada
de	Germany
es	Spain
fr	France
jp	Japan
nl	Netherlands
no	Norway
uk	United Kingdom
tw	Taiwan

If an address doesn't specify a country code, it's more than likely, but not necessarily, in the USA. At present, domain types are usually one of the following; however, the range will expand dramatically as recent changes to the domain registration system filter through:

ac	Academic (UK)
com	Company or commercial organization
co	Company or commercial organization (UK, NZ)
edu	Educational institution
gov	Government body
mil	Military site
net	Internet gateway or administrative host
org	Non-profit organization

What's an IP address?

Every computer on the Net has its unique numerical IP (Internet Protocol) address. A typical address is four numbers separated by dots and looks like: 149.174.211.5 This is its official location on the Internet.

Your computer will be assigned an IP address when you log on. If it's **dynamically**, or **server**, **allocated**, the last few digits could vary each time you connect.

Internet traffic control relies on these numbers. For example, a router might send all addresses beginning with 213 in one direction, and the rest in another. Eventually, through a process of elimination, everything ends up in the right place.

Thankfully, you don't have to use these numbers. Humans are numerically dim so we use domain names instead, by matching up the names and numbers in a table. Isn't it easier to remember "roughguides" than 204.52.130.112?

Not all IP addresses have attached domain names, but a domain name will not become active until it's matched to an IP address. The table is coordinated across a network of **Domain Name Servers** (DNS). Before you can send a message to someone@somewhere.com, your mail program has to ask your Domain Name Server to convert somewhere.com into an IP address. This process is called a **DNS lookup**.

What's bandwidth?

Bandwidth, which is expressed in bits per second (bps), is a term used to describe Internet connection capacity. It affects the speed at which you can download material from the Net. A high **bandwidth connection** can carry more data at the same time than a low bandwidth connection – just as a bigger gauge pipe can pump more water. But unlike water, where pressure can increase flow, data is limited by electron speed. When a connection is at full capacity, it can't be pushed faster, so data goes into a queue – thus forming a bottleneck that slows things down. So even if you have a high bandwidth connection to the Internet, you could be impeded by insufficient bandwidth between you and your data source.

What if?

What if I'm harassed online?

It's possible to be harassed on the Internet by someone sending you unwelcome email, posting hostile replies to your comments in a newsgroup, pestering you in a Chat/Internet Phone channel or publishing something on a Web page. The simplest thing to do is ignore them – on the other hand, if you've provoked the harassment, you might have to take it as a lesson. It's all too easy to **abuse or criticize people by email** (especially work colleagues) in ways you'd never imagine doing in person, or by regular mail. And it's all too easy to send email – and worse, with the mail copied to others adding to the humiliation. So, think before you click! If you strike serious problems with someone you don't know personally, then the best route is to forward the messages or **pass their details to your Internet Access Provider**. Even if your harasser masks their identity, they're probably still traceable. Your provider should contact their provider, who'll most likely warn them or kick them offline.

It's not easy to harass someone seriously via the Net and get away with it. After all, it generates evidence in writing. There have already been convictions for relatively mild threats posted to Usenet newsgroups. Apart from the nature of the harassment, whether you have a case for action will depend on where you're both based. Across US State lines it becomes an FBI matter, while internationally you might have no recourse other than to appeal to their Access Provider. For more, see: http://www.cyberangels.org

What if my children discover pornography or drugs?

If you're at all prudish, you'll get a nasty shock when you hit the Web. You only need type **the merest hint of innuendo** into a search engine to come face to face with a porno advert. In fact, what once wasn't much more than schoolboys trading Big & Busty scans has become the Net's prime cash cow. Most perfectly normal kids will search on a swearword the first chance they get – after all, children are pretty childish. Consequently, if they're the slightest bit curious about sex, it won't be long before they end up at a porno merchant. That's the truth, if you can handle it.

What can you do about it? Well, that depends on whether you'd rather shield them from such things or prepare them for it. There is a large range of **censoring programs** available that attempt to filter out questionable material, either by letting only known sites through, banning certain sites, or withholding pages containing shady words. Internet Explorer and Netscape, for example, can restrict access according to a rating system. For stuff on censoring material, see our Web chapter (p.94). Bear in mind that a smart kid – and no doubt that's what you're trying to raise – might be able to find a way to veto these filters. Whatever the case, if you're worried about your kids, the Net, and sex, then talk to them about it.

As for **drugs**, there's no way to get them from the Net. In fact, they're likely to find out the dangers of abusing them. So when they come across them in real life they'll be informed. And that has to be a good thing.

Will being on the Internet put me at risk?

It's unlikely that someone is so interested in you that they could be bothered trying to worm their way into your PC to read or interfere with your files. So it's more a hypothetical question of whether it's possible for someone to break in. Security is tightening all the time, but yes, though highly unlikely, it's not entirely impossible. Nonetheless, the truth is **it's easier to break into your house** – and burglary is harder to trace.

Most professional Web sites issue you a "**cookie**" file to identify you when you visit. If that bothers you, and it shouldn't really, unless your Net interests are pretty unwholesome, then just switch off the option to accept them. For more on cookies, see the Web chapter (p.93).

What about viruses and rogue emails?

You are far more likely to catch a virus from a corporate network or a friend's floppy disk than the Internet. Still, it pays to run a **virus check** regularly and to keep your virus checker's signature file up to date.

It's almost unheard of to get a virus by **downloading programs** from a reputable site. Sure, there are regular scares that some controls embedded into Web pages could exploit browser security flaws and harm your PC. But fixes generally appear days later. And these flaws are rarely exploited. The two biggest risk areas are

decoding unknown programs posted to **Usenet news-groups**, and running programs sent to you as **email attachments**. Be particularly cautious of Microsoft Word and Excel documents, as they can carry malicious macros. **Never accept a macro** in any document unless the sender assures you they've put it in for a good reason. For more, if you're running Microsoft Office, read http://www.microsoft.com/office/antivirus/

While it's possible for an attachment to contain a virus, plain text email is entirely harmless. Despite this, there's a glut of **hoax letters circling the Net warning you not to open email** with certain subject headings. These are nothing more than chain letters. If you get such a message, **do not forward it to everyone you know**. Instead, direct the sender to: http://kumite.com/myths/ If, however, you receive an email containing an attachment called **Happy99.exe**, alert the sender that they've been infected by a "Trojan Horse". This is a program which contains another, often malicious, program. It won't affect you unless you click on the attachment and run the program. If you do, it alters a key system file that allows it to sneak aboard your outgoing messages. It's easy enough to undo with the latest virus programs or by following the instructions at: http://www.symantec.com/avcenter/

Messages sent in HTML carry the same risks as **browsing the Web**. For example, it's possible to crash a computer by overloading its processing resources. All the same, it's not something you should worry about.

Some ISPs automatically scan your mail attachments for viruses. It's another factor to consider when shopping around for a provider. Here's what's top of the virus pops: http://academy.star.co.uk/public/virustats.htm

Getting online

What's full Internet access?

You can access the Internet – and send email – through several channels. But not all methods will let you do everything. The **World Wide Web**, **IRC**, **FTP**, and **Telnet** – key areas of the Net, which we'll deal with later in this book – require **"full Internet access"**.

You can get full Internet access through an **Online Service** such as CompuServe or America Online (AOL), or from any **Internet Service**, or **Access Provider** (**ISP** or **IAP**). You'll encounter a range of accounts, which may include standard **modem dial-up**, **ISDN**, **ADSL** and **cable**. There might also be a selection of pricing plans and added extras. Regardless of what type of full Internet access you choose, you'll be able to do the same things, though perhaps at different speeds.

What do I need to get started?

You can get to the Net aboard an increasing number of devices from mobile phones to televisions, but the most popular and flexible route is via a home **PC**, hooked to an Internet Service Provider through a **modem**. So if you have a PC, a modem, and a telephone line, all you need next is an account with an ISP, and possibly some extra software to get rolling. This is covered in detail in the following chapters.

Where can I get an email address?

You should get at least one email address thrown in by your Internet Provider with your **access account**. Many providers supply five or more addresses – enough for the whole family. The only problem with these addresses is that they tie you to that provider. If you want to switch providers, you either have to negotiate a mail-only account or obtain an address you can take on the road with you (see p.230). It's a hassle, either way, so choose your provider carefully.

If you already have an email address, say at work or college, but want a **more personal or funky-sounding address**, you can ask any Access Provider for a POP3 mail-only account, try a mail specialist such as Mail-Bank (http://www.mailbank.com) or sign up with a Webmail or redirection service. That way you can choose an address and use it over any connection. To get yourself a free email address, see (p.116).

How can I find someone's email address?
See: "Finding It" (p.160).

Will I need to learn any computer languages?

No. If you can work a word processor or spreadsheet, you'll have no difficulty tackling the Internet. You just have to get familiar with your Internet software, which in most cases isn't too difficult. The hardest part is **setting up for the first time**, but even that's becoming less of an issue as most Access Providers supply startup packs or almost foolproof instructions.

Once online, most people access the Net through **graphical menu-based software**, with a similar feel to most Windows and Macintosh programs. And on the World Wide Web – the most popular part of the Net – **you hardly even need to type**: almost everything is accessible by a click on your mouse.

The one time you might need to use **UNIX commands** – the Internet's traditional computer "language" – would be when using Telnet to log on remotely to a UNIX computer and that's something most of us can avoid.

Can I use the Internet if I can't use a computer?

As mentioned above, even if you can't type, you can still use the World Wide Web – all you have to do is **point your mouse and click**. That's about as far as you'll get though. If you've never had any contact with computers, consider the Internet a real opportunity. Don't think of computers as a daunting modern technology; they're only a means to an end. The best way to learn how to use a computer is to grab one and switch it on.

So, how do I get connected?

Good question, and worth a whole chapter. Read on.

Getting Connected

By now you're probably already in contact with a Net-connected terminal, perhaps through work, study or friends. It's also likely there's somewhere nearby where you can rent Internet time by the hour or even get online free, say at your local library. If you're not in that position or you'd like to set it up at home, you needn't wait. It's possible to get everything you need to be up and running in a day or two. The good news is it's no longer expensive or complicated, and it's beoming cheaper and easier by the day.

You don't need to be a computer expert

Perhaps you're not already hooked up because you find the whole computing world a bit off-putting. Well, this is the perfect opportunity to get over it. The rewards of being online far outweigh the effort involved in learning to use a computer.

Although there's enough information in this guide to get you started on the Internet, if you're entirely new to computers it might be a good idea if you asked someone who's computer literate to sit with you for a couple of sessions. If you don't know anyone suitable, then drop into a **cybercafé** or **Internet center** (see "On the Road": p.234) and ask an attendant to kickstart you onto the World Wide Web. That's their business, they won't laugh at you, so there's no shame in admitting you're green. You should be able to figure out how to surf the Web within a matter of minutes. Finding your way around is another matter, but you're at an advantage – you have this guide.

In addition, if you strike problems remember that the **online community** – other folks on the Net – is always on tap for help as long as you direct your queries to the right area. Just wait and see; before long you'll be sharing your new-found expertise with others.

What you'll need

Before you can get connected, you'll need three things: a **computer** with enough grunt to handle the software, an account with an **Internet Service Provider**, and a hardware device – usually the fastest **modem** you can afford – to connect your computer to the Internet. How you connect can make the difference between pleasure and frustration. You don't necessarily need state-of-the-art computer gadgetry, but no matter what you have, you'll find a way to push it to the limit.

Computer firepower

It's possible to access the Net in some way with almost any machine you could call a computer, but if you can't run your Web browsing and mail software together without a lot of chugging noises coming from your hard drive, you're going to get frustrated.

If you have an old **486 IBM-compatible PC** or **Macintosh 68030** series, equipped with at least **8MB RAM**, it's possible to get online in a fairly limited way by sticking to old software. You'll get further by adding more RAM, but it'll still be a struggle.

You can also connect to the Net with Ataris, Amigas, PCTVs, Psion Organizers, Palmtops, and even the Nokia 9000 series cellular phones, but you'll be severely restrained by the basic software, low storage and tiny screen size. Unless you want to use these devices only for email, you'll be far happier with something faster and more versatile. For the full range of hardware that can connect you to the Net, see: http://www.allnetdevices.com

PC, Mac or Linux?

If you're in the market for a new computer, you will first have to decide between a **PC** (running Microsoft Windows, typically) or a **Mac**. This can be an incredibly confusing question to answer. There's something of a holy war between supporters of the two platforms, as well as a rebellious undercurrent pushing the free **Linux** operating system. Unless you intend to run a Net server, you can overlook Linux for the time being. It's still a bit too geeky for everyday use.

To be frank, **you won't get a straight answer from anyone** on this subject, particularly from the Mac minority, whose members can become **pathologically brand loyal**. Ignore anyone who tries to convince you that either option is without flaw or would deride you for choosing either. And for heaven's sake **don't bring the subject up at a dinner party!**

In other words, if you ask a Mac user for advice, they'll rarely steer you towards anything but a Mac. In some situations that might be good advice, but it will limit your options more than buying a PC. You might find yourself on the sidelines, (or entirely unaware), of the latest action, if that bothers you.

However, if you intend to work with **print standard color**, such as in publishing, get a Mac. Although PCs can now do the same job, Macs are so ingrained within the industry that it's not worth your while to go against the flow. You'll find it much easier to trade files with peers and turn to them for help. By all means check out the hugely promoted **iMac**, but if you want to do anything serious, veer towards the more **expandable G3** range.

While Apple's G3 processors are now comparable, and sometimes superior, to what's offered by Intel (or AMD), you'll probably get more bangs per buck by going down the more popular PC track. PCs have considerably **more (and newer) software**, **games**, and **peripheral options**, and are usually **a bit cheaper** for similar specifications. Since some **95 percent of computers run Windows** you won't feel like the entire industry is plotting against you.

With PCs, brand names mean less than **after-sales service**. PC components often come from several different manufacturers. The crunch comes when something goes wrong. Find out how long you'd be without your computer if it needs repair. Your corner shop might be able to do it on the spot, or help you set up your software. Name brands often offer a range of service agreements ranging from same-day replacement to potentially leaving you stranded for weeks. Don't undervalue a generous guarantee. And consider buying the same set-up as a friend so you have someone to lean on when things go haywire.

Whatever you buy, the Net is a full multimedia experience, so pack it with as much **memory** or **RAM** (32+ MB) as you can afford, a decent **hard drive** (2+ Gig), a fast

CD-ROM or DVD drive (for loading software and playing movies), and check out the advanced options in **sound and video**.

Do your own research

It's well beyond the scope of this book to cover adequately all the pros and cons in the Mac vs PC squabble. If you'd like to research further, pick through this lot and decide for yourself. Caveat emptor!

Comparisons

http://www.statmarket.com
http://www.people.cornell.edu/pages/jcs33/compare.html
http://www.geocities.com/SiliconValley/Sector/9295/

Pro PC:

http://www.netherworld.com/~mgabrys/clock/
http://www.ihateapple.com
http://www.geocities.com/SiliconValley/Platform/2985/

Pro Mac:

http://www.macaddict.com/ammo/
http://www.mackido.com
http://www.ihatewindows98.com

Pro Linux:

http://www.slashdot.org

Once you've decided, check out "Finding a computer bargain" (p.179).

Connecting your computer to the Net

A powerful computer won't make up for a slow link to the Internet. Get the fastest connection you can afford.

Unless you're hooked up through a network, you'll need a device to connect your computer to the telephone line or cable. There'll be a similar device at your Access Provider's end. This device will depend on the type of Internet account. The two main types are **Leased Line** and **dial-up**. Leased Lines are expensive and aimed at businesses that need to be permanently connected. Dial-up suits the casual user. Investigate the Net through a dial-up account before contemplating a Leased Line.

Note: If you're on a network at work or college, don't attempt to connect to the Net without your systems manager's supervision. Networked PCs and Macs can use the same software listed later in this book, but may connect to the Net differently.

Modems – the plain vanilla option

 The cheapest, most popular, but slowest, way to connect is by installing a **modem** and dialing up through the standard telephone network. Modems come in three flavors: internal, external, and PCMCIA. Each has its advantages and disadvantages.

Internal modems are the cheapest option. They plug into a slot inside your computer called a bus. Installation is not difficult, but you do have to take the back off your computer and follow the instructions carefully (or get your computer store to do it). Because they're hidden inside your computer, internal modems don't take up desk space, clutter the back of your computer with extra cables, or require an external power source. On the downside, they lack the little lights to tell you how your call is going, and you can't swap them between computers without removing the case.

An **external modem** is easier to install. Depending on the make, it will simply plug straight in to your computer's serial, parallel, or USB port, making it easily interchangeable between machines (and simple to upgrade). External modems require a separate power source, maybe even a battery. And they usually give a visual indication of the call's progress through a bank of flashing lights (LEDs).

The credit-card-sized **PCMCIA** modems are a mixture of the two. They fit internally into the PC card slots common in most modern notebooks and remove easily to free the slot for something else. They don't require an external power source, but are expensive and won't work with a desktop. Alternatively, you could use any external modem with a notebook by plugging it into an available serial (or USB) port.

The need for speed

Whichever type of modem you choose, the major issue is speed. Data transfer speed is expressed in bits per second or **bps**. It can take up to ten bits to transfer a character. So a modem operating at 2400 bps (2.4 Kbps) would transfer roughly 240 characters per second. That's about a page of text every eight seconds. At 28.8 Kbps, you could send the same page of text in two-thirds of a second.

A 14.4 Kbps (V.32) modem can browse the World Wide Web, but you'll be much happier with something faster. A faster modem might cost a little more, but it will reduce your online charges, and give you more for your money. The modem standard has now reached **56K (V.90)**, which can theoretically download at up to 56 Kbps, and upload at up to 33.6 Kbps. Unfortunately, because of phone line dynamics, you will never get to connect at the full speed, but you should still be able to get well above 33.6 Kbps, the previous speed barrier. If you have an **X2** or **K56flex** modem, upgrade to V.90, if possible. (See http://www.56k.com) Finally, **make sure whatever you buy will work with your computer**. PCs need a high-speed serial card with a 16550 or 16650 UART chip to process any more than about 9.6 Kbps reliably. Most modern PCs (later than 486 DX33) have them as standard, but it's not an expensive upgrade, anyway.

Faster ways to connect

What's good about modems is that they are the right-here right-now accepted worldwide standard and work over the regular telephone system without any excess charges. But they are slow and unstable compared to what's around the corner. If you're into seriously fast connections and enjoy new technology, read on and check the Web addresses given for further details. If you just want to get online in a hurry, skip this section.

ISDN

ISDN is a vast improvement on modem technology, not just for speed, but for superior line handling and almost instantaneous connections – and it is already available.

It provides three channels (1x16 Kbps and 2x64 Kbps) which can be used and charged for in various ways. ISDN Internet accounts don't usually cost more but, depending on where you live, the line connection, rental and calls can cost anywhere from slightly to outrageously more than standard telephone charges. That's up to your telco so it might be worth a call to see what's on offer. Connecting through ISDN, rather than using a modem, you'll need a slightly more expensive device called a **Terminal Adapter**. For details on how to upgrade Windows 95 to support ISDN see:

http://www.microsoft.com/windows/getisdn/

Cable and DSL

Although ISDN guarantees a fast, reliable connection, it's not a patch on the latest generation of broadband alternatives, in terms of speed, and often price as well.

Chances are, if you can get cable TV access, you can also get **cable Internet access**. Cable access offers mega-speed rates (up to 10 Mbps, though more likely considerably less than 1 Mbps) without call charges, but suffers from having to share bandwidth with your neighbors. It's already available as a cable TV sideline in many cities in North America, Holland and Australia, and should become widespread within Europe and Asia soon. So, if you have cable in your street, ask if it's available.

A superior option that's already commercially available across much of the USA is DSL, (eg. http://www.megaspeed.com), most commonly in the form of **ADSL** (Asymmetric Digital Subscriber Line). ADSL is potentially capable of download speeds up to 6 Mbps, and uploads up to 640 Kbps via the normal telephone system without interfering with your voice service. That means you can surf the Net and talk on the phone at the same time over one line. Unlike cable, you don't have to share the line, so your download speeds will be unaffected by your neighbors, though of course you're still at the mercy of your ISP's incoming bandwidth.

As cable and DSL services are permanently connected there's no dialing up necessary, but they require a special modem-like device to connect between your computer and the line. As these speeds are in excess of serial card capacity, you'll also need to install an Ethernet network card.

For more on cable access, see:

http://www.cablemodems.com
http://www.catv.org/modem/

http://www.inside-cable.co.uk and
http://www.home.com

For DSL news, see:

http://www.adsl.com and http://www.xdsl.com

Satellite

If you need zippy delivery and you need it now, your
best choice might be via **satellite**. You receive
through a small TV dish, and send
through a standard dial-up or leased line
account with an Access Provider. So you
can in theory browse the Web at up to 6
Mbps, but send email or upload
material at a standard modem
rate.

DirecPC (http://www.direcpc.com) has
two home user access accounts
with rates of up to 200 Kbps and
400 Kbps. SatNet (http://www.sat-
net.com.au) delivers affordable 400 Kbps download
speeds throughout Australia and NZ.

Satellite access might even become the norm if the
Boeing/Gates-funded global broadband "Internet in the
sky" project has its way. See: http://www.teledesic.com

Doubling up modems

It's possible to bind two or more modems together using
multiple telephone lines in parallel. In theory, this
should give you a bandwidth equal to the sum of the
combined modems, which often works out cheaper than
ISDN. It's simple to set up in Windows 95 or later versions: just right-click on your provider's Dial-up
Networking entry, choose "Properties", and add another
device under **Multilink**.

If you don't see a Multilink option, install the latest Dial-up Networking and Winsock upgrades from: http://www.microsoft.com/windows95/downloads/ or, simply install Internet Explorer (http://www.microsoft.com/ie/).

The hardest part is finding a provider that supports it.

Okay – I have a computer and modem. So, how do I get an Internet connection?

To connect to the Internet, you'll need someone to allow you to connect into their computer, which in turn is connected to another computer, which in turn . . . that's how the Internet works. Unless you have a working relationship with whomever controls access to that computer, you'll have to pay for the privilege.

IAPs and ISPs

A company in the business of providing Internet access is known as an **Internet Access Provider (IAP)** or **Internet Service Provider (ISP)**. The industry has matured steadily over the last few years to the point that most established ISPs deliver reasonable performance and service. However, all providers aren't equal, and it's difficult to tell a good one from a bad one, until you've used them for a while. Try a few before settling, as poor access will jade your online experience. Some, for example, try to squeeze too many folk online, resulting in frequent busy tones when you dial, and slow transfer rates once you're online.

Ask around for personal recommendations, or check local **Internet or computer magazines** (who are forever doing comparative tests of speed, service, and so forth). An added bonus with the computer press is that they often carry cover-mounted disks with all the Net software you'll need to get started – and maybe introductory accounts with reputable providers.

To help with your quest, there's an ISP listing at the end of this book (p.473), along with a **checklist of questions to ask them** – some of which will be important to you, others not, depending on circumstances.

Online Services

You'll no doubt come across disks beckoning you to join an Online Service – such as **CompuServe**, **America Online (AOL)**, or **Microsoft Network** – which offer full Internet access at increasingly commercial rates. Most of these commercial giants offer two separate services: access to the Internet proper and access to their own private network. On the Internet front, they can be appraised in the same way as any other ISP, and are reviewed in the following chapter.

How much will it cost?

Have you ever shopped for a mobile phone? Well, that was easy compared to trying to get the best deal on Internet access. As the gates to the Net are in the hands of small and large business, there's a puzzling array of providers and pricing structures.

The biggest issue is **time charges**. Where local calls are fixed or free, as in North America, Asia, and Australasia, providers began by either restricting the number of access hours included in the monthly charge or charging by the minute. Otherwise, they feared, customers would hog the line all day.

So in the **US** typical charges started at $20.00 per month for the first 40 hours' access and then $2.00 per hour thereafter. However, due to fierce competition, most US providers switched to "all you can eat" accounts for a single monthly fee, usually about $20.00. Most now offer a range of options, starting with a basic low usage account for a few dollars a month.

In the **UK** and other countries where local calls are timed, lengthy connections mean hefty phone bills, and line hogging is not an issue. UK ISPs can negotiate a cut of your phone bill, so it's possible to supply **free access**. Normally, however, they **charge for support through a tolled number** and charges are high. Alternatively, full access with free support costs about £7-12.00 per month.

In **Australia**, where access rates vary as wildly as quality of the networks, untimed accounts are thin on the ground. Costs normally work out between $1-2.00 per hour.

Expect broadband access to be somewhat more expensive, but that's not a rule. Sometimes **cable**, for example, can be just as cheap if you subtract the phone call charges. For instance, the US Internet cable provider, @Home (http://www.home.com), charges between $30-50.00 flat per month depending on the cable reseller. **DSL** usually costs more than dial-up, and is generally tiered into speed levels. Be more wary of cable, satellite and DSL providers that charge an **excess rate per megabyte downloaded**. It can work out prohibitively expensive if you're cruising the Web and downloading software in excess of 30 MB per hour.

In addition to these monthly tariffs many ISPs charge a **once-off setup fee** (usually about the same as a month's access). This often includes a startup software kit, though if you have Windows 98, or a Web browser, you're probably better off not installing their kit. Other providers, especially the Online Services, might offer a **free trial period**, but if you check their pricing for an average year it mightn't work out cheaper overall.

Mind your phone bill: POPs

If you plan to connect through a telephone line, make sure you choose a provider with a **local dial-up number**. And, if you travel, you will want to have a range of access numbers, otherwise you might run up some serious phone bills.

These dial-up numbers are called **Points Of Presence (POPs)**. In the US, if you need to call your provider from interstate, it may offer a free 1-800 number with a flat fee of about 15¢ per minute including the call. If you have free local call access, then make sure your provider has a POP in your local zone. In the UK, unless you restrict your access to nights and weekends, your phone bill will usually outweigh your Internet access bill. Local calls in Australia are flat rate which means it's cheaper to stay online all day than to dial up for a few minutes each hour to pick up mail.

Most telcos offer a discount to your choice of frequently called **"Friends and Family"** numbers. Put your provider on this list, as it's sure to become your most called number. Also ask about the possibility of capped monthly charges to certain numbers. This is commonly offered with timed ISDN.

Online Services

Although AOL and CompuServe provide Internet access, they're more commonly called Online Services rather than Internet Service Providers. This is because their primary interest isn't Internet access, but their own content, which includes all manner of forums, magazines, chat boards, reference databases and news services. These features are available only, to subscribers and not to the general Internet public.

Online Services are, to a certain extent, a relic of the past. The Internet now offers far more than any Online Service could ever hope to produce in-house. Indeed, much of the content within the Online Services is either replicated from the Net or directs you to material located on the Net.

AOL and **CompuServe** are the only major players left standing that consider their exclusive online offerings to be worth more than their Internet access. And now that AOL owns CompuServe we might as well view them as one entity. **Microsoft Network** (http://www.msn.com) and **Prodigy** (http://www.prodigy.com) were once proprietary Online Services but have now evolved into standard ISPs.

Despite the overall trend away from off-Net havens, AOL and CompuServe memberships are still increasing. However, it's generally accepted that they are better at recruiting new members than they are at providing the infrastructure to support them. Consequently they suffer from what's called **high churn rate**. That means their ubiquitous installation disks offering a month's free access succeed in attracting hordes of first timers, but most eventually become disgruntled with the problematic software and slow networks, and move on up to a dedicated ISP. Once they see the Net at full speed, they rarely return.

Try before you buy

Still, if it's to be your first time online, either service can make a gentle introduction. They're well organized, secure, regulated, easy to navigate, friendly, and most of all incredibly simple to get started. You won't have any trouble finding their free installation disks. If you haven't already had one through the mail or on a magazine cover, call them directly and have one sent to you. The latter is the best option because at least you can be sure to have the latest version of their software. They both offer free 30-day trials after which you're either billed at a fixed monthly rate for unlimited access, or a minimum monthly fee plus an hourly rate. Since they're both free for the first month, don't sweat over the choice. Give them both a shot.

What's on offer

CompuServe delivers its fair share of home infotainment, but fancies itself more as a business, professional, and technical service. AOL, on the other hand, is a regular family funshack with something for everyone, from celebrity chats, magazines, games, and sporting results to online stock trading. The one thing they both have in common is that their access software is very much dumbed down for the new user. You might find this a welcome prospect, but it will soon become a shackle that will hinder your progress online. So by all means sharpen your claws on the Online Services but get out on the Net as soon as you can, and compare their network speed, line availability, pricing, software standards (particularly email) and telephone support with a regular ISP.

Travelling companion

If you travel abroad regularly, a CompuServe account can get you connected in over 142 countries. The only catch is it will attract a premium charge over your regular access bill. Call for rates and access details before you set off, otherwise you could be up for a nasty credit card shock on your return.

A reminder

If you're not absolutely delighted with AOL or CompuServe after the free trial period, be sure to cancel your account. Otherwise you'll be billed a minimum monthly charge whether or not you use the service.

Further information

For a free trial and local pricing call:

AOL
☎ 1800 265 265 (Australia)
☎ 888 265 6303 (Canada)
☎ 800 827 6364 (US)
☎ 0800 279 1234 (UK)

CompuServe
☎ 1300 555 520 (Australia)
☎ 800 848 8990 (N America)
☎ 0800 442 374 (NZ)
☎ 0990 134 819 (UK)

Connection
Software

It's standard practice for Access Providers to supply the basic connection software – usually for free. However, because the Internet is constantly evolving, no matter what you get, you'll soon want to replace or add components. It's not crucial to start out with what's state of the art, because once you're online, you can download the latest versions of everything – again, usually for free. Or you can get it in disc form as a cover-mount from one of the many Internet and computer magazine titles: just browse the racks to see who is offering the month's best package.

The connection essentials

What you stand to get from a provider could be anything from a list of configuration settings to a full Internet tool kit.

At the heart of any Net software package is the **TCP/IP** software, known as the stack or in Windows as the **Winsock**, which enables the computer to talk the Net's language. It needs to know your IP address and your provider's DNS server addresses (see p.19), information that you will have to enter, either by running an installation program or manually. It must be set up properly; otherwise none of your Internet programs will work.

Once the TCP/IP stack is correctly configured for your provider, you can pick and choose whatever components you see fit.

Windows 95/98/NT, OS/2, or Mac?

If you're running **Windows 95/98/NT**, IBM's **OS/2**, or Macintosh **OS 8.0 or later**, you already have all the TCP/IP software you need to get started.

In **Windows 95/98**, right-click on the desktop Network Neighborhood icon and check you've installed the **Client for Microsoft Networks**, **TCP/IP protocol** and **Dial-up Adapter**. If not, click "Add" and install each in turn.

Microsoft is the manufacturer in all cases. Then choose Client for Microsoft Networks as your **Primary Network Logon**.

Do not enable **File or Printer sharing** unless you want to let outsiders from the Net into your computer.

Your provider will either supply you with an installation program or give you written instructions on how to set up the finer details. Failing that, have someone talk you through it over the phone. Once that's done the rest is easy.

Earlier systems

If you are running an **earlier version of Windows**, or a **pre-System 8.0 Mac**, you'll need either to **upgrade your operating system** or obtain a TCP/IP program.

Of the several **TCP/IP programs** for **Windows 3.x**, the most popular is **Trumpet Winsock**. It's freely available on the Internet and used as the core of many ISPs' Windows 3.x bundles. It's not actually free, though. If you want to use it after a trial period, you are requested to pay the author. Its dial-up scripting takes a while to figure out, but once you have it going it's rock solid and works with everything. A better choice, if offered, is the version of **Internet Explorer 3.03 for Windows 3.x** that includes its own Winsock. Setting it up is as simple as following the prompts. It's free, if you can get someone to download it for you. It's no longer on Microsoft's site, but you'll find copies of the various versions at: http://www.softhouse.com/resources/windows3x.htm or through **Softseek** (http://www.softseek.com).

Macintosh users need look no further than **MacTCP**, or its successor **Open Transport**, which can be obtained separately from most Access Providers or from your Apple dealer as part of the **Apple Internet Connection Kit**. Open Transport is superior, but will not run on 6800 or 68020 systems. Open Transport has been replaced by **Remote Access** in MacOS 8.0 and later. The best idea is to ask your Apple dealer for advice.

Getting it to dial

Unless you're connecting via a Local Area Network (LAN) you'll also need a **dialer** to automate the dial-up and log-in procedure. You can generally configure this in the same process as **TCP/IP**. This means if you're setting up through a step-by-step wizard, you'll usually enter your TCP/IP configuration, user details, password, provider's telephone number, and then attach a dial-up script (if used), all in one go. Depending on the set-up program you might also be able to configure your mail and news programs in the same process. After it's all configured, you should only need to click on "Connect", or something similar, to instruct your modem to dial. You shouldn't need to enter your dial-up (or mail, if it was included) password again.

Windows dialing

Dialing is the part of **Windows 95** that's gone through the biggest evolution on its path to **Windows 98** via its controversial Web browser program, **Internet Explorer**. If you have the first release of Windows 95, you might need to install a dialing component, as this was originally a Plus pack extra called the "Dial-up Scripting Tool." (There have been so many incarnations since then that it's hard to keep track.) But if you've been supplied with Internet Explorer 4.0 or later, either as part of Windows 98 or otherwise, you'll be able to set it all up in a jiffy through the **Internet Connection Wizard**. If not, your Access Provider will be able to supply you with enough to get you connected. Once online, you can update your Dial-up Networking and Winsock either by downloading the latest version of Internet Explorer (see p.55) or topping up from:

http://www.microsoft.com/windows95/downloads/

Mac dialing

Older Macs need a separate program to enable dialing. The most popular choices are: **FreePPP**, from http://www.rockstar.com; **ConfigPPP/MacPPP**, part of the Apple Internet Connection Kit; and **OT-PPP** for Open Transport, also from Apple. If you don't already have one of these, your provider or Apple dealer should be able to oblige. If you're running a PowerPC consider upgrading to the latest MacOS. Macs are user-friendly in most areas but Internet connectivity wasn't one of the MacOS strong points up until recently. Again, **don't think too hard about it, just ask your Apple dealer for advice**. They'll know it all back to front.

Once you're online visit http://til.info.apple.com for system upgrades and support. Articles 18238 and 24138 in the Tech Info Library explain how to obtain and configure Open Transport.

Dialing different providers

Once your dial-up connection is set up you should be able to forget about it, unless you have to **dial a different provider**.

It's simple to set up **Windows 95/98/NT** to handle multiple providers, or switch to a new one. Just start a new account under Dial-up Networking and then set the TCP/IP under "Properties", or do it all in one go with the Internet Connection Wizard. The same goes for Mac users with **FreePPP**, **MacPPP**, and **OT-PPP**. Just look for the option "New" to start a new account. In the iMac and on MacOS 8.0+, simply open the **Apple Internet Setup Assistant** and follow the prompts.

There's no need in any case to install new software. You just have to change the TCP/IP and dial-up settings. That should take only a few minutes.

Did you get all that TCP/IP stuff?

If you didn't understand a bar of the last few pages on getting connected, don't worry! Internet connection and TCP/IP configuration is your Internet Access Provider's specialty. It's in their interest to get you up and running, so if things go haywire, or you're confused, do things the easy way – give them a call. After all, if you can't get connected, they're not going to get paid.

Setting the settings . . .

There are so many routes onto the Internet, it's difficult to draw up a set of generic step-by-step instructions. That's why we suggest you follow whatever directions you're given on your first sign-up. However, if you have to enter the settings yourself, these are the main ones you'll strike.

TCP/IP SETTINGS
Windows 95/98 – Open Dial-up Networking under My Computer, and click on "Make New Connection" or right-click and choose "Properties" of an existing connection.
iMac – Go to the Apple menu, open the Internet Access folder and click on "Internet Setup Assistant".
IP address: Your location on the Internet. It's likely your ISP's server will allocate this afresh each time you log in. If so, you won't be given a numerical address, you'll be told to choose "server assigned" or "dynamically allocated".
Two DNS server addresses: The servers that convert friendly domain names into numerical Internet addresses. Sometimes these are also dynamically allocated, so you mightn't have to touch any

settings. If not, they'll be numerical, in the form
123.345.123.12

Domain or Search Domain: This will look
something like: provider.net It's not used in Windows
95/98.

SERVER TYPES (Windows 95/98)

Type of Dial-Up Server: Unless instructed otherwise
set this to PPP.

Advanced Options: Unless instructed otherwise,
enable software compression and disable "Log on to
network" and "Require encrypted password".

Allowed Network Protocols: Enable TCP/IP only.

DIALER SETTINGS

User name: Your account name with the ISP.
Dial-up password: Your secret access code.
Dial-up access number: The number your modem dials to access the ISP.

MAIL & NEWS SETTINGS

Outlook Express – Under "Accounts" in Tools menu.
Netscape Messenger – Open Mail & Newsgroups under "Preferences" in the Edit menu.
Email address: The address where you'll receive your mail. Will be in the form someone@somewhere where the somewhere part is a domain name.
Mail login: The name you choose as the someone part of your email address.
Mail password: The secret code you use to pick up your mail.
Outgoing mail server (SMTP): The server that will handle all mail you send. It will be a domain name.
Incoming mail server (POP/IMAP): Where your mail is stored. It will also be a domain name.
News server address (NNTP): Most providers maintain their own Usenet services. This domain address goes into your newsreader preferences. For more take a look at our Usenet chapter (see p.127).

OTHER SETTINGS

Proxy settings: Some providers use a gateway between you and the Internet to manage traffic. These settings go into your Web browser preferences (options) and **any other programs that are affected by the proxy such as FTP and Web search agents.** (See p.92)

IRC server: Not all providers support chat locally, but they should be able to recommend a server to start you off. Enter this into your chat software preferences. For more see p.186.

FTP server: Where to transfer files to and from your ISP's local storage space. This isn't something you configure. You type it into your File Transfer program. (See p.146)

If you need further instructions on tinkering with your TCP/IP settings once you're online, check your provider's home page on the Web. Most ISPs maintain a set of pictorial instructions of what to fill in where for various operating systems. The best thing about these instructions is that they'll be tailored for your situation. If yours isn't so helpful, try another provider:

http://www.dial.pipex.com/support/connect/
http://www.netcom.com/support/
http://www.ozemail.com.au/internet/support/

Right – is that it, or do I still need more software?

The TCP/IP and dialer (Dial-up Networking) combination is enough to get you connected to the Net. But you'll need more software actually to use it. If you have Windows 98, an iMac, or any Mac running MacOS 8.5 onwards you have all you need – at least for the time being. Ask your provider how to configure your Dial-Up Networking (TCP/IP), mail, news and browser rather than install any superfluous software over the top. **Don't believe any provider that insists you need to install their software. Consider switching providers if you get this**

line. Using what comes with Windows 98 or MacOS 8.0+, along with the latest updates downloaded from the Net is always superior.

If you're running an earlier version of Windows or Mac, your ISP should supply some start-up software on a disk, or alternatively instruct you to download it off a local server using a Terminal program such as Hyper-Terminal. If they can't provide the software, they may not be such a great choice in your situation. Still, if you have no other option, you should be able to get it from a computer magazine cover CD.

The one program you'll definitely need is a **Web browser**. In fact, the latest Web browsers (including what comes with Windows 98, iMac and MacOS 8.5+ are so complete you might not feel the need to get any other Internet software. You certainly won't need a **mail** program as the ones that come bundled with browsers are as good as they come – and free. Most people these days also use their browsers (or the programs which come with them) to download other software (see p.146) and read newsgroups (see p.127).

In any case, once you have a browser you can surf around for new programs at will, enabling you to chat, play games and whatever else you desire. Don't worry, they're not hard to find with the whole Internet at your disposal – and they needn't cost a penny. For more on how to choose the right browser, and what it can do for you, read on.

The Web Browser

A Web browser is the most important piece of Internet software you'll ever install. It will serve as the window through which you look at the Net and act as a springboard to almost everything you do online. A couple of years back, the browser was basically a tool for viewing sites on the World Wide Web but today's generation of programs – essentially a choice between Microsoft's Internet Explorer and Netscape – come integrated with a whole assortment of Internet accessories that handle such tasks as email, news, Internet telephony, chat, home page editing, and multimedia playing. That makes your choice of browser pretty crucial.

Choosing a browser

You may not get to choose your own browser initially if you decide to install your ISP's startup kit. If you do, it's likely to be **Internet Explorer**, as most providers and Online Services adopted it during the period when it was free and Netscape wasn't. Now that Netscape is also free, you might even be given both. And if you're using Microsoft Windows 98, you will find Internet Explorer seamlessly bundled into the operating system – the controversial move that resulted in anti-trust action in the US courts – for more on which, see our history of the Net (p.433). Internet Explorer is also on the desktop of every iMac, and Apple running MacOS 8.5+. If you'd prefer Netscape, you'll find it on the install disks.

If you don't have Netscape, it's not exactly hard to obtain – you can download it from the Net (see p.62 – "How to get the latest versions"), or load it onto your system from one of the myriad free disks mounted on computer or Internet magazines.

There's nothing to stop you from having more than one browser on your system. So, if you're serious about the Net, you can try out both programs side by side to see which you prefer or retain both as some sites work better with one or the other.

Unraveling the numbers

Both Microsoft Internet Explorer and Netscape Communicator come in various flavors, catering to Windows 95/98, Windows NT, Windows 3.1, Power Mac, Mac 68k, Unix, and in Netscape's case, OS/2.

You can usually tell which is the **latest release of the program** by its number. For example, in Netscape Communicator, version 4.51 is newer than 4.5. The first number is the series: these are both "4.0x" series browsers (as you'd expect, the "4.0x" series came after the "3.0x" series). The second number, after the decimal point, tells you if it is the **original release** (.0) or an **interim upgrade** (0.1, 0.2, etc) within the series. Such upgrades generally fix problems and add on a few minor features. In doing so, the previous release in that series becomes obsolete, and in the case of betas (test programs), expires.

A **new series release** – which at present happens about once a year – heralds major changes, new features and bug fixes, and usually adds extra system demands.

Thus, if your computer resources are low, you may find an earlier series more suitable.

To make matters just a bit more confusing, developers sometimes release **a new build** of the same program. So you and a friend can both have IE5.0 but if you downloaded it later, you might have a later build that's fixed a few minor bugs. To see a program's build number, choose **About** from the **Help menu**.

System requirements

Browsers consume a lot of **disk space**, especially the full installations of Internet Explorer with all the added accessories.

PC requirements

PC users will need at least a 486 DX66 PC, with **16 MB of RAM** to get either **Internet Explorer or Netscape** to function under Windows 95/98/3.x, and 24-32 MB to run other programs at the same time. Windows NT versions demand at least 32 MB of RAM: depending on which optional components you install, Netscape 4.x requires between 18 and 30 MB of hard disk space, and Internet Explorer 4.x and 5.x, between 40 and 80 MB.

New releases normally write over the old files. So if you're simply upgrading to a newer version, for example, installing IE5.0x over Windows 98, then the increase in disk space might only be marginal. Netscape 5.x (if it's ever released) is expected to buck the trend and be considerably smaller than past releases. If true, the upgrade might actually give you some space back!

Mac requirements

You'll need a **PowerPC processor** to run Internet Explorer 4.5x, Netscape Communicator 4.5x, and later versions of both. Internet Explorer 4.5x will run on **MacOS 7.5.3 or later**, and 12 MB of RAM. Netscape 4.5x requires 16 MB of RAM if running MacOS 7.6.1, and 24 MB of RAM, for **MacOS 8.0** or greater. By the time you read this, version 5.0x of both browsers should be released. Their requirements should be no higher.

Both also have earlier 4.0 series browsers that will run on **68K machines**. Whatever the machine, browser or version number, they'll all work best with Virtual Memory switched on.

Humble PCs

The best choice for older machines running Windows 3.1 is **Internet Explorer 3.03**. It can get by (just about) on 4 MB of RAM and as little as 7 MB of disk space for a browser-only installation, plus it also includes all the TCP/IP dialing software that Windows 3.1 omits. The Mac equivalent also requires somewhat less RAM and disk space than its successor. If that's still too heavy, **Netscape 2.0x** is better than no browser at all.

Alternatively, if you don't mind coughing up (after a free trial period), investigate the lesser-known but distinctly impressive **Opera** (http://www.operasoftware.com) program. This packs a browser, mail sender, and newsreader into only a couple of MB – and it's even slightly quicker than 4.0x and 5.0x series browsers.

You'll find browsers for other platforms, such as **Amiga** and **OS/2** at Browserwatch (http://www.browserwatch.com).

Explorer v. Netscape: what's on offer?

Okay, let's assume your computer is up to running the latest versions of Netscape Communicator and Internet Explorer. What's on offer?

Internet Explorer 5.0x comes close to assembling a best of the Net in its **package of tools** – much more so than Netscape. If you're running Windows, it should also look familiar. Its look is exactly that of Windows 98 and Microsoft's policy (logical as well as commercial) is to integrate the Web browsing experience into Windows.

Thus, in Windows 98 (or Windows 95 with IE4.0x or later), Windows Explorer and Internet Explorer share the same interface – whether you're surfing the Web or ferreting through your hard drive. Installation, too, is a breeze, guided by the built-in **Internet Connection Wizard**, which can also refer you to a local ISP, if you haven't already signed up.

IE5.0x's notable features include: **IntelliSense**, which can automate various tasks such as correcting address typos, filling in forms, remembering passwords, installing upgrades and completing addresses; **Windows Radio Toolbar**, which puts a host of Net radio stations on your toolbar for quick reference; **Media**

Player, which supports most multimedia formats including Microsoft's new **streaming audio** standards; **Offline Browsing**, which can download whole or partial sites at prescribed intervals for you to read offline or enable you to go back over previous sessions offline; **Content Advisor**, which provides a way to bar kids from unsavory Web sites; **Web Accessories**, which allow third parties to extend the features with news tickers, search aids and the like; and the ability to **save complete Web pages as single files**.

Optional extras include: **Outlook Express**, an outstanding Internet email and news program, particularly for those with multiple accounts; **Netmeeting**, an Internet telephony, video conferencing, and collaboration tool; **Microsoft Chat**, a cute comic-based chat client; and **Front Page Express**, a basic home page editor.

Internet Explorer also has **Macintosh versions**, which share a similar appearance, but are written entirely afresh for the MacOS. Its developments and features had tended to lag behind the Windows equivalent until the release of IE4.5, which diverged somewhat and introduced a few new tricks of its own. Although Mac users tend to be **suspicious** of anything Microsoft, many commentators, including Steve Jobs (Apple CEO), rated IE4.5 as the Mac browser of the moment.

Netscape Communicator 4.5x

Netscape's Communicator is based around a browser called **Navigator** that is also available as a **standalone** (in case you'd rather use another mail program). It's available in three editions. If you start with the simplest, you can always patch up to the full kit.

Communicator Base Install contains: the **Navigator** browser; **Messenger**, a fully-featured HTML email program and newsreader; **Composer**, a basic home page editor; and **AOL Instant Messenger**, a skeletal chat tool that alerts you when your buddies are online.

Complete adds **Real Player**, for streaming audio and video; and **Multimedia support** for other formats. There's also an edition with the **Enterprise Calendar**, a basic scheduling program. You'll also be offered a selection of other utilities and multimedia programs created by Netscape's business partners when you go to **Smart Update**.

Communicator can also be set to block access to objectionable Web content via **NetWatch**, which works similarly to Internet Explorer's offering except you have to go online to set it up. Netscape browsers are **notoriously buggy**, particularly the earlier releases. If you find your system crashing frequently, uninstall Netscape and see if Internet Explorer is any better.

Okay – so which one, then?

Both browsers will do the job, so if you've been provided with either – for example IE4.0x through Windows 98 – there's no great hurry to switch. Still, if you're running Windows 98, it's well worthwhile updating to the latest release of Internet Explorer as it's a marked improvement on the shipping version.

At the time of writing, the gap between the two appears to be widening with **Internet Explorer well in the lead on points**. It's much faster, simpler to learn, more stable, and packed with useful features such as searchable history and cache. It also has superior help, better offline browsing, TCP/IP and dialer support, and a richer, more innovative, bundle.

It's hard to imagine this situation will change, but the new-fashioned Netscape 5.0x might yet turn the tables. The next-generation browser is at the mercy of the general programming public at **Mozilla.org** (http://www.mozilla.org). It will aim to be leaner, faster, sturdier, and crammed with more goodies than ever before. That's yet to be seen, and there's every chance it will never see daylight, but it's slated for release about the same time as this book, so keep an eye out for reviews.

If you have the disk space, there's no harm **installing both browsers**, as some Web pages work better with one program than the other. Both browsers will ask you whether you'd like them to be the default, and whether you'd like them to keep asking the question. Take your time in deciding.

How to get the latest versions

If you already have a browser, you can download the latest Netscape release from: http://www.netscape.com and Internet Explorer from: http://www.microsoft.com/ie/

As Internet Explorer is part of Windows 98, you can also update it to the latest version through **Windows Update** (on the Windows 98 Start menu or under the Tools menu in IE5.0x). Or choose "**Product Updates**" from the Help menu in IE3 or IE4. To update Netscape, go online and **choose Software Updates** from the Help menu.

In all cases, the server will automatically interrogate your system to determine which components you need to bring yourself up to date. Then it's just a matter of picking what you want.

Before you start, bear in mind that the entire kits weigh in between 6 and 30 MB. This means **the download could take an hour or more** – depending on which options you pick, how busy the sites are, and at what

Netscape SmartDownload	_ □ X

N Netscape **Netcenter** | Tips to save money. Tools to save time. | **N** Netscape **Netcenter** Go! | Powered by... | Click Here

Click Here

Saving: Communicator 4.6 4.6
From: ftp://ftp-au.netscape.com/.../cc32e46.exe
To: C:\My Download Files\cc32e46.exe
Status: 11449K of 15454K (3.4 K/sec)
Time left: 19 min, 21 sec   74%

Advanced   Pause   Resume   Cancel

speed you connect. Count on about 6 MB per hour with a 28.8 Kbps modem. So, if you're paying by the minute to be connected, you might find it cheaper and more convenient to buy a computer magazine with the browsers (and more) on a CD cover disk. Plus you'll have a backup copy handy if you need to re-install.

Want more information?

For the latest on browsers, reviews, tests, comparisons of new versions on release, tips, and downloads for a wide range of brands and platforms see **Browsers.com** (http://www.browsers.com) or **Browser Watch**: (http://www.browserwatch.com)

More Net software . . .

Once you've installed your browser, you can surf the Web looking for other software. We have selected a few of the best programs from each category in the "Software Roundup" (see p.425). But that's only a smidgen of what you'll find in some of the software guides recommended in our Web directory (see p.259).

Connecting for the First Time

If you've configured your TCP/IP, dialing, and mail software to your provider's specification, you should be ready to hit the Net. Hopefully, you also have a Web browser installed, as the ideal exercise for your very first connection would be to get straight onto the World Wide Web.

Connect that modem ...

Once you're set up, and browser-ready, **connect your modem** (or terminal device) to the phone line, and **instruct your dialer to call**. What you click on will depend on the way you're set up. If you've done it yourself in Windows 95/98, drag a shortcut from the connection in the Dial-Up Networking folder (under My

Connecting to shonkynet	✕
Status: Dialing...	Cancel

Computer) onto your Desktop or your taskbar. That way it's easy to get to in future.

The process is similar on the Mac but differs between system versions. It won't take you long to work it out. Look under the Apple menu. In the iMac, for example, you can connect through **Remote Access** or by clicking on "**Connect To**" within the **Internet Access Folder**.

If your modem speaker volume is turned up (look under your modem Properties), it will make all kinds of mating noises while connecting, like a fax machine. These sounds will cease once the connection's negotiated. At this point your provider's server will need to identify you as a customer, so if you haven't already entered your **user name and password**, you'll have to now. Once that's done, **click the box that says "Save Password"** otherwise you'll have to enter it every time you log in. Make sure you keep this password private – anyone could use it to rack up your bill or, perhaps worse, read your mail (although you should be issued with a separate password to retrieve mail).

Connecting to shonkynet ✕

    Status: Verifying user name and   Cancel
                password...

Now **start your Web browser** and try accessing a few of the addresses from our Web guide (p.247). You'll find instructions on how to browse the Web in the next chapter. If you can access the Web, it's close to plain sailing from now on. If not, you'll need to find out what's wrong. Read on . . .

Troubleshooting

To access all the **connection settings** in **Windows 95/98** (modem, scripting, TCP/IP, phone, and dialer), open Dial-Up Networking (under My Computer), right-click on the connection, and choose **Properties**. To change the log-in settings, simply left-click as if dialing.

If you are using a **Mac with Free PPP** (or equivalent), you can access the settings by opening the **Free PPP** window and clicking on "General", "Accounts", or "Locations". You may also need to adjust the settings in your **TCP/IP file**, which you access through the Control Panel under the Apple symbol (top left-hand corner of the screen). **In the iMac**, look under **Remote Access**, **TCP/IP**, and **Modem** under the Apple menu Control Panel folder.

If you didn't get through

If you **didn't succeed in connecting to your provider**, there's probably something wrong with your dialer or modem configuration. The most common errors are:

No modem detected: Is your modem installed, plugged into the right port, and switched on? To install or diagnose a modem in Windows 95/98, click on the Modem applet in the Control Panel.

Dial tone not detected: Is your phone line plugged in? If not, try disabling Dial Tone Detect or Wait for Dial

Tone under the modem settings. If the option's grayed out in Windows 95/98, you'll either need to re-install the modem with its correct driver (preferable) or manually enter the initialization string X1 into Extra Settings under the modem's Advanced Connection Settings.

No answer: Do you have the right phone number? You can verify your modem's working by dialing a friend's phone. If the phone rings you know your dialer and modem are talking to each other properly.

Busy/engaged: Access providers' lines can be occupied at peak hours such as the end of the working day. Keep trying until you get in: even though you dial a single number, there are several modems at the other end. If it happens often, complain, or get a new provider with a **lower user to modem ratio**.

You got through but were refused entry

If you **succeeded in connecting** but were **refused entry**, check your user name, password, and script (if used). If it **failed to negotiate network protocols**, verify your TCP/IP settings. You might need your provider's help on this one. Keep the settings on screen and phone them.

You're online but not on the Web

If you've **managed to stay connected, but can't access any Web sites**, either your DNS settings are incorrect, you've failed to establish an IP connection, you haven't specified your ISP's proxy properly, or there's a temporary outage. Log off, verify your TCP/IP and proxy settings, and try again. DNS servers go down occasionally, so (unless yours are server-assigned) make sure you specify more than one.

For details on how to troubleshoot Web access see "Finding It" (p.160).

You're on the Web but another program won't work

If your browser's working, but your chat, search agent, newsreader, or FTP client won't connect to any sites, check the individual program's proxy settings. Ask your ISP for the address and port number if you're unsure.

Your connection keeps going down

If everything works fine but **your connection often drops out,** you'll need to check each link in the chain between you and your provider. Unfortunately, there are a lot of links, so it's down to a matter of elimination.

Does it happen only after an extended period of inactivity? Then it could be an automatic defense mechanism in your dialer or at your provider's end.

Do you have telephone Call Waiting? If it's enabled, and you're called while online, those little beeps will knock out your connection.

Pick up your phone. Does it sound clear? Crackling sounds indicate a poor connection somewhere. Modems like a nice clean line.

Do you share a line? Picking up an extension will drop your connection.

Do you have the latest modem driver and firmware revision? Check your modem manufacturer's home page.

As a **last resort** try a different Access Provider, phone line, and modem.

Okay, it works – but it's very slow

When the **Net gets overloaded**, transfer rates slow down: it can happen to the whole Internet backbone at peak usage times, particularly with transoceanic routes. If transfers are slow from everywhere, however, it usually means the problem lies closer to home. It could be that your **provider or office network** has too many users competing online, or too much traffic accessing its Web area from outside. In this case your provider or office needs to increase its bandwidth to the Net.

Access Providers tend to go through cycles of difficult traffic periods. If they have the resources and the foresight to cope with demand, you won't notice. But as it's such a low-margin business, they're more likely to stretch things. Always call your provider when you have complaints with its service. If you're not treated with respect, no matter how trivial your inquiry, take your money elsewhere. There's a prevailing arrogance within the computer industry. Don't tolerate it. You're the customer; they're not doing you a favor.

Finding the bottleneck

If you'd really like to know what's slowing things down, you can arm yourself with some network diagnostic tools from the Net. The staples are: **Ping**, which works like a radar to measure how long it takes a data packet to reach a server and return; and **TraceRoute**, which pings each router along the path to see which one's causing the holdup.

Windows users have plenty of choices for obtaining these programs. **NetScan Tools** (http://www.nwpsw.com) has

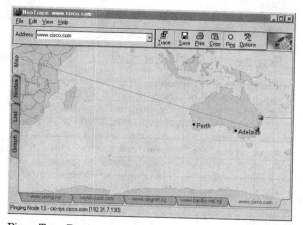

Ping, TraceRoute and loads more. **NetMedic** (http://www.
vitalsigns.com) can tell you exactly where it's breaking
down, whether your provider is falling short, monitor
trends, and send off a complaint report. **NeoTrace** (http:
//www.neoworx.com) adds another level to TraceRoute by
identifying who owns the routers, and then maps it all
out in Hollywood style.

Mac users can enlist WhatRoute: (http://crash.ihug.co.nz/
~bryanc/) for tracing routers, and CyberGauge (http://www.
neon.com) to monitor bandwidth.

The single best piece of advice

If you know someone who's a bit of an Internet
whiz, coax them over to help you hook up for the
first time. Throw in enough pizza, beer, and compliments about their technical prowess, and you'll
have an auxiliary support unit for life.

Surfing the World Wide Web

When you see www.come.and.get.me or suchlike on an advert, business card, or news story, you're being invited to visit an address on the World Wide Web (the Web), the biggest development in communications since TV. You'll have no trouble finding such addresses online as the Web is the genuinely user-friendly face of the Internet.

In fact, you'll find all sorts of interesting stuff once you get started. The Web is such an easy, inexpensive, and flexible platform for expression that it has sparked off more publishing, both professional and DIY, than at any time in history. Consequently, its content spans an exhaustive range of topics across an expanding variety of media formats.

Although getting about the Web is undeniably simple, you'll still need a little help to get off the ground. As preparation, we've dedicated this chapter to explaining **how to set up your Web browser** and point it in the right direction; there's another chapter on **how to find things** once you're there (see p.160); and most of Part Two of this book (see p.245) consists of reviews of **interesting and useful sites**.

What to expect

The Web is the Internet's glossy, glamorous, point-and-click front door: a media-rich assault of shopping, investment services, music, magazines, art, books, museums, travel, games, job agencies, movie previews, self-promotion, and much, much more. It has information on more than a million companies and is accessed by more than a hundred and fifty million users in every corner of the globe from Antarctica to Iceland. It will bring the world to the keyboard of your computer. It's better than the best encyclopedia, and for the most part, it's free. **There's no doubt, if you're not on the World Wide Web, you're missing out.**

How it works

When you enter a Web address into your browser it will retrieve the corresponding page from wherever it's stored on the Internet and display it on your screen. The page is likely to contain a mixture of text and images, laid out like a magazine. But what makes a Web page special is that it can contain links. When you click on a link, something happens. Generally, it brings up another page, but it might do something else like launch a Net radio broadcast, or start a file download.

Clicking on links

You rarely have to enter addresses to get around the Web, because most of the time you'll simply be **clicking on links**. Web pages are written in **HTML** (HyperText Markup Language), which specifically enables documents to **link** to other documents. Clicking on such a link effectively turns the page. This creates a sort of third dimension. If you've used Help in Windows or on the Mac, you'll be familiar with the concept.

Depending on how you've configured your browser, **text that contains links** to other documents (or another part of the same document) is usually highlighted in another color and/or underlined. When you pass over a link (which can be an image as well as text) **your mouse cursor will change from an arrow to a pointing hand** and the target address will appear in a bar at the bottom of your browser.

To pursue the link, simply **click on the highlighted text or image**. A link is only a **one-way connection**, like a signpost. So when you get to the new page, there won't necessarily be a link back. You might imagine that once you've been clicking for a while you could easily get lost. You won't, because there are some simple ways to trace your steps, as we'll explain soon.

Home pages and Web sites

On the World Wide Web, **home page** has two meanings; one refers to the page that appears when you start your browser and acts as your home base for exploring the Web – whenever you get lost or want to return to somewhere familiar, just click on the "Home" button on your browser menu and back you go; the other usage refers to the front door to a set of documents that represents someone or something on the Web. This set of interconnected documents is called a **Web site**.

For instance, Rough Guides' **"official"** home page – found at: http://www.roughguides.com – acts as the publishing company's site index. You can access every page in the Rough Guides site by following links from the home page. Play your cards right and you'll end up at this book's home page.

If a site hasn't been endorsed by whomever it represents it's called an "**unofficial**" home page. This is typical of the celebrity worship sites erected by doting fans. Some film and pop stars have so many they're linked into "Webrings" (http://www.webring.org).

How to read a Web address

Web addresses are formally called **URLs** (Uniform Resource Locators). Every Web page has a unique URL that can be broken into three parts. Reading from left to right they are: the **protocol** (such as http:// ftp:// or news:); the **host name** (everything before the first single forward slash); and the **file path** (everything after and including the first single forward slash). Consider the address: http://www.star.com.hk/~Chow/Yun/fat.html The http:// tells us it's a HyperText file located on the World Wide Web, the domain www.star.com.hk tells us it's in Hong Kong, and the file path indicates that the file fat.html is located in the directory /~Chow/Yun/

Anyone who's serious about their presence on the Web has their own domain name. Typically, a company will choose an address that relates to its business name or activity. It's also common, but certainly not a rule, for such addresses to start with http://www. For example, you can find: Apple computers at http://www.apple.com; the BBC at http://www.bbc.co.uk; and some cheap airfares at http:// www.bargainflights.com

What to do with Web (http) addresses

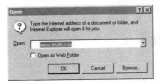

To visit a Web site, you must first submit its address to your browser either by clicking on a link or by keying in the address. The **Address Bar** runs horizontally above the browser pane. In Netscape, when it's blank, it says **Go to** beside it, and when it retrieves a page the wording changes to **Location** or **Netsite** (for sites housed on Netscape servers). In Internet Explorer it says **Address**. You can bring up an alternative box by choosing **Open** or **Open Page** under the File menu. Key the address you're looking for into either box, **hit your enter (or return) key, and wait**.

Your browser will examine the address and work out what to do next. If you've submitted a legitimate Web address it will contact your DNS server to convert the host name into an IP address. You'll see this process happening in the lower right corner of your screen. Once it's converted, the browser will contact the Web site's server and request the page.

It rarely takes more than a minute or two to locate and load Web pages, and if you've a fast connection, it can be a matter of seconds. If all works well, your browser will retrieve the page and display it on your screen. If you receive an error message, try again. If that fails, follow the instructions in "Finding the right Web address" (see p.181).

Take care with capitals

Note that URL path names are **case sensitive**. So key them carefully, taking note of capitals as well as their often bizarre punctuation. Host names are almost always written in lower case, but are actually case insensitive. **Don't bother keying the** http:// **part as your browser will automatically add it on if you omit it.**

Other addresses (non http)

You can also access **FTP** (see p.146), **Telnet**, and **Usenet** (see p.127) from the helm of your Web browser.

To **use FTP**, you just add ftp:// to the file's location. So, to retrieve duck.txt located in the directory /yellow/fluffy from the anonymous FTP site ftp.quack.com you should enter: ftp://ftp.quack.com/yellow/fluffy/duck.txt (In fact, with recent browsers you can omit the ftp:// part as they know that any domain starting with ftp. is an FTP site.)

Telnet works in exactly the same way. So does **Usenet**, except that it omits the // part. Thus, to access the newsgroup alt.ducks key: news: alt.ducks

Addresses starting with file:/// are located on your own hard drive. You can browse your own computer by entering a drive letter followed by a colon (eg, c:).

The main navigation aids

All the main **navigation buttons** are located on the toolbar above the main browser panel. Displaying them is optional, but they're hard to live without. Once you get to know them, choose to display them small and without text. It will free up some screen real estate.

You'll use the **Back** and **Forward** buttons most. To **go back to a page** you previously visited, click the Back button until you find it. To **return to where you were**, keep pressing Forward. And to go back to your start-up page hit **Home**.

You can go back and forward through pages pretty much instantly once you've visited them during a session, as your computer stores the document in its memory. How much material you can click through in this fashion, however, depends on the amount of storage space that's been allocated to **cache** or **temporary Internet files** in your settings. We explain cache later under "Browse Offline" (see p.86).

Two other important buttons are **Stop** and **Reload**. To **cancel a page request**, because it's taking too long to load a site, or you've made a mistake, just hit the Stop button. Occasionally you might have to hit Stop before Back will work. Alternatively, if a page doesn't load properly, you can hit **Refresh** or **Reload** to load it again. You'd also do this if a page changes regularly, and you want to load a new version rather than one that's stored in your session "cache".

Use your mouse

Open Link
Open Link in New Window
Save Target As...
Print Target
Show Picture
Save Picture As...
Set as Wallpaper
Copy
Copy Shortcut
Add to Favorites...
Properties

The next most important navigation controls are in your **mouse button** (the right button on PCs). Just hold it down and try them all out. The menu will change depending upon what you click. For instance, if you click on a link, you'll have the option of opening the target page in a new window or saving it to disk. The latter is sometimes handy if you want to save time loading a large page or image. The saving process goes into the background while you continue in the foreground.

Browse your History

During a session browsing the Web, you can **return to recently visited sites** through the drop-down menus found by either holding down the Back and Forward buttons or clicking on the adjacent down arrows. And you can return to the sites you visit most by scrolling through the drop-down menu where you enter addresses.

These, however, are but a pale imitation of the **History file**. You'll find the main History file under the Communicator menu in Netscape under Tools, or on a toolbar button or under the File menu in Internet Explorer. Think of it as a collection of signposts. You can use it to return to a visited page, rather than clicking the Forward and Back buttons. We'll discuss another use for the History file ahead in "Browse Offline" (p. 86).

Address and form tricks

Browsers are getting smarter with every release. Now, not only do you not have to key http:// but you can sometimes get away with **just putting in a company's name** if its URL starts with www. and ends in .com So to reach Yahoo in Netscape or Internet Explorer, simply key in yahoo and hit enter. Internet Explorer will also **autoscan** the other common root domains (.edu and .org, with and without www.) and then give you the option of looking it up in a search engine (see p.163).

Netscape will also attempt to **guess which URL you're entering** by looking at your History file (see p.84) and **autofilling** in the gaps. If it guesses correctly, you can stop typing and hit enter.

IE5.0x takes this way further with its **IntelliSense** technology. It will present a drop-down list of all the sites from both your History and Favorites that so far match your keystrokes as you type. You can either complete the address or click on one of the selections.

It can also **remember your form entries** (such as search engine terms, user names and passwords) if you choose to enable **AutoComplete**. You'll find various settings, and the option to delete the current data, by clicking the AutoComplete button under the General tab in Options.

If you're bored, you might like to experiment with the **Autosearch** and "**What's related**" features in Internet Explorer and Netscape. Both offer myriad ways to configure automatic searches. For instance, if you **key in a phrase instead of a URL**, they're smart enough to direct the query to a search engine rather than a DNS lookup. They can also offer you a list of related sites courtesy of **Alexa** (http://www.alexa.com). Click on **Show Related Links** under Tools in IE5.0x, and **What's Related** on the Address toolbar in Netscape 4.5x. It looks impressive at first, but power users will get better value by going straight to the search engines and directories (p.161).

How to find a page later

Whenever you find a page that's worth another visit, you should file its location. In Netscape that's called **adding** it to your "**Bookmarks**". Internet Explorer calls it adding to "**Favorites**".

Internet Explorer stores each address as an individual "**Internet Shortcut**" in the same way it makes shortcuts to programs in Windows 95/98. To **arrange your Favorites** into logical folders, choose **Organize Favorites**

from the Favorites menu. You can do the same in Netscape by opening **Edit Bookmarks** in the Communicator menu under Bookmarks or under Bookmarks on the Location toolbar.

When you add an address to your Favorites in IE5.0x, it will ask if you'd like to **make it available offline**. If you agree, it will check the page at whatever intervals you specify to see if it's changed. At the same time, it can also download the page, and others linked to it, so that you can browse the site offline later (see "Browse Offline" – p.86). Netscape can't do that, but you can run through your Bookmarks and see which sites have changed by choosing Update Bookmarks from under Edit Bookmarks.

You can also **save an address as a shortcut or alias** on your desktop. In Netscape, just drag the icon on the toolbar to the left of where it says **Location** or **Netsite** and plonk it down wherever you like. In Internet Explorer drag and drop the page icon to the left of the address or choose **Send Shortcut to Desktop** from under the File menu.

Copy and paste

To copy text from Web pages, highlight the section, choose **Copy** from the Edit or mouse menu (or use the usual shortcut keys), then switch to your word processor, text editor, or mail program and choose **Paste**.

Send addresses to a friend

One of the first things you'll want to do online is **share your discoveries** with friends. The simplest way is to copy the site's address into a mail message, along with a note, or perhaps a section copied and pasted from the page as described above. Alternatively, you can send a link or whole page, by choosing **Send** from under the **File menu** in Internet Explorer and Netscape.

That's straightforward but what if you want to **send a whole list**? Both browsers file addresses into folders for later retrieval, but approach the task from very different angles. Netscape stores them in an HTML file – it's actually a Web page in itself which means you can **put it on the Web**, specify it as your home page, or **attach it to mail** as a single file. Internet Explorer saves each address individually as a shortcut, which makes them less convenient to transfer. To send in bulk, **export** a single folder or the whole list as a Netscape Bookmark file with the **Import/Export Wizard** under the File menu in IE5.0x. Then drag and drop the result into an email message like any other attachment. (See p.108)

Save a page

To save a page, choose **Save as** from under the File menu in any browser. You can usually choose between saving in text or HTML. If you **Save as HTML**, you'll be able to view it only in a browser. Save it as text and you can read or edit it in any text viewer or word processor.

The problem with this method (your only choice in Netscape) is that you'll save only the text, but not the images. So, if you want the images you'll have to save them separately.

IE5.0x offers the option of saving the **complete Web page** or a **Web archive**. The first option automatically saves the images into a separate folder. The latter combines all the elements into a single, transportable file that can be viewed only by IE5.0x or later.

Print a page

To print a page, simply choose **Print** from under the File menu. Note the various layout selections on the pop-up print window. To alter the margins, headers and footers, and other details select **Page Setup**.

Download files

Almost, if not all, your **file downloads** and **software upgrades** can be initiated by a link from a Web page. When you click on that link both Netscape and Internet Explorer will start an **FTP operation** in the background, and let you carry on surfing.

Depending on your settings, once the file is found, you'll be asked where you'd like to save it. If it can log in but can't find the file, or you'd like to browse the FTP site, copy the address using the mouse menu, paste it to the Address bar, and delete the file name from the address. Then you can log into the FTP server and browse it like a Web site. If it's a big file, it might be wiser to pass the job over to a dedicated FTP program that supports Resumes Transfers. Otherwise, if you lose your connection during the download you'll have to start again from scratch.

For more on file transfer, see p.146.

Save an image, movie, or sound file

Web pages often display reduced images. In Web art galleries especially, such images often have links to another with higher resolution. To save an image, select it and then choose **Save as** or **Save Image as** from the File, or mouse button, menu. Windows 95/98 browsers can also save images as **desktop wallpaper**. To save a movie or sound clip, click on the link to it and choose **Save Target as**, or **Save Link as**, from the mouse menu.

Uncover the source

The smartest way to **learn Web design** is to peek at the raw HTML coding on pages you like. Choose **Source** from the View or mouse button menu. For more on Web page design, see p.208.

Change the settings

You can reconfigure Internet Explorer by either choosing "Internet Options" under either the View or Tools menu, "Internet" in the Windows 95/98 Control Panel, or by right-clicking the desktop Internet icon and selecting "Properties". In Netscape, the option is under "Preferences" in the Edit menu. The following are a few things you might change.

Choose your own home page

Browsers come preconfigured with a **default page** – their own, or that of whoever supplied it to you. It will come up every time you start your browser, or whenever you hit "Home". **This is the first thing you should change** in Options (Preferences). You can specify any page you like, even one located on your own hard drive such as your Bookmark file. **It's almost always better to start with a blank page.** That way you don't have to wait for anything to load before you start a Web session and it won't cause problems when you open your browser whilst offline.

How to tell where you've been

An **unvisited link** is like a signpost to a new page. You click on the link to go there. After you've been, nothing changes on the page, but your browser records your visit by storing the URL in a **History file**. It's then called a **visited link**.

You can customize links by displaying them as **underlined** and/or in a **special color**. The default is usually underlined blue for unvisited links and either black, purple or red for visited links. See how this works for yourself. Look at any page. Links you haven't followed should appear blue and underlined. Now click one and load the page. Next, click "Back" and return to the previous page. The link will have changed color.

What's more, **visited links will appear in the new color wherever they crop up**, even on a completely different page that you are visiting for the first time. This can be useful if you're viewing directories and lists, as you can instantly see what you have previously visited.

Visited links eventually expire and revert to their old color. You can set the **expiration** period under Internet Options (Preferences). It's wise to keep the expiry short (no more than 20 days). A big **History file** can dramatically slow things down, especially if you surf a lot. After a month or so, click on **Clear History** in your settings and see if it speeds things up. If it does, reduce your expiry period.

Send email from a Web page

You'll often come across an invitation to **email someone from a Web page**. It mightn't look like an email address – it might be just a name that contains a link. Whatever, it will be obvious from the context that if you want to contact that person you should click on the link. If you pass your mouse over this link it will read something like: mailto: someone@somewhere.com. And then when you click on it, a new message will pop up addressed to someone@somewhere.com Just type your message and send it. Any replies will arrive through the normal email channels.

If it doesn't work, your **browser/mail combination** isn't set up properly. Before you can send email, you have to complete your email details. Generally this is automated in your setup process. If not, you'll have to open your browser and email settings and enter it yourself. You can use any mail program with Internet Explorer. Just choose it from the list under Programs in Internet Options. Netscape forces you to use Messenger. For instructions on setting up mail, see p.96.

Join a newsgroup from the Web

A Web page might **refer you to a newsgroup** for more information. When you click on the link, Netscape or Internet Explorer will open a newsreader in a separate window. You can continue surfing the Web in your browser while you wait for the newsgroup subjects to arrive.

Again you'll need to have your **newsreader set up** to get the link to work. With Internet Explorer, if you're using any Usenet program other than Outlook Express or Internet Mail & News, you'll have to specify it in Internet Explorer under Programs.

For more on newsgroups, see p.127.

Browse Offline

If time online is costing you money, consider spending it **gathering pages** rather than reading. Allow each page you want to read to load fully and it will cache for reading offline later. Then you can run back through your session, after you hang up, by choosing **Work Offline** under the File menu in Netscape Navigator or by toggling the plug icon in the bottom left-hand corner. IE5.0x automatically detects whether you're online.

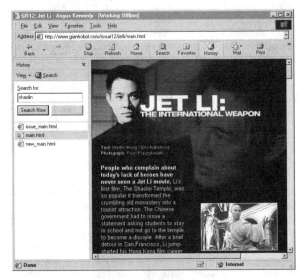

Once in this mode, you can **call up sites** either by typing in their addresses or following links as if you were online, or by clicking on sites in your History file. This works by retrieving files stored temporarily in a folder called **cache** in Netscape and **Temporary Internet Files** in Internet Explorer. Their primary purpose is to speed up browsing. When you return to a page, your browser will check the cache first rather than download its components again from the Net.

IE5.0x is way ahead of Netscape at offline browsing. Clicking IE5.0x's History button will toggle a window on the left-hand side. You can sort the sites by date, name, order of visits, or number of visits. This makes it very easy to backtrack your session. But even better, you can **search the contents of the pages stored in cache**. It's like having your own search engine.

Mind you, these pages won't sit on your hard drive forever – they're governed by your **Cache or Temporary Internet Files settings** and they'll also be overwritten next time you visit that same address. If you wish to archive a page permanently then save it as described earlier.

You'll find your Cache (Temporary Internet Files) settings in your Preferences (Options). While you're there, it's best to select the **option to check for newer versions** just once per session. Then if you suspect the document's changed during a session revisit, just hit **Refresh/ Reload**. Unless you plan to read offline, it's wise to **delete these files every week or two** as, like the History file, if it gets too big, it can slow things right down.

Download entire sites while you sleep

If you'd like to read an online newspaper offline – for example on the train to work – you can set up Internet Explorer to go online while you sleep and download as much of the site as you want. (Handy if your access or phone charges are less late at night and you'd like to browse a large site during working hours.) Just save the site to **Favorites**, choose **make available offline**, and then click on "Customize" to set how many pages to download and when to grab them. To edit or delete your deliveries, choose **Synchronize** from under the Tools menu.

Make the most of your session

Nothing happens instantly on the Net, so **make sure you're always doing at least three things at once**. You might as well download news, mail, and the latest software releases while you browse several sites at once. If you're reading with nothing happening in the background, you're wasting time online.

It's simple to open multiple sites. While you wait for one page to load, open a **New Window** or **New Browser**, and look elsewhere while you wait. For instance, when reading an online newspaper, scan for interesting stories, and then quickly fire them all open in separate windows. Just click each link in turn and select **Open in a New Window** from your **mouse menu**. Then you can read it all instantly, perhaps even offline.

Bear in mind, however, that each process is competing for **computer resources** and bandwidth, so the more you attempt, the higher the likelihood that each will take longer – and that your machine might crash. Mac users will need to allocate extra memory to the browser otherwise it won't be able to open more than three or four windows.

Opera (http://www.operasoftware.com) is the only browser specifically designed to encourage this practice. It can open thirty of forty site windows within the main window, at a fraction of the resources needed in Netscape and IE. In any regard, it's best to experiment first and see how much your setup can take.

Turn off your multimedia

The drawback of the Web's sights and sounds is the time it takes to download them. To speed things up, you have the option of **not showing images and** in Internet Explorer's case, other **multimedia**. You'll find this in the Advanced section of your browser settings.

It's well worth declining images if you're interested only in text. The catch is some pages contain nothing but images with links behind them. If you strike such a page, select the broken image, and choose **Show Image** from your mouse menu on Explorer, or **Show Images** from Netscape's View menu, or change your settings and refresh the page.

If you install IE5.0x's **Web Accessories pack** it will place an **image toggle switch** on your toolbar. Clicking it will turn images on or off.

Plug-ins and ActiveX

Although your browser can recognize a mind-boggling array of multimedia and other file formats, every so often you'll come across something it can't deal with. Generally, there'll be an icon nearby suggesting you grab a **plug-in** or an **ActiveX control**. If not, you'll see a broken image which when clicked on will tell you what you need and where to get it.

A **plug-in** is an auxiliary program that works along-side your browser. You download this program, install it, and your browser will call on it when need be. **ActiveX controls** work similarly, but their scope is far greater. When you arrive at a site that relies on an ActiveX control, it checks to see if you already have it, and if not, installs it automatically after you approve the publisher's certificate. As a rule, don't accept certificates unless you're satisfied the publisher is reputable.

Currently, ActiveX works only under Internet Explorer, or Windows 95/98/NT versions of Netscape when aided by the NCompass ScriptActive plug-in (http://www.ncompasslabs.com).

To **see what plug-ins are already installed** in Netscape, choose **About Plug-ins** from the Help menu. Then follow the link to see what else you can try. Remember, plug-ins consume hard disk and memory, and you can do without most of them, so choose carefully.

Music, video, and animation

There are two plug-in/ActiveX controls you'll definitely need: the **RealPlayer** (which includes **RealAudio** and **RealVideo**) for Internet music and video broadcasts; and Shockwave **Director** and **Flash** for multimedia effects. Whether or not they came with your browser download the latest versions at http://www.real.com and http://www.shockwave.com

Once you have RealAudio you can **sample CDs** before you buy at online music stores, listen to Internet concerts, and tune into live and archived radio broadcasts from all over the world. Shockwave is commonly used to spice up the graphics on elaborate sites, such as movie promotions.

Although Internet Explorer's **Media Player** is capable of playing Real media, it supports only the older standards. So, when you install the **RealPlayer**, make sure it

takes over as your default viewer for all Real media. You'll find the option under the RealPlayer's Preferences.

The reason for this is that Microsoft is developing its own streaming media standard, which at this early stage already looks pretty impressive. It hasn't caught on in a big way yet, but it probably will. For a taster, if you right-click on IE5.0x's toolbar and tick **Radio**, a tuner will appear on a new bar. You'll find a bevy of live stations to listen to while you're online. The fidelity might astound you.

Media Player also supports the much-publicized **MP3 audio standard**. Again, though, it's better to install a dedicated viewer such as **Winamp** (http://www.winamp.com) or **MacAmp** (http://www.macamp.com) for Windows and Mac respectively. Once you do, check out **Mp3.com** (http://www.mp3.com) and **SHOUTcast!** (http://www.shoutcast.com) for live feeds, samples and more info.

For a selection of Net radio sites, music stores, and video broadcasters, see the music and radio sections of our Web guide (p.245).

Java

When **Java** – Sun Microsystems' vision of a platform-independent programming language – arrived, it was instantly pounced upon by the Web community. What once was a static environment quickly sprang to life with all sorts of "animated" applications thanks to its  simple HTML adjunct, **JavaScript**. The main difference between Java and JavaScript is that Java involves downloading and running a small program (called an applet) whereas JavaScript is interpreted by your browser.

Designers can create some cool effects using Java and JavaScript, but if it's not implemented properly it might work inconsistently or even crash your browser. Script that works fine with Netscape can cause Internet Explorer to crash, and vice versa. It's even more pronounced if you're running an old version. If it's causing you too many problems, update your browser version or disable Java in your Internet settings.

To find out more about Java and its latest applications, see **Gamelan** (http://www.gamelan.com)

Proxy settings

Most Access Providers have a server that caches copies of popular Web sites. If you specify this machine's address as your **proxy server**, it should make browsing faster. In some cases, you can't access the Net directly, so specifying it is a must. Ask your provider for its address and enter it into your settings under the **Connection tab** in Internet Explorer's Options (in IE 5.0x, select the connection and click on the settings button), or **Advanced** in Netscape's Preferences.

Cookies

A **cookie** is a small file, placed on your computer by a Web server, as a sort of ID card. Then, next time you drop by, it will know you. Actually, it doesn't quite know it's "you", it recognizes only your individual browser. If you were to visit on another machine or with a different browser on the same machine, it would see you as a different visitor. Or conversely, if someone else were to use your browser, it couldn't tell the difference.

Most Web sites routinely **log your visit**. They can tell a few harmless things like what browser you're using, which pages you've requested and the last site you've seen. This is recorded against your IP address. However, because most dial-up users are issued a different IP address each time they log on, this information isn't useful for building individual profiles. If analysts can log this data against a cookie ID instead, they have a better chance of recognizing repeat visitors. Amongst other things, this makes their lives easier when it comes to looking for sponsorship, which means the site has a better chance of staying afloat.

On the next level, if you **voluntarily submit further details**, they can store it in a database against your cookie, and use it to do things like tailor the site to your preferences, or save you entering the same data each time you check in. This won't be stored on your computer, so other sites can't access it. And most importantly, they won't know anything personal about you – not even your email address – unless you tell them. So unless you have a good reason for hiding your visit to that site, go ahead – accept the cookie. See: http://www.cookiecentral.com

Censor Web material from kids

It's possible to **bar access to certain sites** that might be on the wrong side of educational. Both Internet Explorer and Netscape employ the **PICS** (Platform for Internet Content Selection) system. You can set ratings for language, nudity, sex, and violence. Look under the **Content Advisor** settings, within the Content tab in Internet Explorer's Preferences. In Netscape 4.5x, go online and select **Netwatch** from under the Help menu. AOL also gives you similar control.

There are several third-party programs such as Surf-Watch, ImageCensor, Cybersitter, and NetNanny, which can impose all sorts of restrictions. None, however, is foolproof or particularly satisfactory. See:

http://www.peacefire.org
http://www.censorware.org
http://www.rsac.org

If you're really concerned about what your children are viewing on the Web, you might do better spending a few hours each week surfing the Web with them. After all, banning something will only make them want it more.

Help

If you need step-by-step help using or configuring your browser, refer to your **Help menu**. Microsoft provides excellent help, including all manner of troubleshooting wizards. Netscape's is adequate for basic instructions. If you strike serious **problems with Internet Explorer**, search Microsoft's Knowledge Base at:

http://support.microsoft.com and the Internet Explorer FAQ
http://www.activewin.com/faq/

or try an appropriate newsgroup from:

http://support.microsoft.com/support/news/

For **Netscape problems** check out:

http://help.netscape.com/nuggies/ and http://www.ufaq.org

Email

If you need one good reason to justify hooking up to
the Internet, email should suffice. Once you gather
enough email contacts and get used to communicating
this way, don't be surprised if it becomes your preferred way to get in
touch. You'll be able
to write more and
respond faster –
and that means
you'll probably
become more pro-
ductive. Probably: because email is as time-consuming
as it is addictive. At first you might rediscover the joy
of old-fashioned letter-writing, but because it's so easy
to copy (cc) a message to everyone in your address
book it may invite more mail than you can handle. On
the plus side, though, it will reduce the time you spend
on the phone at work.

Why email will change your life

Email is such an improvement on the postal system it
will revolutionize the way and the amount you communicate. You can send a message to anyone with an email
address anywhere in the world – instantaneously. In
fact, it's so quick that it's possible they could receive
your message sooner than you could print it.

All you need to do is **key an address**, or choose it from your **email address book**, write a brief note, and click **Send**. No letterheads, layout, printing, envelopes, stamps, or visiting the post office. And once you're online your mailer can automatically check in at whatever interval you like. You needn't wait for the postie to arrive. Email is delivered 24 hrs a day, seven days a week, every day of the year.

Email is also better than faxing. It's always **a local call to anywhere, at any time**. No busy signals, paper jams, or failed attempts. Plus you receive the actual text and not a photocopy, or an actual image file and not a scan. So that means you can send **high-resolution color** and **long documents**. As a matter of fact, each edition of this book has been submitted and edited via email.

Email even **beats the phone** at times. You can send a message to a part of the world that's asleep and have a reply first thing in the morning. No need to synchronize phone calls, be put on hold, speak to voicemail, or tell some busybody who's calling. With email, you take the red carpet route straight through to the top. And you don't have to make small talk, unless that's the purpose of the message.

Replacing the post and fax is not email's only strength. You can also **attach any computer file to a message**. That means you can forward things like advertising layout, scanned images, spreadsheets, assignments, tracks from your latest CD, links to Web pages, or even programs. And your accompanying message need only be as brief as a Post-it note or compliments slip.

What's more, with email **everything you send and receive can be filed** in a relatively small amount of disk space. No filing cabinets, no taped phone calls, and no yellowing fax paper. All in writing, and instantly searchable for later reference. Though it doesn't hurt to back up occasionally in case someone steals your computer!

Challenging the establishment

Email is steadily overcoming stuffy business writing. Since email messages are (for the most part) simply text files, there's no need to worry about fonts, letterheads, logos, typesetting, justification, signatures, print resolution, or fancy paper. It distills correspondence down to its essence – words.

But email has gone farther than that – it has encouraged **brevity**. This could be the result of online costs, busy users, or just the practical mindset of the people who first embraced the technology (back in the days before graphical interfaces). Whatever the reason, it's good discipline and it means you'll be able to deal with several times more people than ever before.

Conversely, email is also putting personal correspondence back into letters rather than phone calls. Almost all new users remark on this – and the fact that email often seems to spark off a **surprising intimacy**.

What you'll need

To get started, you'll need a connection to the Net, an **email program (mailer)**, and an **email address**. You don't even need a full Internet connection to use email: as long as you have access to a gateway that leads on to the Net.

You will automatically get an **email address** when you sign up with an Access Provider or an Online Service. If you access through work or someone else's account, you could shop around your local providers for a mailbox-only account or try one of the free email address services on the Net (see p.116).

You should get an **email program** with your Internet access account, most likely whatever comes with your Web browser, but if it's not up to scratch, it's easy to scrap it for another.

Choosing an email program

As your **email program** will become the workhorse of your Net tool kit, you should choose it as carefully as your browser. Still, that need only be one decision, because Netscape's **Messenger** and Internet Explorer's **Outlook Express** are the two best mailers around. They're reliable, user-friendly, cutting edge, and free. Like their respective browsers, it's tough to say which is better. Both are first-class products that improve with each release, but neither is perfect. Outlook Express acts like an independent mail program whereas Messenger clings closely to Navigator.

If it comes down to nitpicking, **Outlook Express** starts quicker, seems more stable, and handles multiple mail accounts superbly. The unique feature is its support for **Hotmail** (see p.116) and other Webmail accounts. In fact, if you don't have an email address you can start a Hotmail account on the spot through the Tools menu. Not surprising if you consider that Microsoft owns Hotmail. If you intend to use more than one email account – and you probably will – Outlook Express is the superior option.

Messenger concentrates more on getting the basics perfect than trying to be clever. That means there's never a hitch carrying out simple everyday tasks such as replying to a message, or forwarding it to someone else. Outlook Express isn't quite as well polished in this regard as we'll explain later.

It's not worth trying to mix and match the browser

suites as neither Outlook Express nor Messenger can be installed without their respective browsers.

Other mail programs

Microsoft has put out some real email stinkers over the years such as **Exchange** (built into Windows 95) and **Outlook 97** (part of Office 97). Exchange should be avoided at any cost, but Outlook 97 can be improved by installing the free Outlook 98 patch upgrade at:

http://www.microsoft.com/outlook/

Outlook 98 is also touted as the next step up from Outlook Express. Although it adds contact, calendar, and task-management tools along with some neat features such as mapping and return receipt, you can safely get by without them. And unless you're using it for internal office mail, ensure you choose the **Internet mail only** installation – it loads faster. Outlook 2000 promises more of the same, but quite simply you can do without the added bulk.

Internet Mail & News, which accompanies IE3.0x, however, is simple, elegant, and ample for the task if you're strapped for disk space.

If you'd prefer a custom-built email program, **Eudora** remains the choice option. It maintains two versions: Light, which is free, and Pro, which is free for thirty days and then you have to pay. If you're presently using Light, check through the features at: http://www.eudora.com and decide if it's worth the upgrade. Probably not . . .

Where to get email programs and tools

If these options can't satisfy your email appetite you'll find plenty of alternative mailers and mail tools at:

http://www.download.com (Mac and PC)
http://www.winfiles.com and http://www.davecentral.com

This includes utilities for polling your accounts and downloading just the headers, selectively deleting mail from your server, and attaching all sorts of multimedia such as video and voice.

Setting up for email

Before you can use your email, you need to fill in a few **configuration details** for whoever supplied your email account (usually your provider). This process is often automated by a wizard or by your Access Provider's software, but take some time to understand your email profile so you can enter it on other machines. For more on email addresses (see p.17).

To **start a new account in Outlook Express**, open **Accounts** under the Tools menu, choose "Add Mail" and follow the prompts. To change the settings select the account and choose Properties.

In **Messenger**, close the browser, open **Profile Manager**, click on **New** and follow the prompts. To change your details later, open **Mail & Newsgroups** under Navigator's Preferences.

The settings

Let's say you're Garret Keogh and your email address is garret@lard.com Open your settings in any mail program and here's what you'll strike:

Name: Garret Keogh
(Who or what will appear as the sender of your mail.)

Email Address:
garret@lard.com
(Where mail you send will
appear to come from.)

Return Address:
garret@lard.com
(Where replies to your
mail will go. Most users
opt for their regular email
address but you could
divert it to a work
account, for example.)

Outgoing Mail (SMTP):
mail.lard.com
(The server to handle
your outgoing mail –
usually your own
provider. If you're on
someone else's machine,
and don't know what to
put, try smtp.site1.csi.com
or mail.geocities.com as a
temporary measure.)

Incoming Mail (POP3):
mail.lard.com
(Where your mail is
stored. This should be
the same as the last part
of your email address,
though often with pop.
or mail. added at the
start.)

Account Name: garret
(The first part of your
email address.)

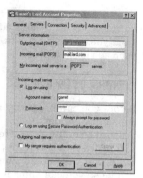

Password: ******

(Careful, don't let anyone see you enter this one.)

Note that the above applies only to **POP3-based mail systems** which at present doesn't include AOL. For more on POP3, including how to upgrade your CompuServe address, see p.232.

Sending and receiving email

You needn't be connected to the Net to **compose an email message**. Simply open your mail program, start a new message, address it either by entering an address manually or by selecting a name from your **address book**, add a **subject**, write the note, and then click **Send**. But before you can actually deliver it you need to **go online**. Sending is usually tied in with receiving (read on for more detail on both operations). Normally you do both at the same time, although it's possible if necessary to separate the two. If you're offline, you'll want to **Send Later**. This is automatic in Outlook Express, but you'll have to choose it from the new message's File menu in Messenger. Then once you're online, you'd choose **Send Unsent Messages** from the File menu.

Outlook Express and Messenger store **unsent mail** in a folder either called the **Outbox** or **Unsent Messages**. Once it's dispatched, it moves into the **Sent** folder. Other programs may do it differently. For instance, Eudora marks unsent mail with a Q, which changes to an S after it's sent.

Incoming mail arrives in the **Inbox** or wherever your filters dump it. When it arrives, you'll hear a sound, get a message and/or see a little envelope in your system tray. That depends on what you configure in your settings. You can change the new mail sound in Windows 95/98 under Sounds in the Control Panel.

Unlike Eudora Light, Outlook Express and Messenger both let you **read mail as it arrives**, as well as preview messages in a separate panel. You can tell which messages are new as they'll be bold and the little envelopes next to them will be closed. Outlook Express displays a number beside each folder to tell you how many unread messages it contains.

Addressing email

Open up a new mail message window, and you'll see a line starting with **To:** which is where you type in your **recipient's address**. Internet email addresses should be along the lines of someone@somewhere where someone is the sender's account name and somewhere identifies the server where they collect their mail.

If you submit a wrongly constructed or a non-existent address, your message should bounce back to you with an **error message** saying what went wrong. This tends to happen within a matter of minutes. Sometimes, however, mail bounces back after a few days. This usually indicates a physical problem in delivering the mail rather than an addressing error. When it occurs, just send it again. If it's your end that's caused the problem, you might have a whole batch of mail to resend.

Sending mail to CompuServe and AOL

To make life a little harder, some addresses – namely **CompuServe** and **AOL** – don't follow the standard someone@somewhere format.

CompuServe members have been able to change their addresses from numbers to names for some time but many members remain unaware of this and stick to the old system. If someone has given you a CompuServe address that looks something like 12345,671 you can convert it to an Internet email address by replacing the comma with a dot and adding @compuserve.com at the end. Thus to send mail to CompuServe member 12345,671 you need to address it to 12345.671@compuserve.com

To send mail to an **AOL nickname** simply tack @aol. com on the end. So to contact Kickme at AOL, address it to kickme@aol.com

With both AOL and CompuServe, you can reply to mail simply by keying **Reply** – more on which below.

The address book

Despite first appearances, Internet email addresses aren't so hard to recall. CompuServe numbers apart, their name-based components are stacks easier to remember than telephone numbers and street addresses. However, there's no real need to memorize them, nor do you have to type in the whole address every time. Not when you have an address book.

Start your address book by putting yourself in. Open it in Outlook Express from under the Tools menu or by clicking on the book icon. In Messenger it's under the Communicator menu. Choose **New Card** or **New Contact** and fill in the blanks. To **import addresses from messages** simply right-click (or click in Macs) on the sender's name and choose **Add to Address Book** from your mouse menu.

You can **send a message to someone in your address book** in several ways, from within the Address Book or the New Message window. Start off by adding every email address you know, and click on all the options until you know it inside out. With most email programs you can **click** or **double-click** on addresses in your address book to create new mail, or with Netscape **drag and drop addresses** into the **To:** or **CC** fields of a new message.

You can also **assign nicknames** to act as shortcuts – and even if you don't the programs are smart enough to help you out. For example, you might only have to enter a few letters of a name, an address or a nickname and it will search the address book for the closest matches. Just be careful it does enter the right address – otherwise it could prove embarrassing.

It's worthwhile experimenting to see which way you prefer. Understanding your address book's capabilities will save you time and tedium in the long run. But the simplest way to address a message is by replying to a previous one. Here's how.

Carbon copies (cc) and blind carbon copies (bcc)

If you want to send two or more people the same message, you have two options.

When you don't mind if recipients know who else is receiving it, one address will have to go in the **To:** field, and the other addresses can also go in this field or in the **CC** (**carbon copy**) field.

Put recipients in the **BCC** (**blind carbon copy**) field if you want their names and addresses masked from all others. However, everyone, including those in BCC, can see who the message is addressed and copied to. To send a bulk mailer without disclosing the list, put yourself in the To: field and everyone else in BCC.

The subject

Let your email recipients know what your message is about. Put something meaningful in the **Subject:** heading. It's not so important when they first receive it – they'll probably open it even if it's blank. However, if you send someone your résumé and you title it "Hi", two months down the track when they're looking for talent, they'll have a hard time weeding you out of the pile.

Filling in the subject is optional when replying. If you don't enter anything, most mailers will retain the original subject and insert **Re:** before the original subject title to indicate it's a reply.

Replying to mail

Yet another great thing about email is how you can quote received mail. To **reply to a message**, simply select it, and click on the **Reply** button or choose **Reply** from under the Message menu. This will automatically copy the original message and address it back to the sender. **Messenger** also offers the option in the right-click (single click on Macs) **mouse menu**.

Depending on your settings (check your Help file or experiment), this new message will contain the original, with **quote tags** (>) prior to each line, or underneath a dotted line perhaps with a bar down the side. It will also contain the **header** of the original message detailing the sender, subject, and delivery date.

To change the quote style in Outlook Express go to the Send tab in Options, and play with the Mail Sending

Formats. Start with the **Send format set to Text** as not all mailers understand HTML. Then you can select to send HTML on a per message basis under the Format menu in the New Message window. Messenger's settings are within Preferences under the Messages tab in Mail & Newsgroups.

You can **include parts or the entire original message**, including the subject – or delete the lot. So when someone asks you a question or raises a point, you're able to include that section and answer it directly underneath or above. This saves them having to refer back and forth between their message and your answer. It also saves keying their address.

Don't fall into the habit of including the entire contents of the original letter in your reply. It wastes time for the receiver and its logical outcome (letters comprising the whole history of your correspondence) hardly bears thinking about.

Note also that the **Reply all** option addresses your message not only to the sender but also to all recipients of the original. That's not something you'll always want to do.

You can normally tell if a message is a reply because the **subject will start with Re:**

Forward a message

If you'd like to share an email with someone, it's possible to **forward it on**. Forwarded messages are just like replies except they're not addressed to the original sender. You'll have to add the addresses manually. Unfortunately Outlook Express treats forwarded messages under the same rules as replies. That means if your replies come with quote tags, your forwarded messages will follow suit. It's better to forward them **inline**,

that is, **beneath a dotted line**. The only way to switch
over in Outlook Express is to re-enter Options. That's
quite a pain. Alternatively, you could **forward the message as an attachment**. This isn't a bad option.

To forward in Outlook Express, select the message
and either select **Forward** or **Forward as an attachment**
from the mouse menu, toolbar, or under the Message
menu. The same for Messenger, except it differentiates
between Forward Quoted and Forward Inline (three
cheers!)

You can tell if a message has been forwarded to you
because the subject line will start with **Fwd:** or **Fw:**

Resend a message

Sending a message again in Outlook Express and Messenger is unnecessarily convoluted. The best way is to
open your Sent box, select the message, forward it
inline, delete the header details, remove the prefix **Fw:**
or **Fwd:** from the subject line, re-enter the recipient's
address and click Send. If you're using Outlook Express
remember to **turn off the quote tags** first!

Signatures and vCards

All mailers let you add your personal touch at the end
of your composition in the form of a **signature file**. This
appears automatically on the bottom of your email, like
headed notepaper. It's common practice to put your

```
   ///\\        //|\\        //\|\\        ///|\
  /`0-0'`      ` @ @\       //o o//         a a
   ]             >          ) | (           _)
   -             -            -             ~
  John          Paul        George        Ringo
```

address, phone number, title, and perhaps round off with a witticism. There's nothing to stop you adding a monstrous picture, frame, or your initials in ASCII art. Except you have more taste than that.

To create and manage your signature(s) click on the "Signatures" tab in Outlook Express's Options, or under Identity in Messenger's Mail & Newsgroups' Preferences.

A **vCard** is an address book entry with as much contact details as you care to disclose. You might like to attach a copy to your mail so your recipients can add it to their address books. To set it up in Outlook Express, edit the Business card section under the Compose tab in Options. In Messenger, choose Edit Card under Mail & Newsgroups' Preferences.

Attaching non-text files to your email

Suppose you want to send something other than just a text message – such as a **word processor document, spreadsheet, or an image** – via email. It's quite feasible, and no longer requires technical expertise. To send a file, look in your mail menu for something along the lines of **Send Attachments** or **Attach File**. Either that or try dragging and dropping the file into the New Message window. It will normally work without a second thought from you.

Well, it's almost that simple. A residual problem, while people are using a variety of mailers, is that both parties' mailers need to support a common encoding standard, otherwise it will appear in gibberish. The most used methods are **MIME** and **UUencode**. It doesn't really matter which you use as long as it works every time, so try a practice run first.

If you have problems getting a file to someone, refer to your Help file on how to specify an encoding method, as it varies between packages. MIME is gaining acceptance across all platforms (it's all that Netscape's older mailers recognize), so if you have the option, set it as the default. Eudora for Macs includes **Binhex**, Apple Single and Apple Double. Always choose Apple Double.

If your mailer doesn't automatically decode attachments, ditch it for one that does. It's not worth the bother. Old office systems like early Microsoft Mail are notoriously fussy. If you're not allowed to use an email program that handles attachments with grace, consider a new job.

Note: Don't ever send an attachment of more than a few hundred kilobytes without prior warning or agreement. Large attachments can take ages to download and even crash meagre machines. It's no way to make friends.

How to send a CD track

If you'd like to share a tune from your new CD try encoding it with **RealEncoder** (http://www.real.com) and attaching it to a message. All your friend will need is the RealPlayer from the same address. Alternatively, if you don't mind a bigger file, you'll get better sound quality by encoding it in MP3. For instructions, see: http://www.mp3.com/faq/making.html

HTML mail and sending Web pages

Not long ago, email was a strictly plain text affair. The odd mailer such as Microsoft Exchange allowed formatting, but it didn't really make an impact until Netscape introduced **HTML mail** as a new standard. Today, if your mailer lacks HTML support you'll feel a bit backward.

HTML mail blurs the distinction between email and the World Wide Web, bringing Web pages right into your mailer. This means Web publishers, particularly magazines and news broadcasters, can send you regular bulletins formatted as Web pages complete with links to further information. It also means you can send Web pages by email. Either drag and drop them into a message or choose Send Page from under the File menu. Just make sure your recipient also has an HTML compliant mailer, otherwise they'll get all the formatting as a useless and time-wasting attachment.

Additionally, although the concept of fancying up your email by adding color, logos, and signatures might seem appealing, it's unlikely to increase your productivity and actually detracts from one of email's strongest features – simplicity. So don't spend too much time worrying about the appearance of your email. Just get the words right.

For a quick lesson in Internet Explorer 4.0's HTML mail see Outlook Expressions: http://www.barkers.org/ie/oe/ and the newsgroup: microsoft.public.windows.inetexplorer.ie5. outlookexpress.stationery

Managing email

If your provider or phone company charges you by the minute to stay connected, it's best to **compose and read your mail offline** (ie, when you are not connected by phone). That way, while connected you're actually busy transferring data, and getting your money's worth. All mailers allow you to send your messages immediately or place them in a queue, as well as to collect mail at regular intervals or on request.

Unless you're connected for long periods, you should select **Choose not to send mail immediately, To check manually (not every x minutes)**, and **Not to check for messages at startup**, otherwise your software will try to send and collect when you're offline. It's best to go online, collect your mail, upload your unsent mail, reply to anything urgent, log off, deal with the rest, and send your new bag of letters next time you go online.

If you have **unsent messages** in Messenger it will ask you if you wish to send them whenever you open or close the program. Choose **No** if you're offline.

Filing

Just as you keep your work desk tidy, and deal with paper as it arrives, try to keep your email neat. Most mailers can organize your correspondence into **mailboxes** or **folders** of some sort and offer you the option of automatically filing sent mail into a **Sent Mail** folder.

It's good discipline to use several folders for filing and to transfer your sent mail into periodic archives, otherwise you'll be creating unwieldy folders containing thousands of messages that are possibly hard to open. Similarly, when you have dealt with mail, either send it to trash (and empty this folder regularly) or put it into a topic folder.

Sorting

To **sort your messages** by date, sender, size or subject, click on the bar at the top of each column. Click again to sort in a different way. Sorting by date makes the most sense so you can instantly see what's most recent.

Filtering

Most mailers can **filter** incoming mail into designated mailboxes, either as it arrives or afterwards. It looks for a common phrase in the incoming message, such as the address or subject, and transfers it to somewhere other than the default inbox. This is indispensable if you subscribe to a lot of mailing lists (see the following chapter) or get a ton of junk office email.

To set up your filters in Outlook Express, open **Message Rules** under the Tools menu. In Messenger, the **Message Filters** are located under the Edit menu.

Etiquette and tracking replies

It's common courtesy – or netiquette – to **reply to email promptly**, even if just to verify it arrived. After all, it only need be a couple of lines. Transfer email that needs attention into a special folder until it's dealt with so you can instantly see what's urgent. Do the same with your Sent box. Transfer the mail that's awaiting replies.

As email is quick, and people tend to deal with it immediately, if you don't get a reply within a few days you'll know what to follow up. Once you've received your reply, you can either archive or delete your original outgoing message.

Sending your first email

The best way to start is to **send yourself some email**. That way you'll get both to send and receive something. If you're dialing in, start this exercise offline with your mailer in **offline mode**.

1. To set up **Messenger**, open Preferences, then Offline, and choose **Ask me**. Restart the program, and choose **Offline**. Open the Mail Servers tab in

the Mail & Newsgroup Preferences, click on the Incoming Mail server and choose Edit. Uncheck the box to check the mail every 10 (or so) minutes.

In **Outlook Express**, open Options, then General and choose not to send and receive messages at Startup, not to check mail regularly, and not **Send mail immediately** under the Send tab.

You can alter all these settings later when you know what you want.

2. Presuming you've completed your server details, the first step is to put yourself into the address book. Next, open up a new message, choose yourself from the address book, give the message a subject, enter something in the body and click **Send** in the **New Message** window. If you're **in offline mode**, that will place your message in a queue to be sent once you go online. Otherwise, it will call up your dialer and try to send it immediately.

3. Now attempt to retrieve/send your mail. If you're offline, that should bring up your dialer. If not and you can't see how to make it happen automatically, call up your dialer manually, log in, and try again. Most mailers pop up a progress window to tell you what's going on.

Once you've sent yourself the message keep checking every 30 seconds until you receive it. It shouldn't take more than a few minutes. Now repeat this exercise until you're confident to face the rest of the wired world.

Get your free email address here

You have an the Internet connection at work – but you don't want your business address for personal mail? No problem. You can score an extra email address and it needn't cost you a thing, though you might have to suffer a little advertising.

There are three main options: **POP3 mail**, **Webmail**, and **mail forwarding**.

Geocities (http://www.geocities.com) has a good deal. It provides a full POP3 address that works with any mailer, plus a free home page in a sort of Web theme village. It might strike you as a bit corny, but it's exceptionally well organized.

Pick of the Webmail is probably **Hotmail** (http://www.hotmail.com): just log in, give a few details and you'll have a mail account in seconds. You can even do it through a menu entry in Outlook Express 5.0x. It's not like normal mail. It's all stored on and sent via the Web. That makes it handy for collecting and sending on the road, especially as you can use the same page to pick up your POP3 mail, but a bit inconvenient for everyday use. At this stage, Outlook Express 5.0x is the only program that supports Hotmail and other Webmail accounts, but the rest are likely to follow suit. As you can give any details you like, it's perfect for anonymous mail – though abusers can still be traced by their IP address.

It seems like just about every major site is handing out **free Webmail** accounts. That includes Excite, Netscape, AltaVista, HotBot and Yahoo. See our Web guide for addresses (p.251)

Internet Connection Wizard

Internet E-mail Address

Your e-mail address is the address other people use to send e-mail messages to you.

◯ I _already_ have an e-mail address that I'd like to use.

   _E_-mail address: [   ]

   For example: someone@microsoft.com

◉ I'd like to _sign up_ for a new account from: [Hotmail ▾]

   < _Back_   [_Next >_]   Cancel

If you already have an email address and simply want something funkier, you can get one ending in anything from @struth.com to @funkymomma.com through a **forwarding service**. What's sent to this address gets redirected to wherever you choose. You're then free to switch providers while retaining a fixed address. See: iName (http://www.iname.com), and NetForward (http://www.netforward.com).

And for a rundown of free email addresses, see: http://fepg.net and http://www.emailaddresses.com

Staying anonymous

Occasionally when sending mail or posting to a newsgroup, you might prefer to **conceal your identity** – for example, to avoid embarrassment in health discussions.

There are three main ways to send mail anonymously. As mentioned in the box on p.116, **Webmail** is one.

The second is less ethical. You can **change your configuration** so that it looks like it's coming from somebody else, either real or fictitious. However, if anyone tries to reply, their mail will attempt to go to that alias, not you. But, be warned, it's possible to trace the header details back to your server, if someone's really eager – and your national law enforcement agency might be if you're up to no good.

The third way is to have your IP address masked by a third party, such as an anonymous remailer. This can be almost impossible to trace. See: http://www.anonymizer.com and http://www.well.com/user/abacard/remail.html

Privacy

Although there's been a lot of fuss about hacking and Net security, in reality email is way more secure than your phone or post. In fact, most new-generation email programs (including Messenger and Outlook Express) have some kind of **encryption** built in. But it's not hackers who are most likely to read your mail – it's whoever has access to your incoming mail server and, of course, anyone with access to your computer. If it happens to be at work, then you can **assume your boss can read your mail**. In some companies it's standard practice, so don't use your work mail for correspondence that could land you in hot water.

If you're really serious about privacy, you may want to investigate **PGP (Pretty Good Privacy)**, a powerful method of encryption which generates a set of public and private "keys" from a passphrase. You distribute the public key and keep the private key secure. When someone wants to send you a private message, they scramble it using your public key. You then use the private key, or your secret passphrase, to decode it. For more, see: http://pgp.rivertown.net

Digital signing and encryption

Internet Explorer, Netscape Communicator, and their associated mailers already support emerging encryption and digital signing standards but it's yet to be seen how they'll be received.

Digital signing proves your identity via a third party certificate. Here's how to get yours. First up, fetch a personal certificate from Verisign (http://www.verisign.com) You can't go wrong if you follow the instructions. Once it's installed, open your mail security settings and see that the certificate is activated. You may choose to sign all your messages digitally by default, or individually. Then send a secure message to all your regular email partners, telling them to install your certificate. Those with secure mailers can add your certificate against your entry in their address books. From then on, they'll be able to verify that mail which says it's from you is indeed from you.

Encryption works similarly, though you'll also need your email partners' certificates to encrypt messages to them. Also, as each certificate only works on one installation, you'll need a different one for work and home. This makes it a bit cumbersome if you're collecting mail on the road. It also means anyone with access to your machine could pretend they're you.

Yes, it's all a bit flaky at this stage. So spend a few minutes in your Help file figuring out the finer details, try it with your friends, and decide amongst yourselves whether it's worth the bother.

Finding an email address – and being found

If you'd like your long-lost childhood sweetheart to track you down by email, you'd better list yourself in a few online email directories. See "Email Search" (p.256) in our Web guide.

For advice on how to find someone else's email address, see our chapter on "Finding It" (p.160).

Coping with spam

If you start receiving piles of unsolicited mail (commonly known as **spam**), contrary to popular advice, **there's not a lot you can do about it**. You can employ various filters but there's really not much point. You might as well let them arrive and delete them on sight. If the option of unsubscribing from a mailing list is offered give it a go. That will stop the messages on any legitimate mailing list, but some unscrupulous marketeers regard any response, no matter how negative, as nothing more than a confirmation of receipt.

The best action is to **avoid exposing your main address** to it in the first place. Most importantly, always mask your email address, or **use an alternative account**, if posting to Usenet or an online forum of any type (see p.133).

To find out more about what steps are being taken to outlaw the practice, see: http://www.cauce.org

Help

If you're frustrated by Microsoft's
Internet Mail & News or **Outlook Express** try
Ed Miller's IMN tips:
http://home.sprynet.com/sprynet/edm/ and

http://www.okinfoweb.com/moe/
or resort to the newsgroups:
microsoft.public.windows.inetexplorer.ie5.outlookexpress or
microsoft.public.internet.mail

For **Eudora**, try: http://www.eudora.com
and the newsgroups:
comp.mail.eudora.ms-windows or
comp.mail.eudora.mac

For **Netscape**, try:
http://help.netscape.com/nuggies/
and the newsgroups:
comp.infosystems.www.browsers.ms-windows or
comp.infosystems.www.browsers.mac

Mailing Lists

If you want email by the bucketload, join a mailing list. This will involve giving your email address to someone and receiving whatever they send until you tell them to stop. Mailing lists fall into two categories: closed (one way) or open. Closed lists are set up by some sort of authority or publisher to keep you informed of news or changes. That could be anything from hourly Antarctic weather updates to product release announcements. They're one way only: you don't contribute. What comes through an open list is sent by its members – and yes, that could be you.

The purpose of most lists is to broadcast news or encourage discussion about a specific topic – anything from alien abductions to Japanese jazz. In some cases, the list itself forms a group, like a social club, so don't be surprised if discussion drifts way off topic or into personal and indulgent rants. You'll see. But you'll also find lists are an easy way to keep up with news and to meet a few peers, maybe in person, too.

How it works

Each mailing list has two addresses: the **mailing address** used to contact its members; and the **administrative address** used to send commands to the server or maintainer of the list. Don't get them mixed up or everyone else on the list will think you're a twit.

Most lists are **unmoderated**, meaning they relay messages immediately. Messages on **moderated** lists, however, get screened first. This can amount to downright censorship, but more often it's welcome, as it can improve the quality of discussion and keep it on topic by pruning irrelevant and repetitive messages. It all depends on the moderator, who is rarely paid for the service. Certain other lists are moderated because they carry messages from one source, such as the US Travel Warnings. Such lists often have a parallel open list for discussion.

If you'd rather receive your mail in large batches than have it trickle through, request a **digest** where available. These are normally sent daily or weekly, depending on the traffic.

As discussions are conducted entirely by email, **the only software needed is your standard mail program**.

Climbing aboard a list

Joining should be simple. In most cases, you **subscribe** by sending a single email message or by filling out a form on a Web page. It depends who's running the list. Once you're on an open list, you'll receive all the messages sent to the list's address, and everyone else on the list will receive whatever you send. Your first message will either welcome you to the list, or ask you to confirm your email address (to stop prank subscriptions). Keep the welcome message, as it should also tell you how to **unsubscribe,** and in some cases set other parameters, such as ordering it in **digest format**.

Subscribing and other list options

Mailing lists are typically run on **Listserv**, **Listproc** or **Majordomo** software. Generally, the list's administrator sets a few options and leaves it up to the program to handle subscription requests automatically, and bounce email out to the list members. So when you want to subscribe or unsubscribe, there's no point writing a courtesy letter as it will only confuse the program. You'll need to find the list's administrative address. Don't send requests to the list address, as it will simply be sent as a normal message to all the list members.

So, let's say you're called Caroline Appleton. Here's how you might subscribe to a list formally called gossip-list:

For **Majordomo:**
To: administrative address
Subject:
Message: subscribe gossip-list

For **Listproc** and **Listserv:**
To: administrative address
Subject:
Message: subscribe gossip-list Caroline Appleton

To unsubscribe, replace the word "subscribe" with "unsubscribe".

And to find out about other list options in any program, send:

To: administrative address
Subject:
Message: help

In-box Direct

You'll find the most organized collection of high-quality closed (or one-way) lists rounded up by Netscape and loosely known as **In-box Direct**. These range from fashion probes like Elle Direct to techie bulletins like PC Week. But they all have one thing in common: they're all sent as Web pages, less the images. This means you need a mail program – like those built into Netscape or Internet Explorer – that reads HTML mail.

The only hitch is you have to join Netscape's NetCenter, which involves filling out far too many details and choosing a password and log-in name. Don't tick any boxes that give Netscape the right to pass on your address, otherwise you'll be panhandled by email forever.

To sign up, go to:

http://home.netscape.com/ibd/

and follow the instructions. It takes weeks to get on some lists, but persevere; it does eventually work. Or bypass this and go directly to each home site and sign up there. In the same way, keep an eye out for interesting lists as you browse the Web. Almost all the best sites have them. For more on **finding a list to join**, see our chapter on "Finding It" (p.160).

Starting your own list

If you'd like to **create your own list** check out

Listbot:	http://www.listbot.com
Coollist:	http://www.coollist.com
Topica:	http://www.topica.com
OneList:	http://www.onelist.com

They're free, and simple to manage from the Web. Or if you want to get serious, ask your provider or network manager to set you up a Listserv, Listproc or Majordomo account on their server.

Privacy

You should consider anything sent to a mailing list to be **in the public domain**. That means discussions could end up archived on the World Wide Web. This isn't usually the case, and may not even be legal, but it's safer not to test it, so take care not to say anything you wouldn't like to see next to your name on the front page of your local paper.

Coping with the volume

Before you set off subscribing to every list that takes your fancy **consider using separate email addresses** for mailing lists and personal mail. Apart from the obvious benefits in managing traffic and filtering, it protects your personal account from spammers. If nothing else, you should at least **filter your list messages** accordingly so your high-priority mail doesn't get buried amongst the junk. Remember, though, when posting to ensure you switch accounts first. It's easy with Outlook Express 5.0x. You can select whichever identity you want to post from through the drop-down window in the From: field. Messenger is less flexible. You can set up a separate identity, but you'll have to close and re-open Netscape to switch.

Vacation alert!

If you're going on vacation or away from your mail for a while, consider unsubscribing from your high-volume lists. Otherwise you might face a serious mail jam when you return.

Usenet
Newsgroups

The Internet is a great place to catch up on the latest bulletins, health warnings, celebrity gossip, sports results, TV listings, film reviews, and all that stuff commonly called "news". You can even have it delivered by email, like a virtual newspaper run. But, don't be confused – that's not what's called "news" on the Internet. In Net-speak, if you're "downloading news", you're retrieving messages posted to Usenet discussion groups. And these can make the regular news look positively out of touch.

Usenet is where the Net community meets to kick around ideas about every subject imaginable. It consists of over 60,000 **newsgroups** each dedicated to a single theme. Whether you're into baseball, be-bop, Buddhism, or brewing beer, there's sure to be a newsgroup chewing over the issues closest to your heart. With an Internet population of over 150 million, you may get access to the world experts (and loonies) in the field. Want to know the recipe for Lard Surprise, who sells Mach3 blades in Kabul, or where to sell that unexploded land mine in your garden? Easy, just find the right newsgroup, post your query, and wait for the results.

It's the Net as virtual community in action: fun, heartwarming, contentious, unpredictable, and ultimately useful – and, after email, arguably the Internet's most valuable resource.

There's a selection of popular and interesting news-groups in our guide to Newsgroups (see p.398). This chapter covers the basics of how to jump in and join in.

How it works

A **Usenet newsgroup** is a bit like a **public notice board** on the Internet. When you send (post) a message to a news-group, everyone who reads that group can see it. They can then **contribute to the discussion publicly** by posting a reply and/or **contact you privately** by email. You won't have a clue who's reading your messages unless they post.

What you'll need

Most Access Providers maintain a **news server**. You'll need to enter its address into your **newsreader** program. Once you've installed your newsreader and downloaded the list of available newsgroups, you can read and post messages – sometimes called **articles** – online, switching between newsgroups as you please. It's possible to read any message, in any group, as long as it remains on your news provider's system. That could be anywhere from a few days to a month depending on the policy your provider has set for each group.

If you're on a very tight budget or live in a remote area without full Internet access, it's also possible to access Usenet through a **BBS (Bulletin Board)** or a **shell account**. You won't, however, have instant access to mes-sages; you'll need to subscribe in advance and wait for them to arrive.

Choosing a newsreader

Newsreaders – the software you use for viewing and posting to newsgroups – are the most counterintuitive and inconsistent of all Internet programs. You can be proficient with one but bewildered by another. That particularly goes for the set of various mutations bundled throughout the history of Microsoft's and Netscape's Web browsers.

If you are running **Netscape Communicator 4.x (Messenger), Internet Explorer 4.x (Outlook Express) or later versions** you shouldn't need to look for another newsreader unless you have high demands. (Earlier versions, Netscape Navigator 3.0x and Internet Mail & News, are satisfactory though not cutting edge.)

However, if you want more power and value from your session, you might consider a dedicated client. For PCs, try **Agent** from Forté (http://www.forteinc.com). It has two versions: Free Agent, which is free, and Agent, the registered, full-featured, Swiss-army-knife edition.

MT NewsWatcher (http://www.best.com/~smfr/mtnw/) is probably the pick of the Mac crop.

You can also access Usenet through a Web interface such as

Deja.com (http://www.deja.com),

Remarq (http://www.remarq.com),

EasyUsenet (http://www.easyusenet.com) or

Talkway (http://www.talkway.com).

These can make a relatively painless introduction, but lack the speed and features of a dedicated Usenet reader.

How to read newsgroup names

Newsgroups are divided into specific topics using a simple **naming system**. You can usually tell what a group's about by looking at its name. The first part is the **hierarchy** (broad category) it falls under. Here are just some of the top-level and most popular (asterisked) hierarchies:

Hierarchy	Content
alt.	Alternative, anarchic, and freewheeling discussion*
aus.	Of interest to Australians
ba.	San Francisco Bay Area topics
bionet.	Biological topics
bit.	Topics from Bitnet LISTSERV mailing lists*
biz.	Accepted place for commercial postings
clari.	ClariNet subscription news service
comp.	Computing discussion*
ddn.	The Defense Data Network
de.	German groups
k12.	Education from kindergarten through grade 12
microsoft.	Microsoft product support
misc.	Miscellaneous discussions that don't fit anywhere else*
news.	Discussions on Usenet itself*
rec.	Hobbies and recreational activities*
sci.	All strands of science*
soc.	Social, cultural, and religious groups*
talk.	Discussion of controversial issues*
uk.	British topics

Note that **newsgroup names** contain dots, like domain names, but they're interpreted differently. Each part of the name distinguishes its focus, rather than its location. The top of the hierarchy is at the far left. As you move right, you go down the tree and it becomes more specific. For instance rec.sport.cricket.info is devoted to information about the compelling recreational sport that is cricket. Also, though several groups may discuss similar subjects, each will have its own angle. Thus while alt.games.gravy might have light and anarchic postings, biz.market.gravy would get down to business.

To find which newsgroups discuss your interests, think laterally and use your newsreader's filtering capabilities to **search its newsgroup list** for key words. Or easier still, search **Deja.com** (http://www.deja.com), the biggest newsgroup directory on the Web.

Getting access to more groups

No news server carries every group. Some groups are restricted to a local geographical area or within one ISP's network. Other groups, which are deemed unpopular or irrelevant, might be cut to conserve disk space, or there might be a policy to ban certain groups and hierarchies. The decision on what you see and what you don't falls with whomever supplies your newsfeed.

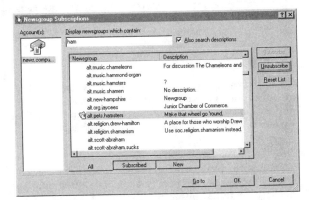

This is not entirely a bad thing as it takes less bandwidth to keep the Usenet file up to date and thus reduces the general level of Net traffic. And **most providers are flexible**. If, say, your provider has arbitrarily decided to exclude all foreign-language and minor regional groups, and you're interested in Icelandic botany and Indian plumbing, you might be able to get the **groups added to the feed** simply by asking. However, sometimes omissions are due to **censorship**. Many providers remove groups on moral grounds, or to avoid controversy. The usual ones to get the chop are the alt.binaries.pictures.erotica (pornography), alt.sex and alt.warez (software hacking and piracy) hierarchies. No great loss.

If you can't get the groups you want from your provider or your account doesn't come with a newsfeed (eg, at work), you needn't resort to another ISP. You could sign up to a **news-only account** with a Usenet specialist, **Remarq** (http://www.remarq.com) or **UsenetServer** (http://www.usenetserver.com), for example, or try a publicly accessible news server with a better selection. Check out: http://www.jammed.com/~newzbot/ and http://www.freenews. maxbaud.net or, if you're really desperate, it's possible to read and post your news for free **via the Web** at **Deja.com**.

Getting started

Before you can get your news you'll need to tweak a few knobs on your **newsreader**. It's hard to give definitive instructions because the features differ so markedly between programs. However, here's what to look for.

Configuring your newsreader

To start with, you'll need to specify your **news server**, **identity**, and **email address** (see opposite). It should be part of your initial set-up routine. If not, to add a new

Usenet service in **Outlook Express**, open Accounts from under the Tools menu, select "Add News" and follow the prompts. In **Netscape Messenger**, open "Preferences" from under the Edit menu, and add your Newsgroup server under Mail & Newsgroups.

Most newsreaders offer a whole bunch of options for how long you want to keep messages after you've read them, how much to retrieve, how to arrange your windows and so forth. Leave those in the default settings and go back when you understand the questions and know your demands. Right now, it's not so important.

Addresses Warning – don't go in naked

Spammers regularly extract all the email addresses from Usenet to add to their bulk mail databases. Consequently most savvy users doctor their addresses in an obvious way to fool bulk mailers but not genuine respondents. For example, henry@plasticfashions.com might enter his address profile as henry@die-spammer-die.plasticfashions.com or henry@remove-this-bit.plasticfashions.com

It's essential to do the same otherwise you'll be bombarded with junk email for years to come. Alternatively, you could use a second address, even under a pseudonym, for privacy's sake.

Building a group list

Before you can jump in, you'll need to **compile a list of the newsgroups** available on your server. Your newsreader should do this automatically the very first time you connect to your news server. It's a big file, so expect to wait a few minutes.

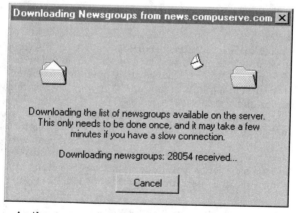

Downloading Newsgroups from news.compuserve.com ☒

Downloading the list of newsgroups available on the server. This only needs to be done once, and it may take a few minutes if you have a slow connection.

Downloading newsgroups: 28054 received...

Cancel

As the newsgroups arrive on your list, they'll either appear in a window titled **New Groups** or go straight into the main list (commonly called All Groups). To **compile your newsgroup list** in Outlook Express, go online and click on your news server entry at the bottom of your mail folder list. In Messenger, go online, select the news server entry in your folder list and click on **Subscribe** under the File menu.

Reading messages

The newsgroup list contains only the group names, not the actual messages. You have to **retrieve the messages** in a separate two-part process. But first you might need to **subscribe** to the group. This simply means putting a newsgroup into a special folder, or marking it in some way, so that it's away from the main list. You might be able to give it priorities, such as automatically updating headers or retrieving all message bodies upon connection, or it might just make it easier to locate.

To **subscribe to a group in Outlook Express**, click on the news server entry and choose "Newsgroups" from the Tools menu, toolbar or mouse menu. When the list appears, select a group, click **Subscribe**, and then **Goto** to commence downloading the message **headers**. The **headers** contain the message subject, posting date, and contributor's name. They can be threaded (bundled together) by subject, or sorted by date or contributor. Once all the headers have arrived, clicking on a message will download its body. You can then read it in the preview panel. If you wish to read the group at a later date, just select it from under the news server folder and wait for the new headers to arrive. To **remove a newsgroup**, choose **Unsubscribe** from your mouse menu.

The process is almost identical in **Messenger**. Choose **Subscribe**, from the File menu, open the folders until you find your group, click on **Subscribe**, then close the window. Click on the group to start downloading headers. Selecting a message will download its body and display it in the preview panel.

Other newsreaders, and probably later versions of

these, will use a different combination of menu choices to go through the same motions. So to get this right, you'll either have to read the **Help File** or randomly click everything the first time. Yes, really: it's the only way. As long as you understand the process, it will all come together, whatever the terms and instructions.

Reading Offline

Reading articles one at a time online is convenient, but not if it's costing you to stay connected or you're tying up your only telephone line. Consider **downloading the article bodies along with the headers** to read offline at your leisure.

This is simple in Outlook Express. Before you go online, choose **Work Offline** from under the File menu, select the group, open its **Properties** from under the File or mouse menu, and make your selection under the **Synchronize** tab. Click on the group when you're next online, and choose **Synchronize** from under the Tools menu to retrieve whatever you've sent. Once you're offline, switch to **Work Offline** mode and browse through the articles as if you're online.

Messenger makes a bit of a meal of the same operation, but it's still possible. One way is to select the group while online, choose **Newsgroup Properties** from under the Edit or mouse menu, then mark your preferences under the **Download Settings** tab. If you choose **Download Now**, it will bring down all the headers. Just follow the prompts.

Contributing to a discussion

When a newsgroup message raises a new topic, it's called **starting a thread**. Replies to that initial message add to this thread. You can configure your newsreader to **sort threads** together to follow the progress of a discussion. But if you follow a group regularly you might find it more convenient to sort by date, to see what's new.

Posting

Posting is like sending email – and equally simple. You can start a new thread, follow up an existing one, and/or respond privately by email. Don't forget if you're replying by email to remove any spam-proofing insertions such as "nospam" or "removethis" from the address.

When you post, most programs automatically insert the newsgroup you're reading in the **Newsgroups**: line. When starting a thread, enter a **subject** that outlines the point of your message. That way it will catch the eye of anyone who's interested or can help. The subject line will then be used to identify the thread in future.

To post a new message in Outlook Express, enter a group and click on the **New Message** toolbar icon or select **New Message** from under the Message menu. The process is identical in Messenger.

To **crosspost** (post a message to more than one group), just add those groups after the first group, separated by a comma, and then a space. Replies to crosspostings are displayed in all the crossposted groups. If you want replies to go to a different group, insert it after "Follow up – To:" For example, to stir up trouble in alt.shenanigans and rec.humor and have the responses go to alt.flame, the header would look like this:

Newsgroups: alt.shenanigans, rec.humor
Follow-up – To: alt.flame

Replying

Replying (or responding) is even easier than posting. You can send your contribution to the relevant newsgroup(s) and/or email the poster directly.

It's not a bad idea **always to reply by email as well as post**, because the original poster will get it instantly. It's also more personal and will save them having to scan through the group for replies. It's quite acceptable to continue communicating outside Usenet as long as it serves a purpose. A lot of new friendships start this way.

Like email, you also have the option of **including part or all of the original message**. This can be quite a tricky choice. If you cut too much, the context could be lost when the original post is deleted. If everyone includes everything, it creates a lot of text to scan. Just try to leave the main points intact.

You'll find the various reply options beside or below your **New Message** menu entries in all newsreaders.

Sending a test post

As soon as anyone gets Usenet access, they're always itching to see if it works. With that in mind, there are a few **newsgroups dedicated to experimenting**. Post whatever you like to alt.test, gnu.gnusenet.test or misc.test You'll get several automatic (and maybe even humanly) generated replies appearing in your mailbox within a few days, just to let you know you're in good hands.

Canceling a message

If you've had second thoughts about something you've posted, select it in the newsgroup and choose **Cancel Message** from under the Message menu in Outlook Express or the mouse menu in Messenger. Unfortunately it won't be instantly removed from every server worldwide so someone still might see it.

Kill files

If you don't like a certain person on Usenet, you can "kill" their mail. If your newsreader has a **kill file**, just add their email address to that, or use your **Filters**. Then you'll never have to download messages they've posted again. You can also trash uninteresting threads in the same way, by setting a delete filter on the subject. But don't make it too broad or you might filter out interesting stuff as well. See: http:www.kibo.com/kibokill/

Decoding binaries (pictures, programs, audio, etc)

As with email, Usenet can carry more than just text. Consequently there are entire groups dedicated to the posting of **binary files** such as images, sounds, patches, and even full commercial programs. Such groups should have .binaries in their address.

Again like email, binary files must be processed, most commonly in UUencoding, before they can be posted or read. You can use a separate program to handle the **encoding/decoding**, but it's far more convenient to leave it up to your newsreader. As postings are restricted to 64 KB, the file could need to be chopped into several messages. Each part will have the same subject heading followed by its number.

Depending on your newsreader, to **retrieve a binary file** you might have to highlight all the parts and decode them in one go. Agent/Free Agent recognizes a set, just by clicking on one part. **Messenger** and **Outlook Express** both decode automatically within the window, but are very slow. You'd be better off with Agent or one of the many newsreaders dedicated to binary decoding.

To decode a multi-part attachment in Outlook Express, select the components and choose **Combine and Decode** from the Tools menu. Messenger, as yet, can't cope with parts. With some newsreaders, you might need to retrieve the message body and decode in two stages. Best to read your Help file to get it straight.

To **post a binary**, just attach it as in email and your newsreader will look after the rest.

> **Warning**: Virus check any programs you download from Usenet. Word documents containing macros should be avoided altogether. And just because you can find **full Playstation CDs** posted to alt.binaries.cd doesn't make it legal for you to burn them to disk – even for your own use.

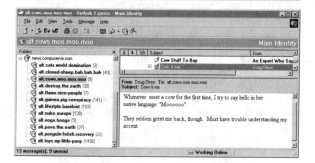

Newsgroup netiquette

Apart from your provider's contract, the Net largely has no formal rules. Instead, there are certain established, or developing, codes of conduct known as **Netiquette** (Net-etiquette). These apply mainly to Usenet.

If you breach Usenet netiquette, you could be ignored, lectured by a self-appointed Net-cop, or flamed. A **flame** is personal abuse. You don't have to breach netiquette to get flamed – just expressing a contrary or naive opinion might do the trick. When it degenerates into name calling, it's called a **flame war**. There's not much you can do to avoid compulsive troublemakers, but if you follow these tips, you should be welcome to stand your ground.

Read the Frequently Asked Questions (FAQs)

Every newsgroup has at least one **FAQ (Frequently Asked Questions)** document. This will describe the newsgroup's charter, give guidelines for posting, and compile common answers to questions.

Many newsgroups carry FAQs on various topics. They should always be your first source of information. FAQs are periodically posted, and usually updated every few weeks. To view a huge selection on the Web, see: http://www.fag.org and http://www.faqs.org

Post to the right group

It's important to **get the feel of a newsgroup** before posting a message. If it's a big group you should get a fair idea within one session, but you might need several. Download all the **relevant FAQs** first, to ensure your message isn't old hat. Some newsgroupies are not too tolerant of repeats.

Next, make an effort to **post in the most relevant group**. If you were to ask for advice on fertilizing roses in rec.gardening you might find yourself politely directed to rec.gardening.roses but if you want to tell everyone in talk.serious.socialism about your favorite Chow Yun Fat film, don't expect such a warm response.

Keep your cool

Never post in anger. You'll regret it later, especially when everything you send is archived at Deja.com. And beware of **Trolls**. These are baits left to start arguments or make you look stupid. If someone asks something ludicrous or obvious, says something offensive or inappropriate, or attacks you personally, don't respond. Let it pass. Tread carefully with sarcasm, too, as not everyone will get it, especially those nationalities with no sense of irony. (This is meant to be a joke, but how can you be sure?)

Less obviously, **NEVER POST IN UPPERCASE** (ALL CAPS) unless you're **shouting** (emphasizing a point in a big way). It makes you look rude and ignorant. And keep your **signature file** short and subtle. Some people believe massive three-page dinosaurs and skyscrapers sculpted from ASCII characters tacked to every Usenet posting gives them cred. Not likely.

Express yourself in plain English (or the language of the group). Don't use **acronyms** or **abbreviations** unless they reduce jargon rather than create it. And avoid overusing **smileys and other emoticons** (see "Net Language" – p.456). Some might find them cute, but to others they're the online equivalent of fuzzy dice hanging from a car's rear-view mirror.

Finally, don't post **email you've received from someone else** without their consent.

Get in there

These warnings aside – and they're pretty obvious – don't hold back. If you can forward a discussion in any way, contribute. That's what it's all about. **Post positively** and invite discussion rather than make abrasive remarks. For example, posting "Hackers are social retards" is sure to get you flamed. But: "Do hackers lead healthy social lives?" will get the same point across and invite debate, yet allow you to sidestep the line of fire.

Overall it's a matter of courtesy, common sense and knowing when to contribute. In Usenet, no-one knows anything about you until you post. They'll get to know you through your words, and how well you construct your arguments. So if you want to make a good impression, think before you post, and don't be a loudmouth.

If you're a real stickler for rules you should read: http://www.idot.aol.com/netiquette/ If all this seems a tad twee, you might appreciate Usenet Tomfoolery at: http://www. elsop.com/wrc/humor/usenet.htm or check Emily Postnews at: http://www.jammed.com/~newzbot/emily-postnews.html

Posting commercial messages

Having such a massive captive audience pre-qualified by interests is beyond the dreams of many marketeers. Consequently you will frequently come across **advertisements and product endorsements** crossposted to inappropriate newsgroups.

This **spamming** is the surest way to make yourself unpopular in Usenet. It usually incites mass mailbombing (loads of unsolicited email) and heavy flaming, not to mention bad publicity. As a rule no-one who uses this technique to advertise is reputable, as with those who send mass emails.

If you'd like to make **commercial announcements**, you could try the groups in the .biz hierarchy; after all that's what they're for. The only problem is no-one reads them because they're chock-full of network marketing schemes. In other groups, tread more subtly with mentions of your new book, CD, or whatever; otherwise you might come in for a hard time. You can still do it, but only in the right groups and in the right context.

Ironically, nobody minds what you put in your **signature**, so if you put in your Web address it might attract a few visitors.

How it gets from A to B

Usenet articles are like email messages but are transmitted in a separate system called **NNTP** (Network News Transport Protocol). Your Usenet provider (eg, your ISP) maintains an independent database of Usenet messages, which it updates in periodic exchanges with neighboring news servers. It receives and dispatches messages anything from once a day to instantly. Due to this pass-the-ball procedure, messages might appear immediately on your screen as you post them, but propagate around the world at the mercy of whoever's in between. Exactly how much newsfeed you get, and what you see, depends on your provider's neighbors and how often they update their messages. Most of the time, these days, it's almost as fast as email.

No provider, however, can keep messages forever, as it needs the space for new ones, so it **expires postings** after a certain holding period. It's usual to delete messages after about four days and even sooner for large groups and **binaries**. Each provider has its own policy.

In addition, some newsgroups are **moderated** which means that postings are screened before they appear. Officially moderated groups are screened by whoever started the group or an appointee, but it's possible, though uncommon, that messages could be censored anywhere between you and the person who posted.

Starting your own newsgroup

With Usenet already buckling under the weight of 60,000+ newsgroups, you'll need fairly specialized tastes to get the urge to start another – plus a fair bit of technical know-how and a monk's patience. It's one of the more convoluted and arcane procedures on the Net.

First off, before you can create a new group – in anywhere but the alt. hierarchy – you need to drum up support. It's a good idea to start a **mailing list** first. To get numbers, discuss the proposal in the newsgroups related to your topic and then announce your list. Once you have a case, and support, you have to put it before the pedantic news.groups for a savaging. Then through a long process that culminates in an election where the number of "yes" votes must be at least 100 more than, and twice the number of, "no" votes.

Starting alt. **newsgroups** is less traumatic. You only need to post a special control message. The hard part is getting people to frequent the group.

For more, see: **So you want to create an alt. newsgroup** (http://www.cis.ohio-state.edu/~barr/alt-creation-guide.html) and **How to write a good new group message** (http://www.gweep.bc.ca/~edmonds/usenet/good-newgroup.html)

Searching Usenet

See our chapter on "Finding It" (p.160).

Downloading Software

Whether you're after a Web browser upgrade, the latest Quake patch, or some obscure CD mastering software, the Internet is the very first place you should look. Just about every program that's released nowadays finds its way on to the Net, and most of the time you can download a full working copy. If not, at the very least, you should be able to order it on disk by email direct from the publisher.

What you certainly will be able to find is all the **Internet software** you'll ever need. And the good news is you can download the pick of the crop, for free. So don't be afraid to replace your starter kit. As Internet software must comply with TCP/IP specifications, units should be seamlessly replaceable, and the only (minor) drawback in add-ons is that you might have to launch them by clicking on their icons and not from the menu in your all-in-one package. That's no big deal.

What you'll need

Before you can download anything, you'll need an **FTP (File Transfer Protocol) program**. You can use a stand-alone dedicated program such as **CuteFTP**, **WS_FTP**,

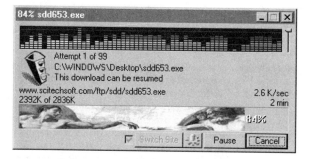

Anarchie, or **Fetch**, but most of the time it's more convenient to use your **Web browser**. Both **Netscape** and **Microsoft's Internet Explorer** browsers are continually improving for FTP, though dedicated programs are still worth checking out for serious use. They have more features. If you're uploading or accessing password-protected sites, you might find one necessary.

We've dedicated a whole chapter to a roundup of **Net software** (see p.425) which includes all the download addresses. You may want to refer to it in conjunction with this section.

Free software from the Net

While the Internet might be a veritable clearing house of freely available software, it's not all genuinely free. There are three types of programs you're allowed to use, at least for a while, without paying. They are called **freeware**, **shareware**, and **beta programs**.

Freeware

Freeware is provided by its author(s) with no expectation of payment. It could be a complete program, a demonstration sample with crippled features, a patch to enhance another program, or an interim upgrade. If you like the program, write and thank the developers.

Shareware

Shareware comes with strings attached, which you accept when you install or run the program. Commonly, these may include the condition that you must pay to continue to use it after an initial free trial period, or that you pay if you intend to use it commercially. Sometimes a shareware program, while adequate, is a short form of a more solid or better-featured registered version. You might upgrade to this if you like the shareware, usually by paying a registration fee, in return for which the author or software distributor will mail you a code to unlock the program or its upgrade.

Beta programs

Betas (and Platform Previews) are distributed as part of the testing process in commercial software development. You shouldn't pay for them as they're not finished products. But they're often good enough for the task, and usually right at the cutting edge of technology. Take Netscape's betas, for example. They've been the most popular programs ever to hit the Net.

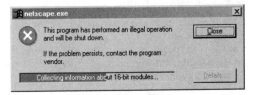

With all betas, expect to encounter **bugs and quirks** now and again and don't be too upset by having to restart the program (or your computer) occasionally – it's all part of the development process. Do report recurring faults to the developers; that's why they let you have it free. If you notice a pattern, email the distributors and ask for a fix. If it's just too buggy, get an alternative.

How to download a file

The most popular way to transfer files across the Internet is by FTP. **Retrieving files by FTP** is straightforward if you have an FTP client with a graphical interface or a Web browser. Dedicated FTP clients are much alike – any of them will do to start. And if you don't like one, you can use it to download another.

Unless you've been granted special permission to log into an FTP server to transfer files, you'll have to use one that permits **anonymous FTP**. Such sites follow a standard log-in. Once you're in, you can look through the contents of a limited number of directories and transfer files to, and sometimes from, your computer.

Many **Net servers** have areas set aside for anonymous FTP. Some even carry massive specialist **file archives**. And most **software houses** provide updates, patches, and interim releases on their own anonymous FTP sites. No single server will have everything you need, but you'll soon find favorites for each type of file. Your Access Provider should have an FTP area, too, where you can transfer files for updating Web pages, download access software, and exchange files with colleagues.

FTP domain addresses

FTP domains are often prefixed by ftp. but that's not a rule. When you're supplied a file location it could be in the form ftp.fish.com/pub/dir/jane.zip That tells you that the file jane.zip is located in the directory pub/dir on the ftp.fish.com server.

Downloading from the Web

Netscape Navigator and **Microsoft Internet Explorer** are superb download clients for both **FTP** and **HTTP** transfers. You can kick off multiple transfers and then surf the Web while you wait for downloads to finish.

That's pretty convenient because most of your file leads will come from Web pages. And not just from specialist software guides either (see our Web guide, p.259). For instance, if you were to read a review of a computer game you can bet your back door it will contain a link to download a demo.

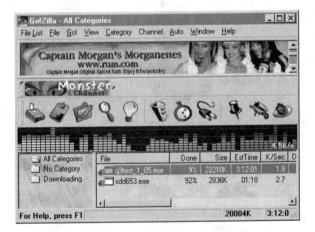

To retrieve it, all you need do is **click on the link and follow the prompts**. You might have to supply a bit of information, but all should be self-explanatory. Once the transfer is initiated (you might have to wait a little longer than it takes to load a Web page), a window will pop up asking you whether you'd like to **open or save the file**. Choose **Save** and browse to where you'd like to put it on your computer. Once that's done a new window will appear with a running estimate of the transfer rate and time to completion. The **Mac version of Internet Explorer** will automatically place all downloads in a **Download folder** unless you specify elsewhere within the Receiving Files section of Preferences. It also combines all downloads into a single Download Manager window.

As with any FTP transfer, if the file has moved, you'll either be defaulted back to a higher directory or face an error message. If the file isn't where it should be, or you want to **enter an unlinked location**, just enter it as a Web address but instead of keying http: use ftp: as the first part of the address.

So, to look for a file at: ftp.chook.com in the path: /pub you enter: ftp://ftp.chook.com/pub Once connected, just click on what you want in the usual fashion.

If you're serious about your downloads, **Go!Zilla for Windows 95/98/NT** (http://www.gozilla.com) is a must. You can assign it to take over whenever it detects a file download of a certain type such as .exe or .zip, or drag and drop links directly into the main window. It can search FTP space looking for alternative locations and tell you which one is quickest. And if you break the transfer it can take over where it left off (as long as the server supports **resume downloads**). Alternatively, try **NetVampire** (http://www.netvampire.com) and **GetRight** (http://www.getright.com)

Resume downloads

As FTP downloads can take some time – hours, even, if it's a big program and your link is slow – it's helpful if your FTP program supports **resume downloads**. Then if you drop out, you can go back and pick up where you left off.

That's a real lifesaver if you're 90 percent through down-loading a 35 MB game demo. Netscape and Internet Explorer are supposed to support resume downloads, but it rarely works in practice. All the more reason to have a dedicated FTP client handy.

Browsing an FTP site

If you'd rather use a dedicated FTP client, it's not much harder. FTP programs use different lingo, so it won't hurt to read its Help or Read Me file. It should tell you what to key in where. Basically, though, the procedure is fairly routine and goes like this:

To retrieve ftp.fish.com/pub/dir/jane.zip
enter the server's address ftp.fish.com as host name
enter anonymous as user name and your Internet
email address (in the form user@host) as a password.

Next, enter the **directory** in which you wish to start looking, in this case /pub/dir Make sure the path and file details are entered in the correct (upper/lower) case. If you enter Dir instead of dir on a UNIX host, it will return an error because UNIX is case sensitive. If you have the file's full location, try entering that as the initial directory. However, don't be surprised if a file isn't where it's supposed to be – system managers are forever shuffling directories. And it's not necessary to get the location exactly right: once you're in, you can always browse around until you find it.

Having entered the details above, you're ready to **log in**. If it's busy, you may not be admitted the first time. Don't let that discourage you. If you can't get in within ten attempts, try again later, perhaps outside the local peak hours. If you're accessing a foreign site, try when that continent is asleep. You're likely to get a better transfer rate.

Once you're accepted, you'll see a listing of the initial **directory's contents**. Look for a contents file called **readme**, **index**, or the like. Read it if you're unsure of the contents, and read, too, any accompanying **text files** before downloading a program. You can usually do that by either clicking on them or selecting **view** or **read** from the menu.

Most FTP programs work in a similar way to Windows' file manager or the Macintosh folder system. That means when you click, something happens. Look at the top of the directory contents. **Clicking on ".."** will send you up a directory level. Directories should stand out from files by having a different color, typeface, folder icon, or at least not having extensions. **Clicking on a directory** will open it, clicking on a file or dragging and dropping it should start the download.

Always select **binary transfer** when downloading. It's usually set as the default. But if you're playing around you might accidentally change it and any graphic, sound, or program you download as **text** will be useless.

Your FTP client should give you a **transfer progress report** to tell you how long it's going to take. You can either sit back and watch the bits zip into your hard drive or relegate it to the background while you do something else, such as explore the Web. But, if the **transfer fails or is canceled**, or your line drops out, you won't be able to pick up where you left off unless your FTP program and the server both support **resume downloads**. Bear this in mind when choosing an FTP client.

Uploading files

FTP isn't just for scoring files, you can **upload** as well. It might be more practical to submit stories, documents, graphics, and applications this way, rather than burden the email system with bulky attachments. For example, suppose you want to submit artwork to a magazine. You could FTP the scans to an area set aside for downloads (often a directory called **incoming**), and then notify your editor by email. The editor could then instruct staff to upload them for approval. If they're okay they could then be processed and moved to an outgoing directory for print house access.

In some cases an area is set aside where files can be uploaded and downloaded to the same directory. Useful maybe if you want to transfer files to a colleague who's having problems with handling mailed attachments (it happens!). It's frustrating waiting for several megabytes of mail attachments to download and decode before you can read your mail. Especially if it has to be resent.

You can upload through your Web browser but it's simpler with a dedicated program. You'll need to log into the site, probably with a legitimate user name and password, switch to the directory and start the transfer.

With most programs it's as simple as dragging and dropping the file. Check your Help file if it's not obvious.

FTP by email

Several services offer **FTP by email**. They can take up to a few days, but may save access charges over slow networks – it might be quicker to download your mail from a local server than to transfer files from a distant busy server. If you're in more of a hurry to get offline than get the file, give it a shot. See: http://www.emailfile.com

File types and compression

There are two good reasons to compress files. One is to decrease their storage demands, the other to reduce transfer times. After you download a compressed file, you must decompress it to get it to work. Before you can decompress it you need the right program to do the job.

In general, it's easy to tell which technique has been used by looking at the file name or where it's located. Unless the site is specifically targeted at one platform, you're usually offered a **directory choice** between DOS, PC/Windows, Mac, and UNIX. Once you've taken that choice everything contained in that directory and its subdirectories will be for that platform only. If not, you can usually tell by the file extensions.

PC archives

PC archives mostly end in .exe, .zip, .lzh, or .arj. The .exe files are usually self-extracting archives, which means they can decompress themselves. To do this, transfer the file to a temporary directory and double-click on it. If you're on a PC, get the latest copy of **WinZip** (http://www.winzip.com), and the latest **Aladdin Expander** (aka **Stuffit Expander**) for Windows (http://www.aladdinsys.com) and place their shortcut icons on your desktop. The great thing about this combination is that it will handle just about everything, including files compressed on Macs. And it's easily configurable to extract archived files automatically just by double-clicking on them in Explorer, or by dropping them onto the Stuffit or WinZip icons.

Mac files

Compressed **Macintosh files** usually end .bin, .cpt, .sit, .sea, or .hqx. The .sea files **self-extract** by clicking on them, the rest by dropping on, or opening with **Stuffit Expander**.

If you're **expanding a Mac file for PC use**, set the options under Cross Platform to "convert text files to Windows format when the file is known to contain text" and "never save files in MacBinary Format".

Internet Explorer will **automatically decode** MacBinary and Binhex files unless you specify otherwise within Download Options in Preferences.

Useful helper programs

All recent Web browsers add support above your standard multimedia software to cope with the most common **audio and video** formats. Anything else is likely to need a browser plug-in or specialist program. If it's something odd, there'll probably be a link to download the player on the Web site where you found the file. Otherwise, browse through the file archives in our Web guide (p.259) for a solution.

How to set up your directory structure

Before you start installing every Internet program you can find, sort out your **directory structure**. Otherwise, you'll make a jungle of your hard drive.

Hard drives are organized into tree-like structures. In DOS, UNIX and Windows 3.x, each level is called a **Directory**. In Windows 95/98 and Macs it's called a **Folder** – they mean the same thing. For simplicity's sake we'll call them directories. The top level of a drive is called the Root Directory. It's for system start-up files only, so don't lob anything in there. No matter what system you're running, you should create the following first-level directories:

Programs

Install all **programs** into their own separate subdirectories under a first-level directory called **Program Files**, **Apps**, or similar. Most Windows programs will install themselves by default in the Program Files directory. It's probably wisest to take that choice if possible, as it's less likely to cause problems later.

Download

Configure your **browser, newsreader and any FTP programs such as Go!Zilla** to download to a common Download directory and create a shortcut (alias) on your desktop to open it. Think of it as an in-tray and clear it accordingly.

Temporary

Once you've downloaded the installation program, extract it to an empty **Temporary directory** and then install it under the Programs hierarchy. Once done, delete the contents of the Temporary directory. If you have space, keep the original installation file in case you need to re-install it. Put it in your Archive directory.

Archive

Rather than clog up your Download folder, create a dedicated **Archive directory** with enough **subdirectories** to make it easy to find things again. As you download new versions of programs, delete the old one.

You could open your archive to your peers through a Windows 98 Dial-Up, or FTP server. It should be the first place to delete files to make space.

Data

Put irreplaceable files, such as those you create, into a **Data directory** tree and regularly back it up onto another medium such as a floppy disk, Zip drive, CD, or even an FTP site. Use WinZip or Stuffit to compress it all into manageable chunks.

Storing files on the Net

Want somewhere to stash your most precious files for safekeeping, to free up some room on your hard drive or backup your iMac? Try **FreeDrive** (http://www.freedrive.com) or **iFloppy** (http://www.ifloppy.net)

Sending a file to a friend

If you use **ICQ** (chat – see p.195) to stay in touch online, rather than attach files by email, try sending them directly using its File option. It's more efficient.

Where to find an FTP client

See "Software Roundup" (p.425).

Finding Files

See the following chapter, "Finding It".

File extensions and decompression programs

The following table shows common **file extensions** and the **programs needed to decompress** or view them.

Extension	Filetype	Program to decompress or view
.arc	PC Compressed archive	PKARC, ARC, ArcMac
.arj	PC Compressed archive	UNARJ
.bin	MacBinary	MacBinary, usually automatic in Macs
.bmp	Bitmap	Graphics viewer, MS Paintbrush
.cpt	Mac Compact Pro archive	Compact Pro, Stuffit Expander
.doc	MS Word document	Word processor such as MS Word or Wordpad
.exe	PC executable	Self executing from DOS or Windows
.gif	Graphic Interchange Format	Graphics viewer
.gz	UNIX Compressed archive	GNU Zip
.hqx	Mac BinHex	BinHex, Stuffit Expander
.jpg	Compressed graphic	Graphics viewer
.lha, .lzh	Compressed archive	LHA
.mpg	Compressed video	Video viewer
.pict	Mac picture	Graphics viewer
.pit	Mac PackIt	PackIt
.ps	PostScript	PostScript printer or GhostScript
.sea	Mac Self-extracting archive	Click on icon to extract
.sit	Mac Stuffit compressed archive	Stuffit Expander
.tif	Tagged image format	Graphic viewer
.txt	Plain ASCII text	MS Notepad, text editor, word processor
.uu, .uue	UNIX UU-encoded	UUDECODE, Stuffit Expander
.z	UNIX Gnu GZip archive	GZip
.Z	UNIX compressed archive	UNCOMPRESS
.zip	PC PKZip compressed archive	PKZip, WinZip, Stuffit Expander
.zoo	Compressed archive	ZOO

Finding It

Once you're installed, setup, online, and the whole thing's purring along to perfection, you'll face yet another dilemma. How on earth do you find anything? Relax, it's not too hard once you've learned a few tricks. Before you can proceed to search for something, you'll need to take into account what it is, how new it is, where it might be stored, and who's likely to know about it. In this chapter, we show you the first places to look, and as you gain experience the rest will fall into place. We also show you how to fix Web addresses that won't work. Assuming you have Web access, the only program you'll definitely need is a browser. You already have one? Fantastic. Well, here's how to wind it out to its full potential.

Become an instant know-it-all

The art of **finding something** pinned up on the world's biggest scrapboard is, without doubt, **the most valuable skill** you can glean from your time online. If you know how to use the Net to find an answer to almost anything quickly and comprehensively, you'd have to consider yourself not only useful, but pretty saleable too. As it stands, most people simply bumble their way around, and that includes a fair share of Net veterans. Yet it's a remarkably basic skill to master once you've been pointed in the right direction. So read this chapter, then get online and start investigating. Within an hour or two you'll be milking the Net for what it's worth. It might turn out to be the best investment you'll ever make!

How it works

The Net is massive. Just the Web alone houses some 500 million pages of text, and millions more are added daily. So if you need to find something – particularly if you want to research it in depth – you're going to need some serious help. Thankfully, there's a wide selection of search tools to make the task relatively painless. The job usually entails keying your **search terms** into a form on a Web page and waiting a few seconds for the results.

We'll introduce you to **search tools** that can locate almost anything on the Web, that is linked to from the Web or archived into an online Web database, such as email addresses, phone numbers, program locations, newsgroup articles, and news clippings. Of course, first it has to be put online, and granted public access. So just because you can access US government servers doesn't mean you'll find a file on DEA Operative Presley's whereabouts.

Let's start by examining the main search tools. You'll find even more listed in the "Search Tools and Directories" section of our Web guide (see p.250).

The main search tools

There are three basic types of Web search tools: **search engines**, **search agents**, and **hand-built directories**. Apart from the odd newspaper archive, they're almost always free. Because they're so useful and popular, most are tacking other services onto the side and building themselves into so-called **portals**, **communities**, and **hubs**. **These expressions are close to meaningless**, really only stating a desire on the site's behalf to attract repeat visitors by making themselves useful. The intention is to get you to choose them as your browser home page. The next few pages discuss each category in detail, and show you how to torture them for answers.

Read me!

As with just about everything on the Net, the easiest way to learn is to dive straight into the search engines and explore how they work. But before you do, it's worth pausing to read the instructions first. Every search engine and directory has a page of Read Me tips on how to use them to their full potential. A few minutes' study will make your searching more effective.

Search engines

Use a search engine when you're looking for specific mention of something on a Web page. Examples: **HotBot**, **AltaVista** and **Northern Light**.

Search engines provide a way to search the contents of millions of Web pages simultaneously. All you have to do is go to the search engine's Web page and **submit keywords**, or **search terms**, into a simple form. It runs these terms past its database and, almost instantly, returns a list of results or "hits". For example, if you were to search on the expression "Rough Guide to the Internet," here's what might come up on top:

1. Welcome to the Rough Guide to the Internet
The Rough Guide to the Internet is the ultimate guide to the Web, complete with a 1500+ site directory.
99% 2/24/99 http://www2.roughguides.com/net/index.html

In this case the top line tells us the name of the page or site. The second is a description excerpted from the page, a relevancy score, retrieval date, and the page's address. If it suits, click on the link to visit the site.

Tip: Don't click on a result, and then hit the Back button if it's no good. Instead, run down the list and open the most promising candidates in new browser windows. It will save you tons of time.

It's important to know you're not searching the Web live. You're merely searching a database of Web pages located on the search engine's server. This database is compiled by **a program that crawls** around the Web looking for new sites, as well as changes to the ones it already knows. How much text is retrieved from each site varies between search engines. The better ones scavenge almost everything.

AltaVista (http://www.av.com)

Excite (http://www.excite.com)

Google (http://www.google.com)

Goto (http://www.goto.com)

HotBot (http://www.hotbot.com)

InfoSeek (http:///www.infoseek.com)

Lycos (http://www.lycos.com)

Northern Light (http://www.nlsearch.com)

Snap (http://www.snap.com)

Webcrawler (http://www.webcrawler.com)

Choosing a search engine

Not all search engines are equal, though some are very similar because they share technologies. **HotBot**, **Snap**, **Goto** and **MSN**, for example, currently use the **Inktomi** system, which means their results won't differ greatly, but that may change over time. What will definitely differ is the way their search forms are presented.

Because the various engines source, store, and retrieve data differently, shop around to see which you prefer. You'll want the biggest, freshest, database. You'll want to be able to fine-tune your search with extra commands. And you'll want the most hits you can get on one page with the most relevant results on top.

Currently, **AltaVista**, **Northern Light** and **HotBot** appear to have the biggest databases. Of these three, AltaVista seems the biggest, fastest, and freshest, but **HotBot is our pick**, as it's by far the easiest to tune, and can return **ten times as many hits per page**. Although **Northern Light** has a bigger database and a unique system of filing returns under subject folders, it's not quite as user-friendly.

Google is a highly promising newcomer, with a large database, an intelligent system of ranking hits by relevancy (popularity), and local cache access to pages that have disappeared since it's crawl or are otherwise

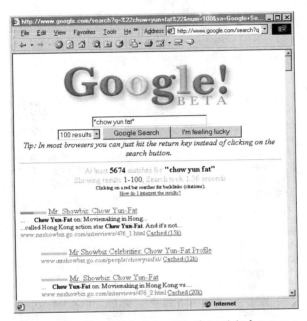

unavailable. Check it out, as it looks set to become a future champ.

InfoSeek has a similar-sized database, and can also give quick, accurate results especially if you're after a single URL, but there are enough other options that you're rarely likely to need it. Most of the rest, such as **Lycos**, **Excite** and **Webcrawler**, and those based around their respective technologies, such as **AOL Netfind**, really aren't worth your time.

If you need **more results**, rather than visit several engines in turn, query them simultaneously using an agent such as **Copernic** (see p.168). You can tell how each engine ranks from the results. For more detailed analysis see **Search Engine Watch** (http://www.searchengine watch.com) which keeps tabs on all the finer details such as who owns what and how they tick.

Limitations

Search engines aren't the be all and end all of what's on the Web. They're only as good as their most recent findings, which might be just a small proportion of what's actually there and, possibly, months old. So just because you can't find it through a Web search doesn't mean it's not there. If you're after something brand new, they may not be much use. You might be better off searching **Usenet** (see p.127) or a news service.

How to word your search terms

Now here's the art. Get this right and you'll find anything. The trick is to think up a search term that's unique enough to get rid of junk results, but broad enough not to miss anything useful. It will depend entirely on the subject, so be prepared to think laterally!

Each search engine has its own quirks which you'll need to learn – otherwise you'll waste a lot of time weeding through poor results. You should try all the main search engines and study their instructions. The main things to glean are how to **create a phrase**, how to **search on multiple phrases**, and how to **exclude certain words**. Let's start with a complex example. Suppose we want to search for something on the esteemed author, Angus Kennedy. Let's see how you'd do it in **AltaVista**. If you were to enter:

angus kennedy

it would return all pages that contain "angus" **or** "kennedy" **or both**. That means there'd be lots of pages about Angus cattle and JFK. We don't want to sift through those so let's make sure the pages contain **both words**. In AltaVista, and most other search engines, you can use a **plus sign (+)** to state that the page **must contain a word**. So let's try:

+angus +kennedy

That's better. All the pages now contain both words. Unfortunately, though, there's no guarantee that they'll be next to each other. What we really want is to **treat them as a phrase**. A simple way to do this is to enclose the words within quotes, like this:

"angus kennedy"

Now we've captured all instances of Angus Kennedy as a phrase, but since it's **a person's name**, we should look for Kennedy, Angus as well. So let's try:

"angus kennedy" "kennedy, angus"

As with the first example we now catch pages with **either or both phrases**. Now suppose we want to narrow it down further and exclude some irrelevant results, for example, others with the same name. Our target writes books about French literature, so let's start by getting rid of that pesky Rough Guide author. To **exclude a term**, place a minus sign (-) in front. So let's ditch him:

"angus kennedy" "kennedy, angus" -"rough guide"

That's about all you need to know in most instances. These rules should work in most (but not all) engines, as well as the search forms on individual sites. Of course, you don't have to know any of this to use Hot-Bot, as it has handy drop-down menus. However, it's good to know if you want to search for two phrases. In this case, choose "any of the words" or "all the words" (whichever's relevant) from the HotBot menu, and enter the phrases within quotes. Alternatively, click on "More Search Options" and fill in the boxes.

For more complex searches in other search engines, look for an **advanced search** link, or refer to the Help file. Observe how they interpret **capitals**, dashes between words, brackets, and the **Boolean** operators such as AND, OR, NEAR, and NOT.

But, there's at least one product that can do all this for you, without you ever having to look at a search engine. Read on.

Search agents

Use a search agent to scan the contents of a limited number of sites. For example, to find new information, to compare prices or stock, or combine the results from several search engines. Examples: **Shopper.com**, **Copernic** and **Apple's Sherlock**.

Search agents, or **searchbots**, gather information live from other sites. For example: metasearch agents such as **Copernic** (http://www.copernic.com), **Dogpile** (http://www.dogpile.com), and **MetaCrawler** (http://www.metacrawler.com) can query multiple search engines and directories simultaneously; bargain finder agents, like **Shopper.com** (http://www.shopper.com), can look for the best deal across several online shops; and Web agents, like **NetAttaché** (http://www.tympani.com), can scan specific sites for pages which have changed or contain instances of an expression. Though many are accessible through a Web interface, the better ones are generally standalone clients.

If you're a serious researcher, once you've tried **Copernic** you'll never want to use an individual search engine again. It's a standalone program that can query several search engines, directories, Usenet archives and email databases, at once. It filters out the duplicates, displays the results on a single page in your browser and even retrieves them automatically for offline browsing. If you're running Windows 95/98/NT, don't pause for thought, **download it now!**

Unfortunately, the Web equivalents aren't as useful. Sure, they can query multiple search resources, but even the best, **MetaCrawler,** will return only up to 30 hits per site. The whole point of searching multiple engines is to get more hits, so you'd be better off starting with HotBot.

You might find the same goes for the bewildering layers of **search aids built into IE5.0x and Windows 98**. Click on IE5.0x's Search button, or "Find on the Internet" from Windows 98's Start menu, and a search form will appear on the left-hand side of your browser. Click **Customize** to choose from an impressive array of search engines, directories, email databases, maps, and more. It looks promising but again you'll probably get better value at the source.

Apple's metasearch agent, **Sherlock**, which comes with MacOS 8.5 and later, also looks promising at first but suffers from the same problems as MetaCrawler. Before you condemn it as entirely worthless, download all the plug-ins from Apple (http://www.apple.com/sherlock/), choose Update Search Sites from under the Find menu and search for a common phrase. Compare the result with Altavista or HotBot and then decide. Perhaps the next version…

Shopping agents are about to take over the Net by storm. **CompareNet** (http://www.comparenet.com), for example, can find you the best product by features and price within a category. Others can instantly compare the price and availability of various products across a number of online stores. Try these for starters:

Shopper.com (http://www.shopper.com)
Virtual Outlet (http://vo.infospace.com)
Bottomdollar (http://www.bottomdollar.com)

There are, in addition, **standalone searchbots** such as **WebFerret**, **WebSnake**, **NetAttaché**, and **WebCompass**, which like Corpernic can query multiple engines and some can scan individual sites. Since they're a bit specialized and questionably useful, we won't discuss them here, but to find out more, check the range at any major file archive such as

Stroud's (http://www.stroud.com),
Tucows (http://www.tucows.com) or
Dave Central (http://www.davecentral.com).

Just because search engines can't find something, doesn't mean it's not on the Web. It just means their trawlers haven't visited that site yet which means you'll have to turn to another, maybe fresher source. Check:

Directories

If you'd like to browse the **range of sites within a topic**, or by other common criteria, it's usually more helpful to refer to a **directory**. For the purpose of this exercise we'll define a directory as **any search aid that's compiled by a human being** rather than a program. It's a loose, unfashionable description but best fits their purpose. Examples: **Yahoo**, **About.com**, **LookSmart** and **Tucows**.

Most **directories** seem to offer something unique. Indeed, they're so diverse that lumping them together is somewhat ambitious. What they do all have in common is that humans, rather than automatons, collate them, often add a comment, and catalog them in some kind of logical fashion. Sites are sorted by subject, date, platform, or even their level of "coolness".

You usually have the choice of browsing directories by **subject group** and sometimes by other criteria such as **entry date or rating**. Or sometimes you search the directory itself through a form, rather like a search engine. Unlike search engines, directories don't keep the contents of Web pages but instead record titles, categories, and sometimes comments or reviews, so adjust your search strategy accordingly. Start with broad terms and work down until you hit the reviews.

Good all-purpose directories include:

Yahoo (http://www.yahoo.com)
LookSmart (http://www.looksmart.com)
Magellan (http://www.mckinley.com)
Lycos (http://www.lycos.com)
Excite (http://www.excite.com)
InfoSeek (http://www.infoseek.com)
Britannica (http://www.britannica.com)

and our own **Rough Guide** (http://www.roughguides.com/net) where we post online the Web sites and reviews in Part Two of this book. **About.com** (http://www.about.com) deserves a special mention, because unlike most broad directories, its topics are researched and introduced by expert guides.

All these directories are useful for finding specialist sites, which in turn can point you to the obscure cauldrons of your obsessions.

Specialist sites and directories

Whatever your interest, you can bet your favorite finger it will have several dedicated Web pages and there's probably a page somewhere that keeps track of them all. Such **mini-directories** are a boon for finding new, esoteric or local interest pages – ones that the major directories overlook. How do you find a specialist directory? Well, you could start by searching a directory that specializes in listing specialist directories such as:

Super Seek (http://www.super-seek.com)
Webdata (http://www.webdata.com)

Specialist sites often maintain a **mailing list** to keep you posted with news and, in some cases, they run **discussion lists** or **bulletin boards** so you can discuss issues with other visitors. If you feel you can contribute to the site in any way email the Webmaster and introduce yourself. That's how the Web community works. You'll find hundreds of specialist sites all through our Web guide, including the most popular in the **Internet Search Tools** category.

Lists

If you're looking for nothing in particular, just something new, entertaining, or innovative, maybe you'll find it in a **list**. For example, most software archives, such as **Stroud's**, maintain a daily list of new releases. Award sites, such as **Cool Site of the Day**, which regularly single out what's new or notable, aren't as significant now that the Web's maturing, but are still worth checking into once in a while to keep you up to date. Or if you'd like to know what's popular, run through the ranks of **100 Hot Websites**. You'll find the addresses for these and loads more in our Web guide section.

Portals, hubs, communities, yawn . . .

The tools for searching the Net have improved exponentially over the last few years, but the methodologies have barely changed. Despite that, they now cluster under a variety of new names courtesy of those very smart people with MBAs. And you can bet those names will continue morphing into even more marketing-friendly nonsense.

You'll almost certainly come across the term **portal**. A site can be classed as a portal if you go there to be directed elsewhere. All search engines and directories are portals. A site is a **hub** if you would go there regularly for news or information contained within the site. The **BBC**, **CNN**, and **ZDnet** spring to mind as examples. But if they make a concerted effort to attract repeat visitors by setting up bulletin boards, discussion lists, chat forums, or free Web space for members, they might prefer to call themselves a **community**.

Finding stuff

If you start your search with the search engines and directories they'll invariably lead you to other sites, which in turn point you closer toward what you're after. As you get more familiar with the run of the Net, you'll gravitate toward specialist sites and directories that index more than just Web pages, contain their own unique content, and shine in specific areas. What's best depends largely on what you're after. When you find a useful site, **store it in your Bookmarks, Hotlist, or Favorites**, so you can return. Here are a few examples, using a mixture of techniques.

Find answers to the most common questions

Where else would you look for answers to the most Frequently Asked Questions than the repository for Usenet

FAQs? If the answer's not in http://www.faq.org, or http://www.faqs.org try Usenet itself.

Find out what others think on Usenet

You want to, but you don't know how. You want one, but you don't know which one. You have one, but you can't get it to work. You want more than just a second opinion. You want a forum on the subject. That's Usenet (see p.127).

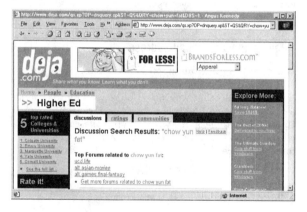

There's no better place to find opinions and personal experiences than Usenet, but it's a lot of text to scan. Although it's sorted into subject bundles, if you had to find every instance of discussion about something, it could take you days. And if it was tossed around more than a couple of weeks ago, the thread might have expired.

With **Deja.com** (http://www.deja.com), however, not only can you scan close to all Usenet now, but a fair chunk of its history as well. That includes over 20,000 news-groups going back, in many cases, to March 1995. You can pursue entire threads and profile each contributor, just by clicking on the results. Which means you can follow a whole discussion, as well as check out who's who and how well they're respected. And on top of that, you can identify which groups are most likely to discuss something and then join the group. You'll get to the bottom of even the most obscure subject.

Like all search engines, Deja.com is pretty self-explanatory, but do yourself a favor and start out by reading: http://www.deja.com/help/help_ps.shtml

Find someone's email address

When you're given an **email address** it's private unless you instruct someone to list it in a **directory** or make it public in some other way. So if you're looking for a long-lost friend's email address, there's no guarantee you'll find it. Nonetheless, it's worth trying the **email directories**, but don't give up if they're not there! The biggest directories are:

Yahoo PeopleSearch (http://people.yahoo.com)
Bigfoot (http://www.bigfoot.com)
WhoWhere (http://www.whowhere.com)

These get most of their data from Usenet postings and visitors, so while they're not in any way comprehensive they're pretty vast databases – and growing by the day. You can also access them from the address books in Messenger and Outlook Express.

If these fail, try searching on your quarry's full name in HotBot (choose "Look for the Person") or Deja.com. Alternatively, if you know where someone works, search their company's Web pages – or (an old standby of detec-

Find People - [28 entries found]

| Look in: | WhoWhere Internet Directory Service | | Web Site... |

People | Advanced |

Name: Chow Yun Fat

E-mail:

WhoWhere?

Name ▲	E-Mail Address
Chow Woan Yun	wychow@mailcity.com
Chow Yan-Fat	edt2@hardboiled.com
Chow Yat Fat	jimmychow@pop3.hknet.c...
Chow Yat Fat Jimmy	chowyf00@stlinux.oli.hk
Chow Yat Fat Jimmy	yfchow00@stlinux.oli.hk
chow yu fat	yfchow@medi.net.hk
Chow Yun	wychow@mailexcite.com
Chow Yun	wychow@myworldmail.com
Chow Yun	chowyunpht@aol.com
Chow Yun Fat	cc201760@anan.nanat.f...

Find Now

Stop

Clear All

Close

Properties

Delete

Add to Address Book

tive agencies), **ring up and ask**.

For other tips, see the **FAQ on finding email
addresses**: http://www.qucis.queensu.ca/FAQs/email/finding.html
and **Yahoo's email search directory**: http://dir.yahoo.com/
Reference/Phone_Numbers_and_Addresses/Email_Addresses/

Find games, hints, and cheats

Try one of the big games sites such as the **Games
Domain**, **Gamespot**, or **Happy Puppy**, or search through
Usenet as explained above. Stuck on a level? Look for a
walkthrough, or ask in Usenet.

Find a product review

Generally the best place to get product advice is from a
newsgroup dedicated to the subject. For example, if you
want to know if some new nuclear flea collar works, toss
it around alt.fleabags Specialist sites and magazines are
always a good source, so check our listings in the Web
guide or see what's under the category in Yahoo. Or, if
you're really lucky, you might be able to find something
in **Product Review Net** (http://www.productreviewnet.com).

Scroll down or click here to Price Comparison Table

TITLE: The Internet : The Rough Guide 1999, Fourth Edition
ISBN: 1858283434
Publisher: Rough Guides Limited
Publish Date: November 1998
Author: Kennedy, Angus J. / Rough Guides (Editor)
Binding: Paperback,4th ed.,432pp.
List Price: US 8.95

Store	Shipping Service	Shipping Time	Shipping Cost	US sales Tax	Price	Total Price US	Click to Buy	Add to Notepad
1Bookstreet	Parcel Post	3-14 days	0.00	0	8.06	8.06	Buy it	memo
Kingbooks	USPS Ground	6-17 days	2.44	0	7.16	9.60	Buy it	memo
A1Books	UPS Ground	4-6 days	3.95	0	5.75	9.70	Buy it	memo
Alphacraze	Regular Mail	3-7 days	3.95	0	6.00	9.95	Buy it	memo
1Bookstreet	UPS Ground	4-6 days	2.70	0	8.06	10.76	Buy it	memo

Find an online shop

Try our Web guide (p.245), both within the Shopping
section and elsewhere. Start with the specialist directories such as **Bizrate** (http://www.bizrate.com), **Shopping
Search** (http://www.shoppingsearch.com), and **Enterprise City
UK** (http://www.enterprisecity.co.uk), and then go through
the big, all-purpose directories like Yahoo and Infoseek,
including their regional counterparts. Alternatively, if

it's something more obscure than books or music, hunt down a relevant newsgroup and ask for advice.

Find a computing bargain

If bargain finder agents have taken off anywhere it's within computer sales. There's no shortage of options but most of them come from the US. Still, that's where it's cheapest, so if you live elsewhere it might be worthwhile importing. Make sure you take the tax, freight and warranties into account. To compare prices, try:

Shopper.com (http://www.shopper.com)
PriceScan (http://www.pricescan.com)
PriceWatch (http://www.pricewatch.com)

Alternatively, place a bid at one of these:

Onsale (http://www.onsale.com)
Ebay (http://www.ebay.com)

Find product support

Whenever you buy anything substantial, see if the company has a Web site offering **followup support** and **product news**. If it's not on the accompanying literature, try putting its name between www and .com and if that doesn't work, look it up in any of the search directories.

Most companies offer some kind of online product support and registration, but if you want advice from other users, go to Usenet.

Find the latest news, weather, finance, sport, etc

Apart from hundreds of newspapers and magazines, the Net carries several large **news-clipping archives** assembled from all sorts of sources. Naturally, there's an overwhelming amount of technology news, but also an increasing amount of services dedicated to what you would normally find on the newsstands – and it's often fresher on the Net. Occasionally there's a charge for access, though that's more usual with the archives rather than what's current. For pointers, check our Web guide under News, Fashion, Finance, Weather, and so forth. **Yahoo Daily News** (http://dailynews.yahoo.com) is a great place to start. And for a list of **news search services**, see: http://searchenginewatch.com /facts/newssearch.html

Find out about a film or TV show

See the Film and TV section of our Web guide or try the entertainment section of any major directory for leads to specialist sites. The **Internet Movie Database**, for example, is exceptionally comprehensive and linked to Amazon in case you're tempted to order the video.

Find the latest software

First off, try one of the specialist file directories such as **Stroud's**, **Tucows** or **Download.com** and look under an appropriate category. Failing that, try coining an appropriate search term and feeding it into the search engines, Usenet archives, and IT press archives such as **ZDNet** (http://www.zdnet.com). As a bonus you'll likely find a description or review to tell you whether it's worth getting.

Once you've found a file, if it proves slow to download, feed the file name into one of the **FTP engines** such as **Filez** (http://www.filez.com), **Shareware.com** (http://www.share-

ware.com), or **FTP Search** (http://www.ftpsearch.com), to find
an alternative FTP site from which to download it.

Find a mailing list

Tracking down a **mailing list** is a cinch. Subject search
any of the directories in the Mailing List section of our
Web guide "**Discussion Directories**", p.258. If that's not
satisfactory, try the same search in a **Usenet archive** and
check the FAQs from groups with hits.

Find something you've forgotten

Don't give up if you can't remember where you saw that
hot tip last week. Just open IE5.0x's History and search
the cache. So long as it hasn't been deleted, you should
even be able to recall it offline.

Find help

If all else fails – and that's pretty unlikely – you can
always turn to someone else for help. Use Deja.com to
find the most appropriate newsgroup(s). Summarize
your quest in the subject heading, keep it concise, post,
and you should get an answer or three within a few
days. Alternatively, try a mailing list.

Finding the right Web address

It won't be long before you encounter a **Web link or address that won't work**. Don't get too perturbed – it's
common and usually not too hard to get around. We
already know that many of the URLs in our Web guide

will be wrong by the time you try them. Not because we're hopeless, they just change. For example, in the five months between the last edition of this book's first and fifth printings, almost 100 sites needed updating. That's the way of the Net. The most useful thing we can do is show you how to find their new homes.

Error codes

When something goes wrong, your browser will pop up a box with a message and **error code, or display a page with an error message** – that or nothing will happen, no matter what you try. To identify the source of the problem, get familiar with the types of errors. Different browsers and servers will return different error messages, but they'll indicate the same things. As an exercise, identify the following errors:

Incorrect host name

When the address points to a nonexistent host, your browser should return an error saying "Host not found" or "Cannot find server".

Test this by keying: http://www.rufgide.com

Illegal domain name

If you specify an **illegal host name** or **protocol**, your browser should tell you. Try this out by keying http://wwwrufguide and then http:/www.ibm.com (noting the single slash before the www). Internet Explorer 5.0 will automatically detect the latter error, and correct it.

File not found

If the **file has moved, changed name**, or you've overlooked **capitalization**, you'll get a message within the page from the server telling you the file doesn't exist on the host. Test this by keying a familiar URL and slightly changing the path.

Busy host or Host refuses entry

Occasionally you won't gain access because the host is either **overloaded with traffic**, or it's temporarily or permanently **off-limits**. This sometimes happens with busy FTP servers, like Netscape's. It's a bit hard to test, but you'll come across it sooner or later. You might also make a habit of accessing foreign sites when locals are sleeping – it's usually quicker.

When no URLs work

Now that you're on speaking terms with your browser, you're set to troubleshoot that problem URL. When you get one, first check that you have a **working connection** to the Web. Try another site, like: http://www.yahoo.com

If it works, you know the problem's with that URL (more on which below). If you can't connect to any Web site, **close and then reopen your browser**. It might only be a software glitch. Otherwise, it's most likely a problem with your Net connection or proxy server (if you're using one).

Check your mail. If that looks dodgy, log off, then back on. Check it again. If your mailer connects and reports your mail status normally, you know that the connection between you and your provider is okay. But there still could be a problem between it and the Net or with your proxy server. Check you have the right proxy settings and if so, disable them. If it still doesn't work, **ring your provider** and see if there's a problem at their end or diagnose it yourself.

To do this, test a known host – say www.yahoo.com – with a **network tool** such as **Ping**, **TraceRoute** or **NetMedic** (see p.69) or try logging in to an FTP site. If this fails, either your provider's connection to the Net is down, or there's a problem with your **Domain Name Server**. Get on the phone and sort it out.

If you've verified that all connections are open but your browser still won't find any URLs, then the problem must lie with your **browser setup**. Check its settings and re-install it if necessary. Finally, make sure you have the right browser for your operating system. For example, 32-bit browsers won't work properly with Windows 3.x. Time to get a new operating system . . .

When one URL doesn't work

If only **one URL fails**, you know its address is wrong or its host has problems. Now that you're familiar with error messages you can deduce the source and fix that address.

Web addresses disappear and change all the time, often because the address has been simplified, for example from: http://www.netflux.co.uk/~test/New_Book/htm to http://www.newbook.com

If you're lucky, someone will have had the sense to leave a **link to the new page** from the old address but sometimes even that pointer gets out of date. Since the Web is in a constant state of construction, just about everything is a test site in transit to something bigger and more glorious. Consequently, when a site gets serious, it might relocate to an entirely new host and forget the old address.

Finding that elusive URL

The error messages will provide the most helpful clues for **tracking elusive URLs**. If the problem comes from the host name, try **adding** or **removing the www part**. For example, instead of typing http://roughguides.com try http://www.roughguides.com Other than that you can only guess. It may only be that the host is busy, refusing entry, or not connecting, so **try again later.**

If you **can connect to the host but the file isn't there**, there are a few further tricks to try. Check capitalization, for instance: book.htm instead of Book.htm Or try **changing the file name extension** from .htm to .html or vice versa, if applicable. Then try **removing the file name** and then each subsequent directory up the path until finally you're left with just the host name. For example:

    http://www.roughguides.com/old/Book.htm
    http://www.roughguides.com/old/book.htm
    http://www.roughguides.com/old/book.html
    http://www.roughguides.com/old/
    http://www.roughguides.com

In each case, if you succeed in connecting, try to locate your page from whatever links appear.

If you haven't succeeded, there's still hope. Try **submitting the main key words** from the URL's address or title to **HotBot** or **AltaVista**. Failing that, try searching on related subjects, or scanning through one of the subject guides like **Yahoo** or **About.com**.

By now, even if you haven't found your original target URL, you've probably discovered half a dozen similar if not more interesting pages, and in the process figured out how to navigate the Net.

Chat

You won't really feel the full impact of having instant access to a cast of millions until you jump into your first chat session. You might even find it a touch spooky at first. The way you can type something in, and within seconds, someone replies. Even if chat doesn't quite sound like your sort of thing, at least give it a go once or twice, just for fun.

You'll find Internet chat opportunities at almost every corner, particularly within the Online Services, and increasingly, on the **Web**. AOL and CompuServe are known for their **chat forums**, which often host interviews with notable **celebrities**. You have to be a member, though, to join in. But don't let that bother you because there are ample chat forums on the Web, and way more again within an entirely separate system called **Internet Relay Chat**, or **IRC**. We'll cover IRC in step-by-step detail over the next few pages, and then investigate some other popular chat techniques such as **Comic Chat**, **ICQ**, **Web chat** and **Internet Telephony**.

About IRC

Since 1988, IRC has played a part in transmitting timely eye-witness accounts of every subsequent **major world event** – including the Gulf War, the LA riots, the Kobe earthquake. the World Cup, and the bombing of Serbia. IRC channels formed during the Gulf War to dissect the latest news as it came in from the wire services. But, as you'll soon discover, politics, crises, and sport are not the only things discussed.

What's IRC? A veritable online Love Boat, say Mr. and Mrs. A. Hunt at: http://www.andyhunt.demon.co.uk

How it works

Unlike Usenet and email, on Internet chat, **conversations are live**. Joining a **chat channel**, **chat room** or **chat forum** is like opening a door into a **room full of people**, or perhaps only one other person. Whatever you say in that channel, is instantly broadcast to everybody else on the same channel, even if they're logged into a server on the other side of the world. You can expect them to reply as instantly as if they were in the same room.

Some channels are identifiably dedicated to **particular topics**, for example, #cricket, #kosovo and #impeachsamaranch, but most are merely **informal chat lines**. While chat might have business potential in areas such as customer support, it's overwhelmingly more orientated to **social banter**. Such idle natter between **consenting strangers** can lead to the online equivalent of **seriously heavy petting**, and inevitably makes it particularly attractive to teens. It can also make it unnervingly confrontational, so tread with caution.

What you'll need

Although chat requires a full Internet connection, you don't really need a particularly fast connection nor a powerful computer. Ideally, you don't want to be paying **timed online charges** either, because it's another medium where, once you're hooked, you'll end up squandering hours online.

Many chatsters have free permanent connections through university or work, so they can afford to be on all day. That's one of the reasons why you'll often find **idle occupied channels**. When you enter a channel and "**beep**" **an occupant**, if they're in the vicinity of the terminal, they should answer. It's also possible they could be chatting or lurking in other channels, reading email, on the Web, or playing an online game, so give them time to respond.

Net software bundles don't always include a standard IRC program. But that's no problem, because there are plenty out on the Net to download. Ircle (http://www.ircle.com) is the most popular on Macs, while mIRC (http://www.mirc.co.uk) rules on PCs. For more, check any of the major software archives in our Web guide (p.259).

Getting started

There's not much to configure on most chat programs. First, you'll need to think up a **nickname** for yourself. That's what will identify you in the channel. So if you make it something rude you can expect to be ignored. Next, you'll have to decide what to enter as your **real name** and **email address**. For the sake of privacy and to avoid potential embarrassment, try an alias first. Finally, enter a chat server address. You'll probably be offered a choice from a drop-down menu, either within your user settings or upon connecting. Experiment with a few and settle on whichever takes your fancy.

If it's not obvious where to enter your details refer to the program's Help files. In fact, it wouldn't hurt to run through any tutorials either. It might sound a bit pedestrian but it will pay off. Chat programs have an array of cryptic buttons and windows that are less intuitive than most Internet programs. And before you start randomly clicking on things to see what they do, **remember people are watching you**.

The servers

There are hundreds of open IRC hosts worldwide; many of them linked together through networks such as **Undernet** and **Efnet**. To ease the strain on network traffic, start with a **nearby host**. The best place to get a fresh list of servers, or indeed any information about IRC, is from the alt.irc newsgroup. But the quickest would be from: http://www.irchelp.org/irchelp/networks/

For starters, choose a host from your chat program's Connect Setup menu or try: us.undernet.org on port 6667.

A caution

Of all the Net's corners, IRC is the one most likely to trip up newbies – mainly because you can't hide your presence. For example, on Usenet, unless you jump in and post, no-one can tell you've been following the discussion. However, the second you arrive in an IRC channel **you'll be announced** to all and your nickname will remain in the names list for as long as you stay.

If you select someone's name in your channel, and click the right button, you'll be able to find out a little bit about them. Cross-reference that, and you might find out a little bit more. So bear in mind: others might be checking you out in the same way.

Never enter an unfamiliar command at someone else's request. At best it could be a harmless prank, but you might inadvertently hand over control of your computer. You certainly don't need that. Think we're being paranoid? Then try a Web search on "hacking IRC". If someone is bothering you privately, protest publicly. If no-one defends you, change channels. If they persist, get them kicked out by an operator.

IRC commands

IRC has **hundreds of commands**. Unless you're really keen, you'll need to know only a few. However, the more you learn, the more you can strengthen your position. You can almost get away without learning any commands at all with modern programs, but it won't hurt to know the script behind the buttons, and you may even prefer it. Your client won't automate everything, so each time you're online test a few more. The Help file should contain a full list. If not, try: http://www.connected-media.com/IRC/

There are far too many commands to list here, but those below will get you started. Note that **anything after a forward slash (/) is interpreted as a command**:

if you leave off the slash, it will be transmitted to your active channel as a message and you'll look like a dork.

```
/AWAY <message>...........................Leave message saying you're not available
/BYE ...................................................................... Exit IRC session
/CLEAR ........................................................... Clear window contents
/HELP ............................................................. List available commands
/HELP <command> ........................................... Return help on this command
/IGNORE <nickname><*><all> ..................... Ignore this nickname
/IGNORE <*><email address><all> ...................... Ignore this email address
/IGNORE <*><*><none> ............................... Delete ignorance list
/JOIN <#channel> ................................................... Join this channel
/KICK <nickname> ......................................... Boot this nickname off channel
/LEAVE <#channel> ...................................... Exit this channel
/LIST <-MIN n> ................................... List channels with minimum of n users
/MOP ............................................... Promote all to operator status
/MSG <nickname><message> .......... Send private message to this nickname
/NICK <nickname> ...................................... Change your nickname
/OP <nickname> ......................................... Promote this nickname to operator
/PING <#channel> ............................................ Check ping times to all users
/QUERY <nickname> ............. Start a private conversation with this nickname
/TOPIC <new topic> .......................................... Change channel topic
/WHO* .................................................... List users in current channel
/WHOIS <nickname> .............................................. Display nickname's identity
/WHOWAS <nickname> ............................. Display identity of exited nickname
```

Step by step through your first session

By now, you've configured your client, chosen a nickname you'll never use again, and are raring to go. The aim of your first session is to connect to a server, have a look around, get a list of channels, join one, see who's on, say something public, then something private, leave the channel, start a new channel, make yourself operator, change the topic, and then exit IRC. The whole process should take no more than about ten minutes. Let's go.

✦ Log on to a server and wait to be accepted. If you're not, keep trying others until you succeed. Once aboard, you'll be greeted with the MOTD (message of the day) in the server window. Read the message and see if it tells you anything interesting.

✦ You should have at least two windows available. One for input, the other to display server output. Generally, the two windows form part of a larger window, with the input box below the output box. Even though your client's point and click interface will replace most of the basic commands, since you probably haven't read its manual yet, you won't know how to use it. So instead just use the commands.

✦ To see what channels are available, type: **/LIST** You'll have to wait a minute and then a window will pop up, or fill up, with thousands of channels, their topics, and the number of users on them. To narrow down the list to those channels with six or more users, type: **/LIST -MIN 6** Now you'll see the busiest channels.

✦ Pick a channel at random and join it. Channel names are always preceded by #, so to join the lard channel, type: **/JOIN #lard** and then wait for the channel window to appear. (Clicking on its name should have the same effect in most programs.) Once the channel window opens, you should get a list of the channel's occupants, in yet another window. If not, type: **/WHO*** for a full list including nicknames and email addresses.

✦ Now say something clever. Type: **Hi everyone, it's great to be back!** This should appear not only on the screen in your channel window, but on the screen in every other person's channel window. Wait for replies and answer any questions as you see fit.

✦ Now it's time to send something personal. Choose someone in the channel and find out what you can about them first, by typing: **/WHO** followed by their nickname. Your client might let you do this by just double-clicking on their nickname in the names window. Let's say their nickname is Tamster. To send a private message, just type:

/MSG Tamster Hey Tamster, I'm a clueless newbie, let me know if you get this so I won't feel so stupid. If Tamster doesn't reply, keep trying until someone does. Once you're satisfied you know how that works, leave the channel by typing: /LEAVE Don't worry, next time you go into a channel, you'll feel more comfortable.

➕ Now to start your own channel. Pick any name that doesn't already exist. As soon as you leave, it will disappear. To start a channel called lancelink, just type: /JOIN #lancelink Once the window pops up, you'll find you're the only person on it. Now promote yourself to operator by typing: /OP followed by your nickname. Others can tell you have channel operator status because your nickname will appear with an @ in front of it. Now you're an operator – you have the power to kick people off the channel, change the topic, and all sorts of other things that you can find out by reading the manual as recommended. To change the topic, type: /TOPIC followed by whatever you want to change the topic to. Wait for it to change on the top of your window and then type: /BYE to exit IRC.

That's it really; a whirlwind tour but enough to learn most things you'll need. Now before you can chat with other chatsters, you'll need to speak their lingo.

The language of IRC

Just like CB radio, IRC has its own **dialect**. Chat is a snappy medium, messages are short, and responses are fast. Unlike CB, people won't ask your "20" to see where you're from but they will use **short-forms**, **acronyms**, and **smileys** (:-). Acronyms are mixed in with normal speech and range from the innocuous (BTW = by the way) to a whole panoply of blue phrases. Don't be too shocked. It's not meant to be taken seriously. And don't be ashamed to use plain English, Urdu or whatever, either. You'll stand a better chance of being understood.

For just a taste of what you might strike, see "Net Language" on (p.456).

IRC netiquette

IRC attracts a diverse bunch. You're as likely to encounter a channel full of Indian expats following a ball-by-ball cricket commentary as a couple of college kids flirting. So long as no-one rocks the boat too much, coexistence can be harmonious. Of course, there's bound to be a little mayhem now and then, but that usually just adds to the fun of the whole event.

However, some actions are generally frowned upon and may get you kicked from channels, or even banned from a server. These include dumping large files or amounts of text, harassment, vulgarity, beeping constantly to get attention, and inviting people into inappropriate channels. Finally, if you make a real nuisance of yourself, someone might be vindictive enough to track you down and make you regret it.

What's on

Although most of what goes on in IRC is spontaneous, it also plays host to loads of organized events, including **celebrity interviews and topical debates**. The big ones tend to hide behind the Online Service curtain but the Net still attracts its share. For a calendar of what's planned across all forms of Internet chat, including the structured Web-based alternatives, such as **Talk City** (http://www.talkcity.com) and **The Globe** (http://www.theglobe.com), see **Yack** (http://www.yack.com).

For a directory of themed, regularly inhabited, and most popular channels across almost 30 networks, see: http://www.liszt.com/chat/

Know who's online – ICQ and Instant Messenger

IRC, Web chat, and Online Service forums are great for meeting complete strangers, but they're not the best for talking privately amongst friends. If you'd like to corner your pals as soon as they pop online get them to grab **ICQ** (http://www.mirabilis.com) or **AOL Instant Messenger** (http://www.aol.com/aim/) which comes with Netscape Communicator. Oddly, both programs are owned by AOL.

These "**buddy lists**" are threatening email as the preferred tool for quick messages – and often lead to impromptu chat sessions if you're both online. But they can be a major source of distraction when your online chums buzz you as you're trying to work. Email puritans also mourn the dearth of deeper discourse.

Web chat

Like almost every other aspect of the Internet, chat too has moved onto the Web. About the only good thing you can say about Web chat it is that it doesn't require a special IRC program. All you need is your Web browser. Web chat is not usually as instant as IRC, as you have to wait a little while for the page to refresh to follow responses. However, if it's done through a Java or ActiveX applet, it can be just like the real thing. For a rundown of the most popular Web chat channels, see: http://www.100hot.com/chat/

Comic chat

Microsoft Chat is certainly worth a quick look. You take on a cartoon character persona, and star in a cute comic strip that's created on the fly. Even if chat's not your scene, it should keep you amused for several minutes. If you have Windows 98, you can install it from under Communications in Windows Setup, or grab the most recent version by going online and clicking on "Windows Update". Otherwise, you'll find it bundled as part of Internet Explorer or available as a standalone from:

http://www.microsoft.com/ie/chat/

And if it really takes your fancy, here's where to find power tips: http://members.tripod.com/ComicChat/

IRC games

Many IRC channels are dedicated to **games**. Sometimes you can play against other people, although more commonly you're up against programs called **bots**. Such programs are written to respond to requests in a particular way, and even learn from the experience. You'll also come across bots in standard chat channels. It might even take you some time to recognize you're not talking to a human.

For more about IRC games, see:http://www.yahoo.com/Recreation/Games/Internet_Games/

Internet telephony

The concept of using the **Internet as an alternative to the telephone network** is getting some quarters quite frisky – mainly because it can **cut the cost of calling long distance** to that of a local call plus Internet charges (at both ends). But it's an area that's well and truly in its teething phase. It works but don't expect the same fidelity, convenience, or reliability, as your local regular phone network.

To place a Net call through your computer, you need a **soundcard**, **speakers**, and a **microphone** – standard multimedia fare. If your soundcard permits duplex transmission, you can hold a regular conversation, like

an ordinary telephone; otherwise it's more like a walkie-talkie where you take turns to speak. As for your modem, 14.4 Kbps is generally ample to the task but the higher the bandwidths at each end the better your chance of decent sound quality.

Alternatively, you might look into a standalone Internet phone device such as **Aplio Phone** (http://www.aplio.com), which looks like an ordinary telephone and works similarly except it automatically initiates a call through each end's ISP. The sound is passable, albeit with slight delay, but you'll need to tally the combined cost of both party's Internet access and local call charges, and factor in the cost of the units at each end, to tell whether its cheaper than a discount calling card.

Phone programs

You have plenty of choice in **Net phone programs**. Some, like **Internet Phone**, are similar to IRC – you log into a server and join a channel. Others, such as **WebPhone**, are more like an ordinary phone and start a point-to-point connection when you choose a name from a directory. It's worth trying a few to see what works best for you.

Microsoft NetMeeting is as good as any. It has **real-time voice and video conferencing**, plus things like collaborative application sharing, document editing, background file transfer, and a whiteboard to draw and paste on. Plus it's free with Windows 98 and Internet Explorer. Grab the latest version through Windows Update or from: http://www.microsoft.com/netmeeting/

Video conferencing

You might like the idea of seeing who you're talking to, but even with ISDN connections and snazzy graphics hardware, **Internet video conferencing** is more like a slide show than real-time video. But if it means seeing live footage of a loved one across the world, perhaps it's worth it. The most popular clients are **Net-Meeting** and **CU-SeeMe** (http://www.cu-seeme.com). For more, see our "Software Roundup" section (p.425).

Chat worlds

There's no doubt virtual reality can look quite cute, but there's not much call for it. The best applications so far seem to be among the plethora of **chat worlds**, **virtual cities**, and **avatars**. These tend to work like IRC, but with an extra dimension or two. So rather than channels, you get rooms, playgrounds, swimming pools, and so forth. To switch channels, you might walk into another building or fly up into the clouds. You might be represented by an animated character rather than a text nickname and be able to do all sorts of multimedia things such as build 3D objects and play music.

This all sounds pretty futuristic and it's certainly impressive at first, but whether you'll want to become a regular is another matter. The most popular are **World's Chat** (http://www.worlds.net) and **The Palace** (http://www.thepalace.com).

If it's action and hi-tech graphics you're after, however, ditch chat, and head straight to the world of **Online Gaming**. Read on . . .

Online Gaming

Computers are entirely brainless. It doesn't take much skill to get through games like Quake II, Half-Life and War Craft in single player mode – just loads of practice. But over the Internet, playing against real people – even strangers – such games take on a whole new dimension. And things become way more serious. In fact, once you've played in multi-player mode, you'll never want to play alone again.

When home computers first appeared in the late 1970s, they weren't good for much else but games like Pong and Breakout. Back then gaming consoles and PCs sometimes let two players compete though joysticks or at either end of the keyboard. As computers became more useful in the 1980s, gaming took a back seat to business software, and game designers focused on players taking turns rather than playing together. Today, multi-player racing and martial-arts games dominate the arcade while at home, players compete on the same games by **connecting their personal computers** together. These machines needn't be in the same room. Or even in the same country. Serious gamers no longer loiter with intent in arcades – they can have more fun at home.

Multi-player capability is becoming standard in most new games, and not just in the action genre. Almost any computer game that can be played by two or more people can be played online – from Snakes and Ladders up. Current hot numbers include: Age of Empires, Com-

manche 3, Caesar's Palace Virtual Casino, ChessMaster 5000, CivNet, War Craft, Diablo, Hornet FA-18, Kingpin, Marathon, Monopoly, Myth 2, NetStorm, Panzer General, Quake II, Tomb Raider II, Total Annihilation, Unreal, and You Don't Know Jack. And some, such as Netwar, Ultima Online, Starsiege Tribes, Team Fortress, Quake Arena, FireTeam, and Unreal Tournament can only be played online.

Finding opponents

To bring in another player to a computer game, you'll need to connect to their machine. The simplest way is via a **serial link**. Just run a null modem cable between your serial ports. It's a fast connection, and quick to set up, but restricts it to two players at cable's length apart. The same can be done over a **telephone line**, using modems or ISDN terminal adapters. Again it links only two players and is limited by the speed of the modem.

To conscript more victims, you need a proper network. A **local area network (LAN)** is best. That's where you connect all the machines via network cards and cables. It doesn't cost much to set up at home, though everyone will have to bring their machines round. Easier still is to use a LAN at work. Just be sure to invite your boss to play, and lessen the flak if you crash the network.

A far easier way to find new opponents, or someone to play you at 4am, is to chime into a public network – such as the **Internet**.

The problem with Internet gaming

Although it's by far the easiest way to meet other players, the Net has its drawbacks for games that require split-second reactions. **Latency** is the biggest issue. That's the length of time it takes data to reach its destination. If it takes too long, it makes a fast game such as Quake unplayable. Then there's **packet loss** – that's where segments of data fail to reach the other end and must be retransmitted. This has the same effect as high latency.

Game designers are now writing latency correction algorithms, which attempt to predict likely moves. The first, built into **QuakeWorld**, works better than you might imagine. However, players with lower latency times, usually those close to the server, will always be at a distinct advantage, giving the game an inbuilt bias.

On the plus side, those who play on their ISP's server or on a non-Internet dial-in server are hardly affected by latency.

What you'll need

And now for the really bad news: 3D games (and these are the most popular), appreciate every bit of speed you can throw at them. If you want to win, you'll need to be more than just a quick draw on the mouse. You'll need a fat connection, a fast processor, plenty of RAM, and most of all, **3D video acceleration**. At the time of writing, the fastest video boards are those bearing nVidia's RIVA TNT 2 chip.

Until recently, serious gamers shunned Macs, due to their substandard 3D graphic support. Consequently, games developers have been concentrating on the greater PC market. Mac versions often appear months after the PC release, if at all. In gaming terms, that makes the platform about as fashionable as last year's top 40. Thankfully, Apple has finally recognized the demand, and beefed up its 3D capabilities. So while PCs still lead in gaming technology, Macs aren't too far behind. It's yet to be seen whether it's too little, too late, to result in more Mac games and earlier releases, but it's unlikely to get worse.

So let's play

Once you're armed, online and ready to duel, you'll need to track down some willing chumps. That's usually not too hard, but how you go about it depends on what game you're playing. If it won't let you start midway, you'll need to meet in some kind of lobby and wait for a game to start. Otherwise, you only need find the nearest available game and jump aboard. A few of the newer games such as **Starseige Tribes** include inbuilt support for finding, and chatting to, opponents, but most require a third-party program.

The best way to start is to download **GameSpy** (http://www.gamespy.com) and **Kali** (http://www.kali.net). These programs enable you to find the closest games, with the lowest lag times, and then automate the connections.

If these don't cater to your game, you might like to investigate some of the **commercial networks**. For example, Mplayer (http://www.mplayer.com), Heat (http://www.heat.net), MSN Gaming Zone (http://www.zone.com), Ten (http://www.ten.net), and World Opponent Network (http://www.won.net) provide Internet-accessible game servers. You log in via your ISP or Online Service, sometimes paying a premium above your regular Internet access charges. In turn your ISP may give priority to your gaming traffic to help smooth play. Then there are **dial-up networks** set aside solely for gaming, such as Wireplay (UK & Aust) (http://www.wireplay.com).

Almost all **Online Services** and many **ISPs** also have local gaming servers for exclusive customer use. Ask when you sign up for access. Some game software houses also set up their own **game servers** as part of the product package, such as **Battle.net** (http://www.battle.net) for Diablo and **Bungie.net** (http://www.bungie.net) for Myth 2.

Quake

id Software's **Quake** was the first major game designed primarily for online play. Over a network, it's usual to switch off the 'monsters' and fight with or against other players. Serious Quakers form clans, complete with their own custom-designed outfits, called skins. Clan members compete side by side against other clans or individuals.

Quake II comes with its own Netplay support for up to 64 players. For more see http://www.bluesnews.com and http://www.stomped.com

Team play

The most recent trend is not to pit you against the world, but to **join a team**. The first generation of team play arrived in Quake's Team Fortress add-on, which enabled you to choose a team, pick a character type, and battle with your team against one or more opposing teams. The mission usually being to capture the enemy's flag. In Myth and Myth2, you can follow a commander who assigns warriors and determines team strategy. Of course, whether you choose to follow their instructions is up to you. Most gamers find team play considerably more rewarding than the old school splatterfests.

Breaker, breaker!

Want to chat with your teammates or opponents as you play? Try **Roger Wilco** (http://www.resounding.com). It works like an Internet telephone, but uses so few resources it shouldn't interfere with your game.

Where to find the real twist tops

Remember those ancient **text-based games** where you'd stumble around imaginary kingdoms looking for hidden objects, uttering magic words, and slaying unicorns? Believe it or not, they're still going strong on the Net. Admittedly, they've come a long way, and blended with the whole Dungeons and Dragons caper, but they're still mostly text-based.

What sets them apart from conventional arcade games is the community spirit. Within each game, participants develop **complex alter egos** enabling them to live out their fantasies and have them accepted within the group. But it can also become an obsession where **the distinction between an alter ego and the self becomes blurred,** and players retreat into the reassurance of the game. If they're dialing in from a home account, it can also cost. In other words, it's about as geeky as it gets. If that sounds your bag, see http://www.godlike.com/muds/ and the newsgroup hierarchies: alt.mud and rec.games.mud

Somewhat up the evolutionary ladder graphically, but along similar lines, **Ultima Online**, the latest in the Ultima fantasy series, throws you into a continuous, evolving virtual world, complete with day and night. The idea is to create not only a battleground, but a social community for thousands of players. Again, unlike strictly competitive games, the object is to play a role and belong rather than win. See http://www.owo.com

For games – and more info

Although you'll come across simple games such as chess, cards or backgammon that you can play through a Web interface, the best games are way too big to download as a Java applet. They're so big you might even balk at downloading demo versions from the Web. Check out the **Specialist gaming magazines**, such as PC Gamer (http://www.pcgamer.com), PCPlayer (http://www.netgamer.net), PC Zone (http://www.pczone.com). They're often the best place to find out what's hot in online gaming. Not just because gaming companies send them software evaluations early, but because they invariably come with a free CD-ROM full of games. Although you can generally get demos off the Net sooner, with most decent games weighing in at over 20 MB, it's a worthy saving in download time. Especially when you'll flick most of them out after a few minutes.

On the Net, the best source of news and downloads are the main games Web sites (see p.304).

Creating Your Own Web Page

It won't take long exploring the Web before you'll get the itch to have a go yourself, and publish your own Web page. You don't need to be anyone particularly important, or a company with something to sell. You just need three things: something to say, some way to convert it into HTML, and somewhere to put it. Finding a location isn't too hard or expensive. The logical place would be your Access Provider's server. Better providers usually include a few megabytes' storage as part of a subscriber account. If not, we'll show you where to get it free. Though, if you're serious, you should get your own domain name and shop around for the best deal on server space.

Once you have the space, you can publish anything you like from the way you feel about your hamster to your Mad Cow con-

spiracy thesis. Or you can use it to publicize yourself, push causes, provide information, sell your products or entertain. But before you leap out of the closet and air your obsessions or money-making schemes, do check you're not breaking any laws of decency or trade. Your Web space provider will know.

How it works

Dozens of programs claim to simplify the procedure of **converting text into HTML**. These days most attempt to make it a **WYSIWYG** (What You See Is What You Get) desktop-publishing affair. However well they succeed, you'd still be advised to spend an afternoon **getting to grips with how HTML works**. The good news is that, unlike computer programming in general, it's dead easy, if rather tedious. It basically boils down to writing the page in plain text, adding formatting codes called tags (see section below), inserting instructions on how to place images, and creating links to other pages.

There's a small catch in that, like all Net protocols, HTML is under constant review – particularly by Microsoft and Netscape – so although a drawn-up standard exists, the latest **HTML enhancements** don't always work equally well on all browsers. Yes, as ever with the Net, the whole affair is quite a muddle.

Getting sorted

The quickest way to get familiar with how HTML operates is to **create a simple page from scratch**. You won't need any complex compiling software – a text editor, or word processor, will do. However, an **HTML editor** can help by automating much of the mark-up process so you don't have to type in all the tags manually.

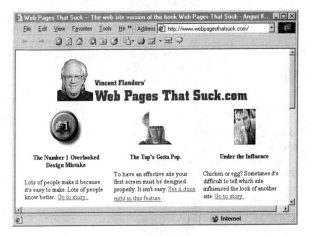

There are plenty of HTML editors, but your choices narrow down fast if you know what kind of Web pages you want to create. Some editors excel at converting word-processed documents and spreadsheets; others specialize in basic page-creation using step-by-step wizards; some score best on image manipulation and mapping; others are competent all-rounders with easy toggling between code views and page views. Experiment at first with one of the free, basic editors bundled with the full editions of either **Netscape** or **Microsoft's browsers**. Alternatively, learn HTML from scratch by using clean, friendly, free, or cheap software such as

SiteAid (http://www.siteaid.com).

Professional HTML editing programs incorporate site maintenance software which automates uploading, identifies old, key, and orphan pages, and generally eases the daunting job of managing huge sites. Most hide the HTML code behind What-You-See-Is-What-You-

Get (WYSIWYG) interfaces. Some also enable code rookies to incorporate fancy bells and whistles easily into their pages using the latest forms of HTML and JavaScript.

Small site owners don't need to shell out for these extra capabilities. But if your online publishing ambitions extend beyond a home, contact, and links page, investigate the following packages:

Microsoft FrontPage (http://www.microsoft.com/frontpage/),
HomeSite (http://www.allaire.com),
Dreamweaver (http://www.macromedia.com),
Adobe GoLive (http://www.adobe.com).

If you're serious about Web design, you'll quickly discover that not one WYSIWYG editor offers full control over HTML – and you'll eventually end up grappling with raw code. So resign yourself to learning HTML. The rest of this chapter will give you enough basic information to start experimenting.

Tags

Next time you're online, examine the HTML that makes up any Web page. Choose "View Source" from your browser menu to see the raw code. The first thing you'll notice is that the text is surrounded with comments enclosed between less-than and greater-than symbols, like this:

```
<BOLD> My budgie rocks! </BOLD>
```

These comments are known as **tags**. Most tags come in pairs and apply to the text they enclose. A forward slash signals the end of their relevance, as in: </BOLD>.

The Code

Want to make a simple Web page? Easy. Create a new blank page in a text editor, name it **test.html**, then type in the following:

```
<HTML>(identifies the document as an HTML file)
<HEAD><TITLE>(the title goes in here)</TITLE></HEAD>
<BODY>(everything else goes in here)</BODY>
</HTML>(defines the end of the document)
```

Congratulations, you've created a Web page! Note that it has two parts: a **head** and a **body**. The head contains the title, which is displayed in the top bar of your browser. The body defines what appears within the browser window. Everything else is a refinement.

Backgrounds and colors

You can specify styles and formats for the entire page by defining them within the <BODY> tag. For example, <BODY BGCOLOR="#FFFFFF"> changes the page's **background color** to #FFFFFF, the RGB (Red, Green, Blue) code for white. HTML editors work out these numbers for you. Most browsers also recognize literal words such as "blue", "red", and "purple".

You can also **define the color** of four types of text within the body tag: the standard text (TEXT="RGB"), the text that links to other documents (LINK="RGB"), the linking text that has been visited already (VLINK="RGB"), and linking text that is being clicked (ALINK="RGB"), where RGB is your chosen RGB color code.

You aggregate these definitions within the tag. So, applying all the above would look something like this:

```
<BODY BGCOLOR="#FFFFFF"
TEXT="#000000
LINK="#0000A0"
VLINK="#008000"
ALINK="#FF0000">.
```

Playing with text

To **change text size**, use:

```
<FONT SIZE="x">(text here)</FONT>
```

where x is an increment above or below a standard font
size (between "–7" and "+7"). You can also change sizes
with the **heading** tags, where <H1> is the largest heading size and <H6> is the smallest. Unfortunately, with
basic HTML, your control here is limited: the actual size
the text appears depends on the type and configuration
of the viewer's browser.

HTML ignores multiple spaces, tabs, and carriage
returns. To get around that you can **enclose text**
within the <PRE></PRE> (preformatted text) tag pair.
Otherwise, any consecutive spaces, tabs, carriage
returns, or combinations produce a single space.
However it's more conventional to **enclose para-
graphs** with <P> and </P> creating two line breaks
above and below. You can also create extra spaces
with   To create **single or multiple line breaks**,
use:

Browsers automatically **wrap text** so there's no need
to worry about page widths. To **center text** use:

```
<CENTER>(text here)</CENTER>
```

and to **indent** from both margins use:

```
<BLOCKQUOTE>(text here)</BLOCKQUOTE>
```

Three simple but effective ways to **emphasize text** are to use bold, italic (though beware; this can be hard to read on the Web), or colored type. To make text **bold**, enclose it within

    <B>(text here)</B >

To **italicize**, use: <I>(text here)</I>
To change **color**, use

    <FONT COLOR="RGB">(text here)</FONT>

where RGB is the RGB color code.

Viewing your page

To **see how your page would look on the Web**, open it up as a **local file** in your browser. Look under the File menu for "Open" or "Open Page". Alternatively, drag and drop it into your browser window. And then to **see changes while editing**, hit "Refresh".

Images

Placing **graphics** on a Web page is easy. Planning and creating them is an art form. The smaller they are in bytes and the fewer you use, the quicker your page will load. So it's wise to reduce their file size first using either an online facility like Gifcruncher (http://www.gifcruncher.com) or a file reduction program such as JPEG Optimizer (http://www.xat.com). If you have access to PhotoShop, splash out on Adobe's professional ImageReady (http://www.adobe.com). With practice, you can **reduce byte size** considerably without sacrificing quality.

The simplest way to **display an image** is to place it within the <IMG> tag, like this: <IMG SRC="(image location here)"> This displays it full size and bottom-aligned with adjacent text. The picture will appear faster if you insert dimensions between IMG and SRC. You also put page layout commands here. For example:

```
<IMG HEIGHT=300 WIDTH=400 ALIGN=TOP VSPACE=60
HSPACE=70 BORDER=100 SRC="image.gif">
```

would define image.gif as 300 pixels high by 400 wide, align its top with the tallest item in the line of adjacent text, give it a border 100 pixels wide and separate it from the text by 60 pixels vertically and 70 horizontally.

Now, before making plans for a full-screen online photo album, bear in mind that your visitors will have to wait (often considerably) for each separate image to load. That means the smaller they are, and the less of them, the faster they'll get to your text. Try to keep the combined image size under 30 KB. The worst thing you can do is embed your site directory within an imagemap so that your visitors have to wait for it to load before they can move beyond your top page. The reasons should be obvious.

Alignments

You can specify all manner of **alignments** including:

    ALIGN=right

Aligns image with left margin. Text wraps on right.

    ALIGN=left

Aligns image with right margin. Text wraps on left.

ALIGN=texttop

Aligns top of image with tallest text in line.

ALIGN=middle

Aligns the baseline of text with middle of image.

ALIGN=absmiddle

Aligns the middle of text with middle of image.

ALIGN=baseline

Aligns the bottom of image with the baseline of the current line.

ALIGN=bottom

Aligns the bottom of image with the bottom of the current line.

Plain text versions

It's good practice to include an **alternative text version** for browsers with images switched off (or with sluggish connections). To do this, insert ALT="description of image" anywhere between IMG and SRC. This is crucial if the image describes a self-contained link.

Lines

Create a **horizontal rule** using <HR> or, more precisely,

<HR WIDTH=X% ALIGN=Y SIZE=Z>, where

X is the percentage proportion of page width,
Y is its positioning (CENTER, LEFT, or RIGHT) and
Z is its thickness.
The default is 100 percent, CENTER and 1.
Or you could insert an image of a line or bar.

Lists

HTML offers three principal types of **lists: ordered, unnumbered**, and **definition**.

Ordered lists

Ordered lists are enclosed with the <OL></OL> pair. Each item preceded by <LI> is **assigned a sequential number**. For example:

> <OL> On the command, "brace! brace!":
>> On the command, "brace! brace!":
>> <LI> Extinguish cigarette
>> 1. Extinguish cigarette
>> <LI> Assume crash position
>> 2. Assume crash position
>> <LI> Stay calm
> 3. Stay calm
> </OL>

Unnumbered lists

Unnumbered lists work similarly within the <UL></UL> pair, except that <LI> **produces a bullet**:

> <UL>Suspected carcinogens
> Suspected carcinogens
> <LI>Television
> • Television
> <LI>Red gummy bears
> • Red gummy bears
> <LI>Toast
> • Toast
> </UL>

Definition lists

Definition lists are enclosed within the <DL></DL> pair.
The <DT><DD> pair **splits the list into levels**:

```
<DL>
   <DT>Best screenplay
   Best screenplay
   <DD>Eraserhead II, Son of Henry
   Eraserhead II, Son of Henry
   <DT>Best lead actor
   Best lead actor
   <DD>Chow Yun Fat, Duke Nukem
   Chow Yun Fat, Duke Nukem
</DL>
```

Links

The whole idea of HTML is to add a third dimension to
documents by **linking them to other pages**. This is
achieved by embedding **clickable hot-spots** to redirect
visitors to other addresses. A hot-spot can be attached to
text, icons, buttons, lines, or even images. Items containing links usually give an indication of where the link
goes, but the address itself is normally concealed. Most
browsers reveal this address when you pass your mouse
over the link.

You can direct hot-spots to anywhere on the Net.
Here's how to:

Create a link to another Web site

<A HREF="http://www.roughguides.com">Rough Guides</A>
Clicking on "Rough Guides" would load the Web page at:
   http://www.roughguides.com

Create a link to a local page

```
<A HREF="trap.html">Step this way</A>
```

If the file trap.html is in the same directory as the file which links to it, clicking on "Step this way" will launch it.

Embed links in images

```
<A HREF="fish.html"><IMG SRC="fish.gif"></A>
<A HREF="bigfish.gif"><IMG SRC="fish.gif"></A>
```

In both cases, the locally stored image fish.gif contains the hot-spot. The first case launches the local Web page fish.html while the second would display bigfish.gif, which could be a different image – for example a more detailed version of fish.gif

Invite mail

```
<A HREF="mailto:bigflint@texas.net">bigflint@texas.net</A>
```

Clicking on "bigflint@texas.net" brings up the viewer's email program, with the email address field automatically filled in. Although you don't have to, it's best to spell out the full email address in the visible text, since the link won't work with all browsers.

Route to a newsgroup

```
<A HREF="news:alt.elvis.sighting">Find Elvis</A>
```

Clicking on "Find Elvis" would bring up articles in the alt.elvis.sighting newsgroup.

Commence a Telnet session

```
<A HREF="telnet://pctravel.com">PCTravel</A>
```

If the browser is configured to launch a Telnet client, clicking on "PCTravel" would initiate a Telnet session with pctravel.com

Log in to an anonymous FTP server

```
<A HREF="ftp://ftp.bennett.com/paul/packet.exe">Packet Plus</A>
<A HREF="ftp://ftp.microsoft.com/">Microsoft</A>
```

Clicking on "Packet Plus" would commence the download of packet.exe while clicking on "Microsoft" would bring up a listing of the root directory of ftp.microsoft.com

But wait, there's more

Once you're comfortable with HTML logic, you can glean advanced techniques by **analyzing other Web pages or plundering their code**. Just find a page you like and from your browser menu, call up "View Source". You can cut and paste selections into your own pages, or save the file and tweak it with a text or HTML editor.

That's about all you'll need to know in about 90 percent of cases, but if you're adventurous there are no bounds to the things you can do with a Web page. At the first level there are dozens more (fairly straightforward) tags to create **tables, frames, forms, moving text,** and assorted tricks. Then there are multimedia options such as **audio, video, animation,** and **virtual reality**. And at the top level there's **form processing** and **interactive pages**.

As you move up the levels of sophistication, you'll start to move out of the basic HTML domain, into DHTML, XML and more complex **scripting and programming languages** such as **JavaScript, ActiveX, Java, PERL, CGI,** and **Visual Basic**. You may also need access to the special class of storage space reserved for Web programs, known as the **cgi-bin directory**.

If you see a feature you like, and you can't work out how it's done by looking at the source code, ask the site's Webmaster, or search the Web for a good DIY document. There are plenty of books on the subject, but beware, the technology's moving so fast that they date instantly.

Java

Among the most over-hyped things to hit the Web in the past few years is **Java**. It's not a mark-up code like HTML, but a hard-core programming language designed to be interpreted by any computer. That makes it perfect for the Web as you can place an **applet** (Java program) on your site and activate it from your Web page. Netscape Navigator and Internet Explorer have in-built Java interpreters, so visitors don't need any extra software to view it. As for writing applets yourself; if you think C++ is a laugh, it's probably right up your alley. Good luck.

JavaScript

JavaScript, a Netscape innovation, extends the Java concept to HTML. Because it sits entirely within the HTML of the Web page, you can pinch the code from other pages, just like regular HTML. It can add tricks, which are usually just that: tricks. But if you want to, say, create personalized messages for each visitor to your site, display a clock, or spawn twenty pop-up windows, look at **Javascripts.com** (http://www.javascripts.com) and **WebCoder** (http://www.webcoder.com). Just keep in mind that most of your visitors would rather you didn't.

Free Web space

Need some free Web space for your handiwork? Then visit **Free Web space** (http://www.freewebspace.net) for overviews of free sites. Or head straight to the grand-daddies of vanity publishing: **Tripod** (http://www.tripod.com), **GeoCities** (http://www.geocities.com) and **Fortune City** (http://www.fortunecity.com)

You'll get all the space you'll need there plus free homebuilding tools to make the process of editing and uploading pages a breeze. The catch, in case you're wondering, is pop-up windows advertising your host's services, varying levels of support and performance, and dubious site lifespans.

Be king of your own domain

Say you run a shop called Top Clogs and you'd like to flog your clogs over the Web. Don't even consider an address like: http://members.tripod.com/~clogs/topclogs.htm to be taken seriously; only http://www.topclogs.com will do.

Before you make any plans check

Websitez (http://www.websitez.com) **to be sure your name's not already taken**. Once that's established, you'll need to pay for three things: **to register a domain name**; the use of two **domain name servers** to direct traffic to wherever your site's located; and the right to store your pages on someone's **Web server** (unless you have your own). You can register the name by approaching the orignal registration body **Internic** (http://www.internic.net) or **name specialists** such as **NetNames** (http://www.netnames.com). Alternatively **Register.com** (http://www.register.com) is a particularly good deal as it will register you at Internic through a friendlier form, supply the required **temporary DNS details** and store your address until you're ready to use it without charging a premium over Internic's standard rate. It's wise not to submit your primary email address as you can expect a little junk email advertising Web services in return.

Once you have your address, you can point it towards your Web space. You'll find this whole procedure confusing the first time, so it's a good idea to have your Web space provider look after the operation. If you're shopping for space, try your ISP first and compare it with the prices and services listed at http://www.tophosts.com and http://www.findahost.com. Check out the bandwidth and phone support thoroughly. You don't want to be stuck on a slow server and you want to be able to talk to support staff at the busiest times of day. Generally the best deals are located in the US. However, it helps to locate close to your target audience as your pages will load quicker.

Your own Web or FTP server

Once your computer's connected to the Net, it can also act as a **Web** or **File Transfer Protocol (FTP) server**, just by running the right software. You can even run your own server on a regular dial-up account, though of course your pages or files will only be accessible while you're online. And if you're using PPP, you'll have a different IP address each time you log in, so you won't be able to pass it on until you're online. This is functional enough if you just want to demo a couple of Web pages to a colleague or friend. However, if you want a serious Web presence, you'll need a permanent connection to run your own server.

Servers are remarkably simple to install – read the Help file and you'll be up within half an hour. But take the time to set up your **security options** to allow only appropriate access to appropriate directories. That means things like making your Web pages read-only and your FTP incoming write-only. Otherwise you might get hacked.

Uploading your site

The most common way to deliver files to a Web server is by FTP. Hence, the pricier HTML editing packages normally incorporate an FTP-uploading facility. They also usually synchronize the content to ensure you have the same files live and locally, as well as check for broken links and dead files.

If yours doesn't, and you're building a serious site, it's worth getting an advanced FTP client like **FTP Voyager** (http://www.ftpvoyager.com) and a **link validator** such as **Alert Linkrunner** (http://www.alertbookmarks.com/lr/). This combination will cater to a variety of servers, sites, directory structures, HTML editors and uploads.

How to publicize your site

Once you've published your page and transferred it to your server, the real problems begin. How do you **get people to visit it?**

Before you crank up the publicity campaign, consider how you'd find such a site yourself and whether, if you stumbled across it, you'd bother stopping or returning. Most of all, decide whether publicity now would be good, or whether teething problems need to be solved before you take out **full-page adverts in *The New York Times*.**

On a basic level, most people will arrive at your site by taking a **link from another site** or by **typing in the URL**. That means if other pages link to yours, or people can find your address written somewhere, you'll stand a chance of getting traffic. Look around the Web for sites of parallel interest to your own and send them email suggesting **reciprocal links**. Most will oblige.

The best publicity machines of all are the **search engines and directories**. Before you submit your URL to them (and you should), find out how they work. Establishing whether they accept brief reviews, if they scan your page for key words, or if they index your site in full. For how they tick, see Search Engine Watch at http://www.searchenginewatch.com

Whether you register or not, the biggest search engines should eventually find your site. You can skew their results in your favor by putting the appropriate key words and phrases in the <head> of your HTML pages in the following format:

<TITLE>A few words that succinctly describe your pages</TITLE>
<META NAME="DESCRIPTION" CONTENT="A sentence which introduces your site when it appears in a search listing.">
<META NAME="KEYWORDS" CONTENT="words and phrases which describe every aspect of your site">

To test your meta tags, try: http://www.webpromote.com

To save time tracking down all the various engines, several services such as

Addme! (http://www.addme.com),

Broadcaster (http://www.broadcaster.co.uk) and

Net Submitter (http://www.suzton.com/SubmitSpider/)

will **send your details to multiple engines and directories** at once. And if what you're doing is **new**, ask Yahoo to create you a new category. Once you've done all that, the online tool, **RankThis!** (http://rankthis.webpromote.com), can tell you how you're ranked, though for a fuller service you'll want to invest in

Web Position Agent (http://www.webposition.com).

Next, generate some off-Web interest. Announce your site in relevant **newsgroups and mailing lists**. You can get away with posting the same message periodically in Usenet, and as many times as you like if it's part of a signature file, but don't post to a mailing list unless you have something new to say.

Don't forget about the old world, either. **Include the URL** on your stationery, business cards, and in all your regular advertising. And flash it in front of everyone you can. Finally, if it's really newsworthy, send a press release to whatever media might be interested. And just quietly, it mightn't hurt to throw a party, invite some journos, and wave some free merchandise about.

But before you tell anyone, install a behind-the-scenes **visitor counter** (see http://www.getscript.com). Now you've built it, see if they come.

Where to next?

For more about HTML, Web programming, and publicity, try the following sites:

WebMonkey (http://www.webmonkey.com)
Web Developer's Virtual Library (http://www.stars.com)
CNET's Builder.com (http://www.builder.com)
Developer.com (http://www.developer.com)
Link Exchange (http://www.linkexchange.com)

You should find everything you need either on or linked to these sites, while for HTML editors see our "Software Roundup" (see p.425). And to check your site's health, for example how it looks in different browsers and whether all the links work. drop in to the **Web Site Garage** (http://www.websitegarage.com).

On the Road

Wherever you travel, if you can get to a phone line, you can get to your email. Unlike a phone number, fax number, or postal address, you can take your email address anywhere, picking up and sending your mail as if you were at home. Read on and we'll show how the Internet can liberate you from your desk.

Going portable

Anyone who's serious about work mobility has a **laptop (notebook) computer**, often as a desktop replacement. After all, almost anything you can do on a desktop you can do on a portable. And although at present they're still more expensive than their bulkier equivalents – and lag slightly in chip, video, and sound technology – that margin is rapidly closing. When shopping around, here are a few things to look out for:

Weight: No matter how small a laptop might seem in the shop, it's a different experience carrying it over your shoulder for a few hours. Get one that's thin and light.

Power: If you plan to use it on a plane, in your car, or anywhere away from a power socket, go for long battery life (lithium ion is best) and consider a spare. Also ensure your power adapter supports dual voltage (100-240 V and 50/60 HZ). They usually do, but check anyway.

Modem: A built-in modem's an added bonus, but PCM-CIA models sometimes have better specs, plus you can swap them between machines. Make sure it supports V.90 and that it'll work with a cellular phone. There are also several PC cards that combine a **cellular phone and modem**, if that sounds useful.

Something most travelers don't consider is whether their modem is approved internationally. Technically, you could be breaking the law if you're caught using a non-approved modem. If you're trotting the globe, check out 3Com's Global Modem PC cards. They have built in digital line guards, tax impulse filtering, widespread approval, and software to tweak your modem to the tastes of almost every country's telephone network. See: http://www.3com.com

Network card: Modems are convenient but nowhere near as fast or as cheap as hooking into a corporate network. If you're on business, visiting a branch office, ask the IT manager to fill in your network settings. Now, that's luxury but only practical if you plan to spend extended time there. Otherwise it's back to the phone jack.

Warranty: Having a notebook go down with all your mail and data onboard is one of life's least rewarding experiences. If you can have a replacement shipped to you anywhere in the world the minute you have problems you'll never regret having paid a bit extra.

Scaling down

If the risk of having your technological triumph shorted by tropical rain, or filched from your daypack, makes your skin creep, look at taking something smaller and/or cheaper. Exactly what, depends on how small or cheap you want to go, and why you need it. There are plenty of options, but many are little more than expensive novelties.

You can reduce size and weight without losing features, by moving towards **sub-notebooks** and **palmtops** that can run Windows programs. Don't expect big savings though. If price is the key, or you just need a powerful organizer, try something like the **Psion Organiser**, **3Com Palm Pilot**, or one of the many other **PDAs**, which combine basic office programs with Net connectivity, and can upload later to your main machine.

Scaling down further, you can collect your email, and surf the Web (just), with a **Nokia 9000 mobile phone**. Or, if you only need to receive mail, see what your local paging services have to offer. These, however, work only within one country.

Wireless access

While you can hook GSM-ready PC card modems to cellular phones and dial your Access Provider, it's slow and usually prohibitively expensive. A better option is to connect your Palm Pilot, Notebook, or PDA to a dedicated wireless ISP through a CDPD (Cellular Digital Packet Data) PC card or similar device. Rates and services vary, but it's not hard to find unlimited access for a reasonable monthly charge. Well, in the US anyway. The rest of the world hasn't quite caught on yet. For more see:

http://www.goamerica.com
http://www.airbridge.com
http://www.novatelwireless.com
http://www.metricom.com
http://www.wirelessweek.com
http://www.wirelesstoday.com

An address that moves with you

Road Trip '97

Once you have a **reliable fixed email address**, no matter where you roam, people can reach you. Put it on your business card and say, "If you want a swift reply, email me." You might shift house, business, city, or country, but your email address need never change, so, take care when choosing your address as it might become your virtual home for years to come. For more on email addresses, see (p.116). Here's how to use the various types on the move:

POP3 and IMAP

Almost all ISP mail accounts these days are **POP3** (ask your provider if you're unsure), which means that if you can get onto the Internet, you should be able to collect your mail.

If you're taking **your computer** with you, it's doubly easy. You mightn't even have to change your mail settings – only your dial-up configuration, and possibly your outgoing mailserver.

To collect mail using an email program on **another computer**, you need to enter your **user name**, your **incoming mail server** address, and your **password**, when prompted. To send email you also need to enter your **identity** (who you want your mail to appear it's come from) and your **return address** (your email address). Although you can sometimes use your regular **outgoing mailserver** address, you'll get a faster response if you use the one maintained by the ISP through whom you're dialing. So if the machine you're using has one set, leave it be.

If your connection's slow or difficult, you can **configure your mail program** to download the first 1 KB or so of each message and then select which you want to read. Alternatively, if your mailserver supports **IMAP** (a superior form of POP mail which allows you to manage mail on the server – again, ask your provider), you can download just the headers. So when you're up in a plane paying 14¢ per second to download at 2400 bps you can leave all those massive mail list digests for later.

One day, you'll also be thankful that you **maintain an alternative address for priority mail**.

Webmail

With **Webmail accounts** such as **Hotmail** and **YahooMail**, you can send and collect email on any machine with access to the Web. If you don't already have an account, stop by their sites (see p.116 – "Get your free email address here") and you'll be granted one free, right away.

What makes Webmail so different, is no matter what computer you're on, you won't need to change any settings; you just log into your account using a Web browser. Plus, you can scan through your headers first and retrieve only what interests you.

The problem with Webmail is that you need Web access, which can make things slow or impossible over low bandwidth connections. It also has zero prestige – if that's an issue – so try not to use a Webmail address as your permanent business address.

This easiest way to collect your POP3 mail

If you're using a machine only briefly, you needn't tamper with the email program. You can do it all through the Web. You can configure Hotmail to collect your POP3 mail and retain the headers in your mailbox. It's worth setting up a dummy account just for this purpose, and forgetting about it until you need it. Alternatively, if you're in a real hurry, try MailStart (http://www.mailstart.com). Just enter your **long email address*** and password to collect your mail on the fly.

Messages aren't deleted from the server so they'll still be there next time you collect.

* Your long email address is your mail account name @ your incoming mailserver name. For example, the long email email address of angus@easynet.co.uk is angus@mail.easynet.co.uk (mail.easynet.co.uk is the incoming mailserver address)

CompuServe's global connection

CompuServe's biggest drawcard is its globally scattered **dial-up points**. You can dial in direct to a CompuServe number in pretty much any country in the world.

Hats off to CompuServe, too, for providing an extra and bizarre way to collect your mail. You can call a toll-free number, punch in your account number and PIN, and have your **mail selectively read back to you over the phone**. This service also doubles as an international phone calling card. In CompuServe, GO Globalconnect

Converting CompuServe to POP3 mail

Apart from being impersonal and hard to remember, the biggest problem with CompuServe's numbered mail is that you can't collect it through an Internet mail program such as Outlook Express or Messenger. So not only do you miss out on the latest mail advances like HTML and encryption, it's not easy to pick up from another machine. Thankfully, that's been solved with its parallel introduction of POP3 mail.

Converting your account requires changing your email number to a personal name, activating a new POP3 account, and redirecting your old account if required. Just follow the instructions at GO Popmail or http://www.csi.com/communications/ That will you give you two addresses: one ending in compuserve.com, the other in csi.com If you wish, you can continue to collect the former as before. Call support if you're unsure.

AOL Netmail

You can now collect your AOL mail from any computer by firing up your Web browser and pointing it at:
http://www.aol.com/netmail/

Telnet

Many universities and workplaces don't maintain POP3 mail accounts. If that applies to you, you might have to use **Telnet** to log in. Once you get over the indignity of not being able to point and click, it's not so bad. You can access Telnet in Windows 95/98 by opening **Run** on the **Start** menu and typing telnet. Collecting this way will involve logging into your mail server over the Net, supplying identification, then typing commands into a UNIX mail program. **You can also read your POP3 email by Telnetting to your mailserver** on port 110 (you'll have to add this in manually in Windows), entering user then your user name, pass then your password, and list to list your messages. To read messages selectively, type retr followed by the message's number. This can be handy when you're operating over a very low bandwidth or limited by software, for example with a palmtop. Ask your ISP or systems manager for further instructions.

How to stay connected

Keeping in touch needn't mean expensive long-distance calls home to your provider. It's possible to travel the world on a single **ISP account**, dialing locally wherever you are. Depending on your deal and where you travel between, that should work out considerably cheaper – though if you need to dial in only every few days, then calling long distance with a discount calling card may be both practical and economical. Only you can tell what suits you best, but these are your most likely options:

Cybercafés and Net terminals

When you're traveling without hardware you have to use someone else's machine. If you can't get to one through a friend or work, look for somewhere to rent Internet time. That's most commonly available through so-called **cybercafés**. These are basically coffee shops or bars, with a few Net-connected terminals up for public use. Lately, though, the concept of mixing cakes, coffee, and computers is giving way to **communication centers** complete with fax, discount phones, and printing. Whatever the case, you can generally buy half-hour blocks of Net time.

If you're new to the Net, these also make the ideal places to test-drive it under supervision. Or if you're after a temporary account on your travels they can point you to a provider. Most of all, though, they're an easy access point to do your email, and coincidentally meet other wired travelers.

Whether you're using a cybercafé or someone else's computer, the procedure is the same. Either open the browser and do your stuff through Mailstart or Hotmail (see p.116) or look for a **mail program**. In the latter case, open the settings, and fill out your details as described earlier (under "POP3" – see p.230). Then set it to "leave mail on server", and "CC" yourself everything you send. That way when you get back to your main machine, and download for the first time, you'll have a record of all your correspondence. Once you've finished, delete all your mail (don't forget the "sent" box), and change the settings back.

To **find a cybercafé** before you leave, try Yahoo or the following directories:

The Cybercafe Search Engine
(http://www.cybercative.com)

Internet Café Guide
   (http://www.netcafeguide.com)
Cybercafés of Europe
   (http://eyesite.simplenet.com/eurocybercafes/)
Cybercafe Guide
   (http://www.netcafes.com)

Even easier, just ask at any backpacker's guesthouse once you arrive. Even if there's only one cybercafé in town, you can bet it will be close to the main tourist district. And keep your eye out for **Netbooths** in places like airports, major hotels, or shopping malls. They're like public phones, except with a computer screen instead of escort ads.

National ISPs

Most of the **ISPs in our directory** (see p.474) have national coverage or at least multiple dial-up points across a country. But this doesn't mean they'll have local call access everywhere – it may be restricted to major urban areas. Before you sign with a provider, ensure it covers your territory at local call rates. Many ISPs, particularly in the US and Australia, have a national number charged at a higher rate. Check that first and do your sums. All our listed UK providers have local call access throughout Britain.

International ISPs

Several **Online Services** and **ISPs** have **international points of presence** (POPs). These include:

AOL: Although AOL has POPs in more than 100 countries, many are serviced by third-party networks. Outside the UK, North America, Australia, and select European cities, you'll be hit with a surcharge. For full details, log onto AOL and type Global

APC: Set up mainly to link non-governmental organizations and social activists worldwide, APC is represented by GreenNet in the UK, IGC in the US, and Pegasus in Australia. APC members in more far-flung places like Ethiopia might not have full Internet access, but you could get your mail forwarded if you plan ahead. See: http://www.apc.org

CompuServe: Nothing will get you up and running faster when you land in a new city than a CompuServe account. Like AOL, though, it relies on a variety of networks once you stray a little. Once again, pricing varies between countries. It's never going to be as cheap as a local ISP but you can treat it like any ISP, forgo its software, and dial through, say, Windows Dial-up Networking. However, at the time of writing, not all countries offer full IP, and some require a different dial-up script. If you intend to visit any such countries you'd better keep a CIM installation CD handy. Then it's just a matter of picking the network from a drop-down menu. Of course, if it's not full IP you won't be able to browse the Web, or pick up your POP3 mail. But you will be able to use compuserve.com mail. Best to do your research before you set out. You'll find all you need to know at: GO Phones

EUNet: The leading Europe-based ISP, EUNet maintains local POPs in over 150 countries. Charges are US$40.00 or around £24.00 sterling, for the first 90 minutes then 12¢, or around 7p, per minute thereafter. See http://traveller.eu.net

IBM Internet Connection: Big Blue subscribers get full reciprocal Internet access in over 50 countries – though charges vary between regions. Outside the US, it's aimed more at the corporate user so don't expect a cheery welcome. See http://www.ibm.net

Microsoft Network: MSN has scaled back its operation worldwide and now offers reciprocal access only in the US, UK, and Japan. For access numbers, see http://free.msn.com/msncom/numbers/

Netcom: Local call access is offered throughout much of North America, and the entire UK, plus global roaming through iPass (see below). More details at http://www.netcom.com and http://www.netcom.net.uk

Prodigy: With ventures in China, Africa and Latin America, you'd expect reciprocal access from Prodigy; however, as yet it hasn't been announced. At this stage, it's restricted to North America. If you're venturing into the regions above, though, it might be worth calling to see if you can secure a local account before you leave. See http://www.prodigy.com

UUNet: UUNet/Pipex Dial subscribers can pay extra for a month (or more) reciprocal international access – in selected cities in North America, Europe, Australia, and Asia. For more, see http://www.dial.pipex.com/services/roaming/

Global roamers

Another way of ensuring international access is to join an ISP that belongs to a **global roaming group**. This means you can dial into any ISP in the group. You'll be charged by the minute for the convenience which is fine for email but if you plan to surf the Web abroad, it might be better value signing up with a local. See **GRIC** (http://www.gric.com) and the **i-Pass** Alliance (http://www.ipass.com) for their lists of participating ISPs.

Jacking in

No matter what your account, you'll get nowhere fast if you can't **get your modem talking** to the phone system. This is where it can get a bit technical, especially when you're abroad, so be prepared to roll up your sleeves. Here's what you should know:

Foreign plugs

If you think the variety of power plugs is crazy, wait until you travel Europe with a laptop and modem. There are six different varieties of phone jacks in Germany alone. Nevertheless, thanks to wired travelers, the US **RJ11 plug** is becoming somewhat of a world standard. Trouble is, some countries use this plug but connect the two wires to different pins. So, before you set out, get a **lead/adapter** that plugs into your modem at one end with a US-wired RJ11 plug/socket at the other. As long as you travel with this setup, you'll have no trouble finding an adapter at a local airport, electrical store, or market. To prepare in advance, grab a plug bundle such as TeleAdapt's Laptop Lifeline (http://www.teleadapt.com).

Dial tone detect

It's a rare modem that's smart enough to recognize every foreign dial tone, and if it's been instructed to **wait for a tone before dialing**, you mightn't get anywhere. If dial tone errors persist, or your modem refuses to dial, switch this setting off. It's usually as simple as checking a box in your dialer. If not, you'll need to insert the **Hayes command X1** into the modem's initialization string. Refer to your modem manual for more on initialization strings.

Then there is the question of **pulse or tone**? Pick up a phone and dial. If it sends beeps, set it to tone dialing. If it makes clicking sounds, set it to pulse.

Manual dialing

Sometimes you need to dial with a **phone in parallel**. For example, if you have to go through an operator or calling card company, or if the phone system won't recognize your modem's tones. If that's the case, **turn the dial detect off** and set it to dial a short number, say 123. Have it ready to dial with one key press or mouse click. Now, dial your provider with the phone. When the other modem answers, press or click to fire off your dialer. As soon as you hear the two modems handshaking, hang up the phone and you'll be away.

Public phones

In the US, Australia, and Asia (though rarely at present in Europe), an increasing number of phones at airports, convention centers, and hotel lobbies have **modem ports** – generally RJ11 sockets. If not you can use an

acoustic coupler, which you just strap over the handset. **Roadwarrior** (http://www.warrior.com) and **TeleAdapt** have units that will transfer at up to 28.8 Kbps.

If the handset has a carbon microphone, give it a tap first to loosen the grains, but don't expect better than 2400 bps. However you connect, you'll need to dial manually (see above).

Planes

Don't set your hopes too high on surfing the Net at 35,000 feet. Yes, with the wide-scale introduction of satellite telephony in planes, it's possible. But, at present it's limited to a speed of 2400 bps, with 9600 bps some way on the horizon. At a cost up to US$10.00, or around £6.00 sterling, per minute, you'd use it only for the most urgent email.

Digital PBX

Most offices and hotels run their own **internal PBX phone systems**. What matters to you is whether the extensions are hooked to the exchange using **digital** or **analogue** techniques. If it's digital, your modem won't like it. At worst, it could turn to toast. You can't always tell at first, so when you're shopping for a PCMCIA modem, look for one with a **digital line guard**. If you strike a digital system, look around for an alternative line. Try the fax line, for starters. Otherwise, you might need an acoustic coupler or a device like TeleAdapt's **TeleSwitch** or Road Warrior's **Modem Doubler** to tap you in between the handpiece and the phoneset.

Hard wiring

More often than not, hotel phones are wired directly into wall sockets. If you don't have an acoustic coupler, you'll have to tap in. In that case, before you set out, pick up a **telephone line tester** and a **short patch cord** with an RJ11 female socket at one end and a pair of alligator clips on the other. You can get both from TeleAdapt, Road Warrior, or any good computer store. If you can't get a patch cord it's easy enough to make – just find an extension lead, cut off the male end, and crimp clips to the right two wires (usually the red and green, but use your line tester for confirmation). You'll find clips at any electronic store.

When you're ready to operate, fish around for something to unscrew that will expose wires. Inside the mouthpiece is sometimes a good bet. Once you've tapped in, check the polarity with the line tester. Keep trying wires until you get the green light. That's all there is to it. Just plug in to your new extension and dial.

Dropouts

If you keep losing your connection, it could be something simple. First check that **call waiting** is switched off. Those beeps that tell you someone's waiting will knock out your modem every time. Next, **unplug any phones that share the same line**. Some phones draw current from the line every few minutes to keep all those numbers stored in memory.

Maybe the **secret police** is bugging your line. Don't laugh, it happens in certain countries. After all, if your hotel cleaner spots you hunched on the floor tapping in messages, jacked in through a nest of clips and wires, don't say you won't look a bit suspicious. Mostly, however, it's just a noisy line and there's nothing you can do.

Tax impulsing

A few countries – Austria, Belgium, Czech Republic, Germany, India, Spain, and Switzerland, among them – send metering pulses down the line to measure call times. Unless your modem is approved in these countries, the pulses will slow down or knock out your connection. Better PC card modems, and certainly all those approved in the above countries, have filtering built in. If not, you can fit a filter, such as TeleAdapt's **TeleFilter**, between your modem and the line.

Faxes and voicemail

Although thanks to email, the fax's days are clearly numbered, many still cling to this antediluvian protocol. But what do you do if your fax is in Houston, and you're in Hochow? **Jfax** (http://www.jfax.com) has the answer. It can allocate you a phone number in one of several cities worldwide. Any fax sent to this number is converted to an email attachment and redirected to your email address. It can also take voicemail messages, forwarding them on as highly compressed audio files. Or if you want it **free**, and don't mind handing out a Midwestern US fax number, try **Efax** (http://www.efax.com), which works similarly.

Most **Online Services** offer this, or a similar, service, as do several large ISPs such as **UUNet** (http://www.uu.net) and **PSInet** (http://www.psi.net).

Further info

As the world wakes up to the era of computer mobility, you'll see loads of new products and new opportunities.

For **general news** read:
Mobilis (http://www.volksware.com/mobilis/)
On the Road (http://www.roadnews.com).

For tips on how to **connect worldwide**, see:
Help for World Travelers (http://www.kropla.com)
Laptop Travel (http://www.laptoptravel.com)

For **adapters, insurance, advice, and support** see:
TeleAdapt (http://www.teleadapt.com)
Road Warrior (http://www.warrior.com).
Port (http://www.port.com)

For reviews on the full range of **Net devices**, see:
AllNetDevices (http://www.allnetdevices.com

PART TWO

The Guide

World Wide Web

Usenet Newsgroups

Software Roundup

World Wide Web Sites

No-one knows the precise number of addresses accessible from the Web. If you were to try to work it out you'd have to factor in not only every Web page, but everything capable of being linked to or from any Web page. That would include every newsgroup on every news server, every chat room, every music sample, and potentially every computer hooked to the Internet in any way. The Web proper, though, is the most popular part and it's what we'll deal with in this guide. As you'll see from the following listings, it's more than just the world's biggest library, it's something you'll have to experience for yourself to understand.

Technically, Web site addresses start with the prefix http: – anything else, although accessible from the Web, really belongs to another system. What sets the Web apart is the way you can move around by clicking links. Most Web sites have links to other sites strewn throughout their pages. Plus, as a bonus, they often devote a section to listing similar sites (or simply ones they think might interest visitors). Just look for a section called "Links". Of course if you take such a link, you'll arrive at another site which could link to even more related sites. So even though there are only about a couple of thousand sites reviewed in the following pages, they'll lead you to millions more.

Finding what you want

The keys to finding your way around the Web are the **Internet search tools and directories**. They're listed first. See "Finding It" (p.160), for how to use them.

How to get there

To reach a site, carefully enter its **address** (taking note of any capital letters) into your browser's **URL, Location, or Address** bar. This is normally located directly underneath the menu. Although formal Web addresses start with http:// you don't need to enter this bit unless you have a very old browser. **So if the address is listed as** http://www.ibm.com **simply type** www.ibm.com

An easier way to get there

You'll also find this entire listing on the Rough Guides' Web site. So rather than type these addresses individually, simply browse this chapter, get an idea of what you'd like to see, go online, type: www.roughguides.com/net/ and follow the links from there.

How to find a site again

When you see something you like, save its address to your **Bookmarks**, **Favorites**, or **Hotlist**. To find it later, simply click on its name in the list. Or you could read it offline by saving the page to disk or switching to Offline mode. For instructions, see p.86.

When it's not there

Some of the following sites will have moved or vanished altogether but don't let that deter you. For advice on how to track them down, see p.181. The easiest way is to enter the title, subject, and/or related subjects, as keywords into one of the search engines such as HotBot, AltaVista, or Northern Light. Once you've mastered the Internet Search Tools and Directories, you'll be able to find anything. So, wax down your browser and get out there!

Web Sites Directory

Most human life has found its way onto the World Wide Web in some form so it doesn't easily lend itself to **categorization**. We've adopted the following headings to make our listings easier to navigate. However, they do tend to blur into each other at the slightest opportunity. So, if you're into music, you might want to explore "Music", "Entertainment", "Ezines", "Shopping", and "News, Newspapers, and Magazines". If you're up for fun, check under "Comedy", "Entertainment", "Weird", "Games", and so on. To search the Net by **subject or keyword**, try out some of the tools in our "Search Tools and Directories" section.

PART ONE: SEARCH TOOLS AND DIRECTORIES

Let's start with the most useful addresses on the Net: the main search engines and directories. Armed with these, you should be able to find just about anything you might want. Get to know them all in depth, compare their services, and come to your own conclusions about which is best for what. Save these addresses in your Bookmarks, Favorites, or Links bar, as you're sure to return often.

Start off with **Yahoo** and **About.com**. These are the most useful directories: Yahoo, because it's the biggest; About.com because it offers a little more guidance. Next, move on to the search engines.

Try **HotBot** first. Get to know its drop-down menus and you'll be able to find anything. **AltaVista** and **Northern Light** are bigger and faster, but aren't quite so easy to tune. **Google** is the fastest, but not quite as big.

Finally try **Deja.com**. If you haven't already fired up your newsreader, you'll soon find out what Usenet is all about. Browse the ratings, and then search for answers to whatever's puzzling you.

Most of these sites have international versions, personal editions, free Webmail, multimedia searches, chat communities, and a host of other services tacked on – usually fed from other sites. So much, that it's quite possible to spend your entire session within their bounds.

THE SEARCH POWERHOUSES

About.com
http://www.about.com

Cozy directory built by a team of "expert guides". Often the best place to find the best sites within a category.

AltaVista
http://www.av.com

Massive multilingual search engine that's somewhat nobbled by returning only ten results per page. Perfect when you're in a hurry and you expect a result in the first few hits.

Deja.com
http://www.deja.com

Here's where to come when you're looking for opinions, advice, first-hand experiences, or the right newsgroup to join. Search Usenet archives going back several years or browse the user surveys. Arguably the Net's greatest treasure.

DMOZ Open Directory Project
http://dmoz.org

Netscape's Yahoo killer still has a long way to go to live up to its ambitions of being the world's largest hand-built directory. At this stage, it's merely another place to look.

Excite
http://www.excite.com

Poor search engine, but a reasonable site directory. Comes in several international editions all padded out with a plethora of services such as TV listings, news, weather, stock quotes, people finding, email lookup, flight booking, maps, and yellow pages.

Google

http://www.google.com

New, speedy, search engine without any excess fluff. Try it!

HotBot

http://www.hotbot.com

Still our pick of the search engines, though its freshness is a concern. The drop-down menus make complex searches easier.

InfoSeek

http://www.go.com

Search the Web, Usenet, and various newswires, plus loads of other services similar to Excite, but blessed with the Walt Disney stamp. The Web search is fast and gives accurate results, but not enough of them. Appears to be paying more attention to its site directory.

LookSmart

http://www.looksmart.com

Massive, though orderly, Web directory from the Reader's Digest. Every link includes a comment. **Snap** (http://www.snap.com) is similar.

Lycos

http://www.lycos.com

Like Excite: give the search engine a miss and stick to the directories, MP3 search, newsfeeds, and assorted Webcandy.

Northern Light

http://www.nlsearch.com

Search a massive Web database and/or special collection of newswires, journals, books, and magazines. Results listed and sorted into sensible folders.

Yahoo

http://www.yahoo.com

The closest the Net has to a central directory. Big and easy to navigate by subject, but light on reviews. Loads of specialist stuff such as national and metropolitan directories, weather

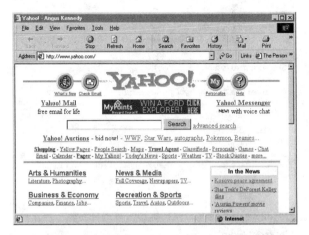

reports, kids' guides, seniors guides, yellow pages, sport scores, plus outstanding news and financial services. And don't overlook the local area Yahoos, which often include a few sites not in the main directory. There's also regional content such as TV listings. Drop by daily!

OTHER DIRECTORIES AND SEARCH AIDS

Argus Clearinghouse
http://www.clearinghouse.net

Directory of specialist Web directories that's hardly exhaustive, but meticulously maintained. Crack open the most interesting categories and bookmark anything that might be useful later. You never know. See also: http://www.allsearchengines.com & http://www.webdata.com

Ask Jeeves
http://www.askjeeves.com

Ask questions in plain English for replies that are often more intriguing than useful. Searches several engines plus its own database simultaneously.

Britannica Internet Guide
http://www.britannica.com

Reviews and rates sites by category. Not that big, but it's top quality.

Disinformation
http://www.disinfo.com

Archives the dark side of politics, religious fervor, new science, and the current affairs you seldom read about in the dailies.

Electric Library
http://www.elibrary.com

Simultaneous search of databases of newspapers, magazines, newswires, classic books, maps, photographs, and major artworks.

EuroSeek
http://www.euroseek.net

Multilingual European Web search and directory.

Internet Sleuth
http://www.isleuth.com

Search over 2000 Web and specialist databases, more than one at a time. All the same, it's usually more efficient to search the sites directly. You could use this listing to find them.

MetaCrawler
http://www.metacrawler.com

Bug several Web search engines at once. Limited to thirty results per engine, which in many circumstances renders it useless. See also: http://www.mamma.com

Search Engine Watch
http://www.searchenginewatch.com

Don't believe any search engine's hype about it being the biggest or freshest. Don't even believe what you read in magazines. Here they give you the truth. See also: http://notess.com/search/stats/

Search Terms
http://www.searchterms.com

Ranks the hundred most popular search terms.

Scour
http://www.scour.net

Search for images, audio, or video relating to keywords. If
you'd prefer them completely wholesome, try:
http://www.arriavista.com

Starting Point
http://www.stpt.com

Another general directory which aims at best of genre.

Tracerlock
http://www.peacefire.org/tracerlock/

Emails you whenever AltaVista finds a new hit on your terms.

Webgator
http://www.inil.com/users/dguss/wgator.htm

Become an online private dick.

WebTaxi
http://www.webtaxi.com

A quick way to find regional directories, though Yahoo lists
more.

Women
http://www.women.com • http://www.wwwomen.com
http://www. iVillage.com

Rival guides to the Web's man-free zones.

BUSINESS AND PHONE DIRECTORIES

Big Book
http://www.bigbook.com

Lists over sixteen million North American businesses, plus street maps, reviews, and free home pages.

Big Yellow
http://www.bigyellow.com

Millions of North American business listings, plus links to international business directories and people finders.

Electronic Yellow Pages
http://www.eyp.co.uk

UK business phone directory.

Scoot
http://www.scoot.co.uk

Search for a British, Dutch, or Belgian business by product, name, business type, and/or location. Returns all the contact and payment details, plus Web pages if available.

Switchboard
http://www.switchboard.com

Trace people and businesses in the US. Also try: http://www.anywho.com

Telstra Yellow Pages
http://www.yellowpages.com.au

Australian business phone directory complete with street maps.

World Pages International Directories
http://www.worldpages.com/global/

Find a phone number in almost any country.

EMAIL SEARCH

If you want your email address made public you'll need to submit it to these directories individually. Likewise don't expect to find someone who hasn't done the same. The downside is it can lead to spam.

Bigfoot
http://www.bigfoot.com

Internet Address Finder
http://www.iaf.net

WhoWhere?
http://www.whowhere.com

Yahoo People Search
http://people.yahoo.com

LISTS AND PICKS

100 Hot Websites
http://www.hot100.com

The hundred most visited Web sites each week, overall or by category. Not necessarily accurate, but close enough.

Cool Site of the Day
http://cool.infi.net

CSOTD still comes up with something fresh each day, but that wasn't what made it so popular. Before Beavis and Butthead Inc took over, it was about giving Web designers new ideas. If that's what you're after, try CSOTD founder Glenn Davis's Project Cool: http://www.projectcool.com

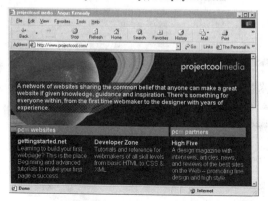

Cruel Site of the Day

http://www.cruel.com

    Something horrid daily.

Losers.org

http://www.losers.org

    Here's a list you don't want to make.

Netsurfer Digest

http://www.netsurf.com/nsd/

    Subscribe to receive weekly site updates and reviews.

Top Ten Links

http://www.toptenlinks.com

    Vote to create top ten site lists under various categories.

Useless Pages

http://www.go2net.com/internet/useless/

http://www.worstoftheweb.com

    The sludge festering at the bottom of the Net.

Web100

http://www.web100.com

    Reviews and ranks the Web's one hundred "top" sites in several categories.

Wired Cybrarian

http://www.wired.com/cybrarian/

    Wired's selective directory of essential references. No longer updated, but still a handy list.

DISCUSSION DIRECTORIES

Forum One

http://www.forumone.com

    Search almost 300,000 Web-based discussion groups.

Liszt

http://www.liszt.com

    Find a mailing list, chat channel, or newsgroup on your favorite topic.

Publicly Accessible Mailing Lists
http://www.neosoft.com/internet/paml/

Thousands of specialist email discussion groups organized by name or subject, with details on traffic, content, and how to join.

Reference.com
http://www.reference.com

Search Usenet, thousands of mailing lists, and Web forums.

SOFTWARE GUIDES

Andover.Net
http://www.andover.net

Several of the Net's finest file directories. That includes software downloads in Dave Central and Slaughterhouse; a fair-sized image library and tools for Web design in Mediabuilder; and the right source code for the job at FreeCode.

Browser Watch
http://www.browserwatch.com • http://www.browsers.com

All the latest on browsers and plug-ins.

Cool Tool of the Day
http://www.cooltool.com

A new Windows or Mac program of merit each day.

Download.com
http://www.download.com

The latest notable downloads in all categories, for PC and Mac, from CNET.

Filez
http://www.filez.com

File search engine for most platforms. Includes descriptions.

Hotfiles
http://www.hotfiles.com

Mac and PC shareware reviewed by ZDNet.

InfoMac HyperArchive
http://hyperarchive.lcs.mit.edu/HyperArchive/HyperArchive.html

HTML dip into the InfoMac Macintosh software pig trough.

Jumbo Shareware

http://www.jumbo.com

Mammoth shareware archive for all platforms.

The Mac Orchard

http://www.macorchard.com

Daily-updated, user-reviewed Internet Software for Macs. See also: http://www.mactimes.com/puremac/

Shareware.com

http://www.shareware.com

Search several major file archives for all platforms.

SoftSeek

http://www.softseek.com

PC downloads reviewed.

Stroud's Consummate Winsock Applications

http://www.stroud.com

Mostly Windows Internet applications posted and reviewed as released. Highly regarded but misses quite a lot and many of the reviews are looking dated.

Tucows

http://www.tucows.com

Another esteemed Internet applications archive with mirrors all over the world. Covers all platforms, even PDAs. For similar, see: http://www.filedudes.com

Version Tracker

http://www.versiontracker.com

Keep your Mac up to date.

Walnut Creek CD-ROM

http://www.cdrom.com

Download direct from this massive shareware archive or get it all at once on CD-ROM.

Winfiles

http://www.winfiles.com

Best place to find obscure Windows programs, for just about every task, as they're released.

OTHER INTERNET STUFF

Beseen
http://www.beseen.com

Add a free quiz, search form, hit counter, chat room, bulletin board, or guest book to your Web site.

Coalition against Unsolicited Commercial Email
http://www.cauce.org

Enlist in the war against junk email.

Em@ilfile
http://www.emailfile.com

Rather than wait for a file to download, have it sent to you via email.

FAQ Consortium
http://www.faqs.org

The place to find all the Frequently Asked Questions from Usenet newsgroups. Look here before you post.

Free Email Addresses
http://www.emailaddresses.com
http://www.geocities.com/SiliconValley/Vista/8015/free.html

Get 'em while they're hot.

Free Webspace
http://www.freewebspace.net

Guide to the free home-page maze.

GIF Wizard
http://www.gifwizard.com

Determine which images on your Web site need compression and by how much. It can fix them instantly.

Hackers.com
http://www.hackers.com • http://www.hideaway.net

Crawl through the Net's very underbelly. Hackers, crackers, phreakers, and warez traders – it's business as usual here in Geek Alley.

Hotmail
http://www.hotmail.com

Get a free address from the biggest Webmail donor within a

few minutes. Need 100 percent privacy? Then sneak over to:
http://www.hushmail.com

Internet Traffic Report

http://www.internettrafficreport.com

Monitor the state of the world's main Internet arterials.

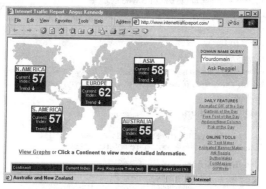

MailBank

http://www.mailbank.com

Rent a cheap personalized Web/email address combination
from a range of more than 12,000 domains.

MailStart

http://www.mailstart.com

Collect your POP3 mail instantly simply by entering your
email address and password. Perfect for cybercafés.

Name Registration

http://www.networksolutions.com • http://www.register.com

Register your domain through Network Solutions if you have
all the DNS numbers, otherwise use Register.com to hold
your name until you're properly hosted. If that seems too
hard, and it shouldn't, try a third-party specialist such as
NetNames at: http://www.netnames.com All sites will tell you
instantly whether your choice has been taken. Alternatively,
you might prefer a regional domain, which ends in a country
code. See: http://www.uninett.no/navn/domreg.html Finally,

URL4Life at: http://www.smartredirect.com offers a free
redirection service until you sort out some serious space.

NetMind
http://www.netmind.com

Alerts you when a Web page changes.

NewzBot
http://www.jammed.com/~newzbot/

Find a news server that will let you tap in free.

NUA Internet Surveys
http://www.nua.org/surveys/

Leading Internet survey results as they're announced. More
stats and Web marketing news at: http://cyberatlas.internet.com

Scambusters
http://www.scambusters.org

Bulletins exposing the sharks who prey on gullible Net
newbies.

Top Hosts
http://www.tophosts.com

Rates commercial Web space providers.

Web page design
http://www.gettingstarted.net • http://www.stars.com
http://www.builder.com • http://www.webmonkey.com
http://www.developer.com • http://www.webpagesthatsuck.com

Everything from building your first page to professional site
management.

Web Publisher's Advertising Guide
http://www.markwelch.com/bannerad/

Compares and reviews banner ads and other site revenue
schemes.

World Wide Web Consortium
http://www.w3.org

Read hard-core technical specs on the Web's next generation.

Yahoo Clubs
http://clubs.yahoo.com

Too lazy to start a newsgroup? Then start a club. No holds
barred.

PART TWO: WEB SITES
SUBJECT GUIDE

First off, a disclaimer. This isn't meant to be a definitive guide to the best Web sites. That just isn't possible any more. There are too many sites, and besides, it's a matter of personal taste or interests. That said, we think you'll find this selection broad enough to get you well and truly on your way. So, get clicking!

ART, MUSEUMS, AND PHOTOGRAPHY

24 Hour Museum
http://www.24hourmuseum.org.uk
Locate British museums and galleries that might tickle your fancy.

24 hours in Cyberspace
http://www.cyber24.com
Collective output of over a thousand photographers and a hundred photojournalists documenting the impact of the digital revolution on February 8, 1996, everywhere from the Sahara to Times Square.

A Life Garden
http://alifegarden.com
Adopt a virtual organism and set it loose in a hostile critter-eat-critter environment. Also try: http://www.technosphere.org.uk

American Museum of Photography
http://www.photographymuseum.com
Exhibitions from back when cameras were a novelty.

Anime
http://www.bigfire.com • http://otakuworld.com
Monstrous archives of Japanese cartoon art and software.

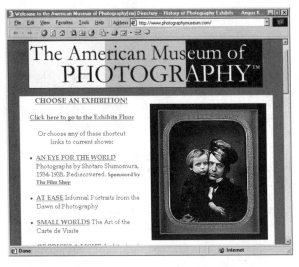

ArtAIDS Link

http://www.illumin.co.uk/artaids/

Internet equivalent of the AIDS patchwork quilt. Upload your own tribute to this ever-growing mosaic of love, loss, and memory.

The Art Connection

http://www.art-connection.com

See what's for sale in a selection of London's top commercial galleries.

Art Crimes: Writing on the Wall

http://www.graffiti.org

Spraying for recognition.

ArtMuseum

http://www.artmuseum.net

Infrequent exhibitions of modern classics from major galleries like the Whitney and the US National Gallery of Art.

Cartoon Bank
http://www.cartoonbank.com

Every cartoon ever published in The New Yorker.

Chankstore Freefonts
http://www.chank.com/freefonts.html

Download a wacky Chank Diesel display font free each week.

Clip Art
http://www.clipart.com • http://www.clipartconnection.com

Bottomless cesspit of the soulless dross that's used to inject life into documents and overhead transparencies.

Cartoon Links
http://www.cartoon-links.com

Simple directory of comic art Web sites and newsgroups.

Central Intelligence Museum
http://laf.cioe.com/~dna/

Spy toys and an active imagination on parade.

Core-Industrial Design Resources
http://www.core77.com

Industrial design exhibits, jobs, chat, and tips on how to get seen.

Dancing Baby
http://www.viewpoint.com/features/baby/

Here's who to blame for that ambling ankle-biter.

Dia Center for the Arts
http://www.diacenter.org

Web exclusives from "extraordinary" artists, plus the low-down on the NY Dia Center's upcoming escapades.

Dingbats
http://dingbats.i-us.com

For when you just can't get enough symbol fonts.

Dysfunctional Family Circus
http://www.spinnwebe.com/dfc/

Write your own twisted Family Circus captions.

Elfwood
http://www.elfwood.com

Sketches and tales from a gaggle of junior fantasy and sci-fi buffs.

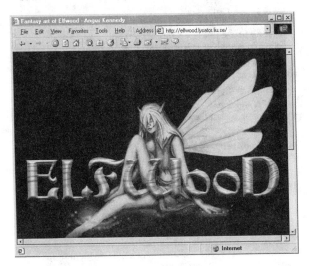

The Exploratorium
http://www.exploratorium.edu

Kid-friendly online exhibitions from San Francisco's Exploratorium.

The Font Fairy
http://www.printerideas.com/fontfairy/

Stuff your sack with free fonts.

Great Buildings Collections
http://www.greatbuildings.com

Shuffle knowingly through 3D models of some 750 of the world's most notable structures.

Grove Dictionary of Art Online
http://www.groveart.com

Freeload on the definitive art reference for 24 hours. After that it costs more than you'll want to pay.

Interactive Collector
http://www.icollector.com

Auction house that specializes in artworks and prize collectibles such as celebrity cast-offs.

Internet Type Foundry Index
http://www.typeindex.com

Typeface news, plus a directory of font and design resources.

Joke Wallpaper
http://www.jokewallpaper.com

Corny backgrounds for your desktop.

King Features
http://www.kingfeatures.com

Dip into the archives and bring yourself up to date with Juliet Jones, Popeye, Zippy, The Phantom, Blondie and the bulk of King's comic strip stable. For Dilbert, Peanuts, Tarzan and all of the United Media family, see: http://www.comics.com

Labelcollector.com
http://www.labelcollector.com

Fabulous collection of vintage bottle and fruit crate labels. Sadly, these are only the thumbnails, but if you like what you see you can buy the originals.

Library of Congress
http://www.loc.gov

Research tools, exhibitions, library services, current hot bills, and an unparalleled multimedia showcase of American history. Described as one of the seven wonders of the Internet.

Life
http://www.pathfinder.com/Life/

View *Life* magazine's picture of the day, then link through to some of the world's most arresting photographs. If that's not enough, there's even more over at **Time's Picture Collection**: http://www.thepicturecollection.com.

LIFE Online: Picture of the Day – Angus Kennedy

File   Edit   View   Favorites   Tools   Help   Address http://www.pathfinder.com/Life/pictday/pictday.html

LIFE PICTURE OF THE DAY

LIFE Homepage
Picture of the Day
This Day in LIFE
Cover Collection
Features
LIFE Magazine

search   GO

Subscribe to LIFE
E-Mail LIFE
lifeedit@life.timeinc.com

OTHERNEWS
The TIME 100:
Heroes and Icons

TIME.com

Ricky Martin
Salsas 'Today'

A 30,000-FOOT-TALL SMOKE CLOUD shrouds Bellingham, Washington on June 10 after a gasoline pipeline leak catches fire in a nearby creek. Two boys were badly burned in the blaze.

Internet

Museum of Modern Art NY

http://www.moma.org

They say if you only ever visit one modern art museum . . . well, here's a sample.

Photodisc

http://www.photodisc.com

Sixty thousand-odd royalty-free images all yours to plunder free, but if you need high-resolution you'll have to pay.

Production Book Online

http://www.pb.com.au/pb/

More than 18,000 pages of Australian advertising, film, TV, and multimedia contacts.

Red Meat

http://www.redmeat.com

Dark comic humor from deepest Middle America.

The Secret Garden
http://www-personal.umich.edu/~agrxray/
Stunning gallery of
X-rayed flowers.

Spumco's Wonderful World of Cartoons
http://www.spumco.com
Animated
Shockwave movies
from the creators of
Ren & Stimpy.

Stelarc
http://www.stelarc.va.com.au
No-one hangs naked from a hoist suspended only by flesh-piercing hooks (while onlookers from the Net control their robotic third arm) with more grace than Stelios Arcadiou.

Stick Figure Death Theater
http://www.sfdt.com
Stickcity citizens meet their sticky ends. Like a minimalist Itchy & Scratchy.

Vincent Van Gogh Gallery
http://www.vangoghgallery.com
So, where else could you see his entire works in one place?

World Wide Art Resources
http://wwar.world-arts-resources.com • http://adam.ac.uk
http://www.artcyclopedia.com
Find just about everything that could be considered a bit arty.

Museums around the World
http://www.icom.org/vlmp/world.html
Massive list of museums with Web sites.

Year in the Life of Photojournalism
http://www.digitalstoryteller.com/YITL/
Tag along with voyeuristic pros and see what they do in their day to day.

BOOKS AND LITERATURE

If a squintillion Web pages aren't enough to satisfy your lust for the written word, then maybe you should use one to order a book. You'll be spoiled for choice with hundreds of shops offering millions of titles for delivery anywhere worldwide. That includes bumper showings from most of the major chains alongside exclusively online book havens such as Amazon and IBS. The superstores typically lay on all the trimmings, such as user ratings, reviews, recommendations, sample chapters, author interviews, bestseller lists, press clippings, publishing news, secure ordering, and sometimes even gift wrapping. Try these for size:

Major Chains

Barnes & Noble (US)	http://www.bn.com
Blackwells (UK)	http://www.blackwells.co.uk
Borders (US)	http://www.borders.com
Dillons (UK)	http://www.dillons.co.uk
Dymocks (AUS)	http://www.dymocks.com.au
Hammicks (UK)	http://www.thebookplace.com
McGills (AUS)	http://www.mcgills.com.au
Waterstone's (UK)	http://www.waterstones.co.uk

Only on the Web

Alphabet Street (UK)	http://www.alphabetstreet.com
Amazon (UK)	http://www.amazon.co.uk
Amazon (US)	http://www.amazon.com
BOL (UK & Europe)	http://www.bol.com
Bookpages (UK)	http://www.bookpages.com
Buy.com (US)	http://www.buy.com
Internet Bookshop (UK)	http://www.bookshop.co.uk

While Barnes & Noble and Amazon may rightly jostle over the title of "world's most ginormous bookstore", you'll find they all offer a staggering range, usually at

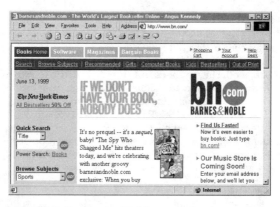

substantial discounts. But because books are heavy, these savings are often offset by freight. And naturally, the further away you are , and the sooner you want it, the more it adds up. Finally, before you check out in a frenzy, see that you have the best deal:

AddAll	http://www.addall.com
Best Book Buys	http://www.bestbookbuys.com
BookFinder	http://www.bookfinder.com
PriceScan	http://www.pricescan.com

Atomic Books
http://www.atomicbooks.com

The director of *Pink Flamingos*, John Waters, frequents this Baltimore shop in search of "insane books about every kind of extreme". Thanks to a Web-linked storecam you can spy such clientele as you order online. For more trashy treasures, see: http://www.fringeware.com/shop/ and http://www.loompanics.com

Banned Books Online
http://www.cs.cmu.edu/Web/People/spok/banned-books.html

See which books have riled the righteous, and why, by reading the contentious extracts. Many titles are now considered classics.

Bibliofind
http://www.bibliofind.com

Track down old, used, and rare books offered by thousands of
booksellers worldwide.

BookCloseouts
http://www.bookcloseouts.com

Host to some five million books slightly
past their shelf life – including this one's
first edition!

Bookwire
http://www.bookwire.com

US book trade news, bestseller lists, and
author road schedules with content
from the Publisher's Weekly and
Library Journal. For UK publishing
news, see: http://www.thebookseller.com

CrimeBoss
http://www.crimeboss.com

Shock comic covers from the mid-20th
century.

The Damnedest Thing I Ever Saw
http://www.thedamnedestthing.com

Push your credibility to the edge.

Dave's List of Words that are Fun to Say
http://members.tripod.com/~DeathInPlaid/list.html

Read them aloud for the time of your life.

The Internet Public Library
http://ipl.sils.umich.edu

Browse online books, magazines, journals, and newspapers.

Literary Kicks
http://www.charm.net/~brooklyn/LitKicks.html

Shrine to the Beats with a mass of fine audio and text on
Kerouac, Corso, Ginsberg, Cassady, and all in the Beat orbit.

MysteryNet
http://www.mysterynet.com

Hmm, now what could this be?

Online Books

http://www.cs.cmu.edu/books.html

Find complete texts tucked way in obscure archives.

Poetry Society

http://www.poetrysoc.com

UK halfway house for budding poets and their victims.
Americans will find more reasons to rhyme at:
http://www.poets.org

Project Gutenburg

http://promo.net/pg/

Fifty years or so after authors croak, their copyrights pass
into the public domain. With this in mind, Project
Gutenburg is gradually bringing thousands of old texts
online, along with some more recent donations. As great as
that sounds, in practice you might prefer the convenience of
hard copy.

Pure Fiction

http://www.purefiction.com

For pulp worms and writers alike. Packed with book
previews, author interviews, and hundreds of links to the
sort of stuff you need to get off the ground and punch out
your first bestseller.

Shakespeare

http://the-tech.mit.edu/Shakespeare/

The Bard's complete works online.

The Slot: a Spot for Copy Editors

http://www.theslot.com

Soothing words of outrage for grammatical pedants.

Sun Tzu's The Art of War

http://zhongwen.com/bingfa.htm

The world's oldest military treatise and Yuppies' surrogate
bible. Oh well, battles do have their casualties.

Tech Classics Archive

http://classics.mit.edu

Hundreds of translated Greek and Roman classics.

Text files
http://www.textfiles.com

Chunks of the junk that orbited the pre-Web Internet. For a slightly more modern slant, see: http://www.etext.org

Urban Legends
http://www.urbanlegends.com

Separate the amazing but true, from the popular myths.

The Yarn
http://www.theyarn.com

A story with two options at the end of each chapter: Your choice will either lead you to a new chapter or you'll be invited to contribute your own. It makes for some wild plot twists.

BUSINESS

AccountingWeb
http://www.accountingweb.co.uk

Impeccably neat hub for British accountants and company searches.

Advertising Age
http://www.adage.com

Newsbreaks from the ad trade.

Bizymoms
http://www.bizymoms.com

Crafty ways to cash up without missing the afternoon soaps.

Business Index
http://www.dis.strath.ac.uk/business/

Low-key, but selective, index of business news sources and company databanks.

Clickz
http://www.clickz.com

What's new in Web marketing trends, including new site reviews from an ad campaigner's perspective.

Companies Online
http://www.companiesonline.com

Get the score on over 100,000 US public and private companies.

Direct Marketing World
http://www.dmworld.com
> How to junk mail and influence people.

Entrepreneurmag
http://www.entrepreneurmag.com
> Get rich now, ask us how.

The Foundation Center
http://fdncenter.org
> Companies who might happily spare you a fiver.

Friends and Partners
http://solar.rtd.utk.edu/friends/home.html
> US 'n' Russian joint venture to help foster business between the old foes.

Garage.com
http://www.garage.com
> Matchmaking agency for entrepreneurs and investors founded by Apple's Guy Kawasaki. For more help milking funds for your online white elephant, see:
> http://www.moneyhunter.com

Guerilla Marketing
http://www.gmarketing.com
> Get ahead by metaphorically butchering your competitor's families and poisoning your customer's water supply.

IBM Patent Server
http://www.patents.ibm.com
> Sift through US patents back to 1971, plus a gallery of obscurities. Ask the right questions and you might stumble across tomorrow's technology long before the media. For UK patents see: http://www.patent.gov.uk

Internet Magazine's Marketing Hotlist
http://www.internet-sales.com/hot/
> One-stop guide to UK Web marketing news, stats, and tools.

Killer Internet tactics
http://www.killertactics.com
> How to murder brain-dead Web surfers using simple HTML scripts.

MediaFinder

http://www.mediafinder.com

Media profile and contact directory. Lists newspapers,
magazines, mailing lists, catalogs, newsletters and more,
sorted by subject focus.

Patent Café

http://www.patentcafe.com

Protect your crackpot schemes and perhaps even see them
through to fruition.

Small Business Search

http://www.smallbizsearch.com

Guide to online business tools.

Super Marketing: Ads from the Comic Books

http://www.steveconley.com/supermarketing.htm

The ads that kept you lying awake at night wishing you had
more money.

COMEDY

Bonk Industries
http://www.telegate.se/bonk/
Surreal dig at corporate propaganda. Here's another:
http://www.thecorporation.com

Brain Candy
http://members.aol.com/WordPlays/words.html
Famous last words, epitaphs, proverbs, insults, quotes, mind games, and the like.

Citizen's Self-Arrest Form
http://www.ou.edu/oupd/selfarr2.htm
Time to give yourself up, son.

Comedy Channel
http://www.aentv.com/home/chcomedy.htm
Live and archived stand-up routines in RealVideo.

Complaint Letter Generator
http://www-csag.cs.uiuc.edu/individual/pakin/complaint/
Someone getting on your goat, but stuck for the right words? Just mince their details through here for an instant dressing down.

Dobe's Punny Name Archive
http://www.eskimo.com/~dobe/
Thousands of unwise baby names.

Doonesbury Electronic Town Hall
http://www.doonesbury.com
Daily strips and archives from Gary B. Trudeau.

Forward of the day
http://www.zdnet.com/yil/content/depts/forward/
Get it here before it lands in your inbox.

Funny – The Comedy Directory
http://www.funny.co.uk
Small, but selective, guide to the top Web humorbases.

Hamsterdance
http://www.hamsterdance.com

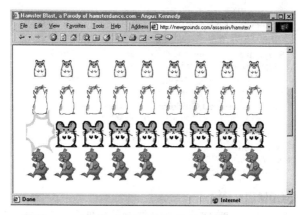

1999's answer to the dancing baby. Get even at:
http://www.newgrounds.com/assassin/hamster/

Humor Database
http://www.humordatabase.com

Thousands of jokes searchable by age, topic, keyword, or
popularity. Tons more at
http://www.humournet.com • http://www.humor.com,
http://www.looniebin.mb.ca • http://www.goofball.com

Jester: the Online Joke Recommender
http://shadow.ieor.berkeley.edu/humor/

Rate a selection of jokes and then receive more based on what
it thinks you'll find funny.

Pranksta's Paradise
http://www.ccil.org/~mika/

Larks and laughs at the expense of others compiled from the
Usenet archives of alt.shenanigans

Pythonline
http://www.pythonline.com

Terry Gilliam-illustrated Monty Python mayhem, juvenilia,
and humor, plus where they all are now.

Rec.humor.funny
http://www.netfunny.com/rhf/
> Archives of the rec.humor.funny newsgroup, updated daily.

Surrealist Compliment Generator
http://pharmdec.wustl.edu/cgi-bin/jardin_scripts/SCG/
> It mightn't make a shred of sense, but hey, at least it's positive.

Tony's Illustrated Guide to Unpleasantness
http://www.geocities.com/SouthBeach/Marina/1743/
> Refresher course in insults.

Uploaded
http://www.loaded.co.uk
> Monthly emissions from the journal of British lad culture.

COMPUTING

Pretty much every PC brand has a Web site where you can download software, get support, and find out what's new. It won't be hard to find. Usually it's the company name or initials between a www and a com. So you'll find **Dell** at: http://www.dell.com, **Compaq** at: http://www.compaq.com, **Hewlett Packard** at: http://www.hp.com, and so forth. Consult Yahoo if that fails. If you're in the market for new computer bits, check out the best price across US online vendors at **Shopper.com**: http://www.shopper.com, **Price Watch**: http://www.pricewatch.com or **PriceScan**: http://www.pricescan.com. Bear in mind, if you live outside the US, it might be taxed upon arrival.

Apple
http://www.apple.com
> Essential drop-in to update your Mac, and pick up the latest release of Quicktime. To top up with news, software, and brand affirmations, see: http://www.macaddict.com http://www.tidbits.com • http://www.macintouch.com http://www.macnn.com Don't even think of looking at http://www.ihateapple.com It will only upset you.

Beyond.com
http://www.beyond.com
>Bumper range of PC and Mac software available for international shipping or sometimes direct download.

CNET
http://www.cnet.com
>Daily technology news and features, plus reviews, games, and downloads, along with schedules, transcripts, and related stories from CNET's broadcasting network. Worth reading weekly as a lightweight way to keep up with what's what in computing.

Computer Humor: True Helpdesk Stories
http://helpdeskfunnies.cyberjuice.com
>Customers: they might always be right, but they sure do ask the dangdest things.

Easter egg archive
http://www.eeggs.com
>Would you believe there's a flight simulator in Excel 97, a basketball game in Windows 95, and a raygun-wielding alien in Quark Xpress? They're in there all right, but you'll never find them on your own. Here's how to unlock secrets in scores of programs.

FreeDrive
http://www.freedrive.com • http://www.ifloppy.net
>Free storage space on the Net that's perfect for backups.

Free-Help
http://www.free-help.com
>Ask an expert to sort out your computer problems, though Usenet might be quicker. See also: http://virtualdr.com or http://www.tek-tips.com/

HotWired
http://www.hotwired.com
>Net's best source of breaking technology news plus archives of Wired magazine and a few ezines that are verging to the left of the Tired/Wired column.

MacFix-it

http://www.macfixit.com

Diagnose what's ailing your Mac. Some things are known to conflict: http://www.mac-conflicts.com

Microsoft

http://www.microsoft.com

If you're running any Microsoft product, and the chance of that seems to be approaching 100 percent, drop by this disorganized scrapheap regularly for upgrades, news, support, and patches. That includes the latest free tweaks to Windows, Office, and particularly all that falls under the Internet Explorer program. Grab the lot, and watch your system directory blossom.

Modem Help

http://www.modemhelp.com

Solve your dial-up dramas for modems of all persuasions including cable, ISDN, and DSL. And be sure to check your modem maker's page for driver and firmware upgrades, especially if it's X2 or K56flex. See also: http://www.56k.com

Need to Know

http://www.ntk.net

Weekly high-tech wrap-up with a sarcastic bite.

Newslinx

http://www.newslinx.com

Subscribe to get the top Net technology stories, aggregated from around 50 sources, delivered to your mailbox daily.

PC Mechanic

http://www.pcmech.com

http://www.pcvelocity.com/hardware/howto/computer/build.shtml

Step-by-step instructions on how to build, or upgrade, your own computer. It's easier than you'd think.

PCWebopaedia

http://www.pcwebopedia.com

Superb illustrated encyclopedia of computer technology with loads of helpful links.

Scantips

http://www.scantips.com

Become a scan-do type of dude.

Slashdot.org

http://slashdot.org

News for those who've entirely given up on the human race.

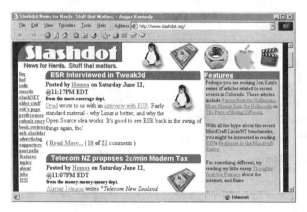

Tom's Hardware Guide

http://www.tomshardware.com

How to overclock your processor into the next millennium,
tweak your bios, and upgrade your storage capacity to
attract members of the opposite sex. More courtship rituals
at: http://www.anandtech.com or http://www.arstechnica.com or
http://www.ugeek.com

Virus Myths

http://www.kumite.com/myths/

If anyone sends you a virus-warning email insisting you
forward it on to everyone you know, send them here instead.
For help with real viruses such as Melissa and Happy99.exe,
see: http://www.symantec.com/avcenter/

Windows Annoyances

http://www.annoyances.org

Fixes and replacements for many Windows "features" and omissions from the author of the O'Reilly book of the same name.

Windrivers

http://www.windrivers.com

Driver file updates and hardware reviews compiled by a Windows fanatic of such maniacal proportions he even named his son "Gates". More Windows news and assistance at: http://www.windows98.org • http://www.wugnet.com/wininfo/ and http://www.win98central.com

Woody's Office Portal

http://www.wopr.com

Beat some sense out of Microsoft Office.

Yahoo! Computing

http://www.yahoo.com/Computers/

The grandpappy of all computing directories.

ZDNet

http://www.zdnet.com

Computing info powerhouse from Ziff Davis, publisher of PC Magazine, MacUser, Computer Gaming World and scores of other IT titles. Each magazine donates content such as news, product reviews, and lab test results; plus, there's a ton of prime Net-exclusive technochow. The best place to start researching anything even vaguely computer-related.

EMPLOYMENT

If you're looking to move on up, beware that if you post your résumé online there's every chance your boss will find it – embarrassing at the very least. Be aware the same situation could arise if you posted it before you started.

America's Job Bank

http://www.ajb.dni.us

Taps into over 1800 US State Employment Service offices.

Careers Online (AUS)

http://www.careersonline.com.au

Generate a résumé online, get career advice and see what's on
offer in the Australian hard labor market. Don't ignore the
classifieds: http://www.newsclassifieds.com

Cool Works

http://www.coolworks.com

Seasonal jobs in US resorts, national parks, camps, ranches,
and cruise lines.

EagleView

http://www.eagleview.com

Post your details to hundreds of Fortune 500 companies.

Ioma's Salary Zone

http://www.ioma.com/zone/

Is it worth $50.00 to find out exactly how much you're
worth? Maybe, but keep it secret just in case your boss finds
out you're overpaid!

Kaplan Careers

http://www.kaplan.com/career/

So you've scored the interview, now let's see if you'd get the
job. No go? Then maybe you could ask the headhunter for
advice: http://www.asktheheadhunter.com

Jobs at Microsoft

http://www.microsoft.com/Jobs/

Earn hard cash for your soul.

Jobsite (UK)

http://www.jobsearch.co.uk

Browse or search for British and European jobs across a
wide spectrum of fields. See also: http://www.jobsearch.co.uk •
http://www.reed.co.uk and http://www.jobsunlimited.co.uk

Monster Board (Worldwide)

http://www.monster.com

Search for professional employment in several countries.
The biggest on the Net, and many say the best. See also:
http://www.topjobs.com • http://www.hotjobs.com,
http://www.careermosaic.com • http://www.joboptions.com,
http://www.futurestep.com and http://www.careerbuilder.com

The Riley Guide

http://www.rileyguide.com

Messy directory of job-hunting resources.

Yahoo Employment

http://employment.yahoo.com

As ever, Yahoo is in on the act, and as ever, does it
superbly. This arm, however, handles only US placements.
Key "employment" as a search term, though, and you'll be
awash with options spanning the globe.

ENTERTAINMENT

Aloud (UK)

http://www.aloud.com

Book UK music, festival, and event tickets online. For
theatre tickets, see: http://www.whatsonstage.com and for **what's
on listings** see: http://www.eventselector.co.uk

Avenger's Handbook

http://www.ekran.no/html/revenge/

Armory of nastiness compiled from alt.revenge – the definitive
meeting place for suburban terrorists. John Steed would
never stoop this low.

Big Green Button

http://www.geocities.com/Hollywood/5945/bgb-main.html

Whatever you do, don't push it. Or this one for that matter:
http://www.pixelscapes.com/spatulacity/button.htm

ContestGuide

http://www.contestguide.com • http://www.contestworld.com

Enter loads of competitions. See also:
http://www.intervid.co.uk/prize/

Celebrities

http://www.celebsites.com • http://www.celebrityweb.com
http://www.fansites.com • http://www.webring.org

Stalk your idols online.

Center for the Easily Amused

http://www.amused.com

Hundreds of sites where thinking's banned.

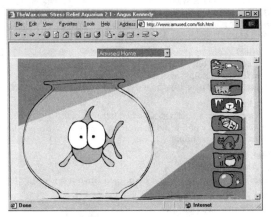

CultureFinder (US)

http://www.culturefinder.com

What's on guide to classical music, theatre, opera, dance, and
visual arts in around a thousand US cities.

Dialect Translator
http://www.shortbus.net/dialect.html

Translate your text into Valley Girl, Swedish Chef, or Jive.

Driveways of the Rich & Famous
http://www.driveways.com

Asphalt on the senses.

Dumpster Dive
http://www.connect-time.com/cgi-bin/dumpdive.cgi

Dig in and find a gift for a friend.

Guess the Dictator/Sitcom Character
http://www.smalltime.com/nowhere/dictator/

Assume a character, and answer yes/no questions until the
computer figures you out.

Hidden Mickeys
http://www.hiddenmickeys.org

Subliminal Mickeys hidden around Disneyland? Must be
something in the drinks. And all those rumors you've heard,
well here's which ones are true: http://www.snopes.com/disney/

Holler!
http://metalab.unc.edu/hollerin/

Learn how to holler by listening to a whole lot of hollerin'
galoots. Quite possibly the most annoying site on the Web.

Lockpicking
http://www.indra.com/archives/alt-locksmithing/

They laughed when I told them I was learning to burgle, but
when they came home . . .

Net Casino
http://www.casino.com

Apply for an offshore debit card, then flush it down the Net.

Obsessive Fan sites
http://countingdown.com/fans/

Levels of adoration that only dog owners take for granted.

Sassy's Dogbite Service
http://www.sassydog.com

Bite first, ask questions later.

Sony

http://www.sony.com

News, support, product blurbs, media clips, previews, and colorful allsorts from Sony's huge stable of movies, music, broadcast, publishing, video, Playstation, and electronic toys. It's like ten major sites under one roof, with hundreds of corners to explore. See for yourself.

The 80s Server

http://www.80s.com

And you swore they'd never come back. Meanwhile, the decade before still won't go away: http://www.rt66.com/dthomas/70s/70s.html

Text to speech converter

http://www.bell-labs.com/project/tts/voices.html

Enter your profanity, hit return, and it will speak the phrase back for the mirth of all within earshot. Try spelling phonetically for greater success. Or maybe you'd prefer it in Morse beeps: http://www.babbage.demon.co.uk/morse.html

Ticketmaster

http://www.ticketmaster.com • http://www.ticketmaster.co.uk
http://www.ticketmaster.com.au

Book event tickets online in the US, UK, and Australia.

Twenty Questions
http://come.to/20Q/

It can guess what you're thinking within twenty questions. Try it, you'll be amazed.

Uri Geller's Psychic City
http://www.urigeller.com

Test your ESP, fail dismally, and then find out why you need the services of the champion cutlery curler himself.

Useless Knowledge
http://www.uselessknowledge.com • http://www.funtrivia.com

Just the sort of stuff you didn't want to know, but are glad you do.

Webcams
http://www.earthcam.com • http://www.coolbase.com/peepingtom/
http://www.live-cam.com.ar

Spend a night peeping through the Net's many cameras, then rest content that you've sat with pioneers at the very cutting edge of technology. Tick that off the list and get on with life.

EZINES

It's a fine distinction as to what's a Net magazine (ezine) and what's a magazine posted on the Net; those below are largely the former. The best lists of electronic journals and ezines are the

Ezine List: http://www.meer.net/~johnl/e-zine-list/ and
Factsheet5: http://www.factsheet5.com

See also "News, Newspapers, and Magazines" (p.336)

Anorak
http://www.anorak.co.uk

Irreverent daily dip into the UK tabloids and broadsheets.

Bittersweet
http://www.bittersweets.org

Short and sharp reflections on lost loves, somewhat reminiscent of **99 secrets**: http://99secrets.com

Chick Click

http://www.chickclick.com

Coalition of the most notable independent grrl-powered Web
sites including: Disgruntled Housewife, GrrlGamer,
Smartypants, Mousy, Amazoncity, Riotgrrl, DJDazy, Hellfire,
and Bimbionic. You'll know straight away if it's your scene.

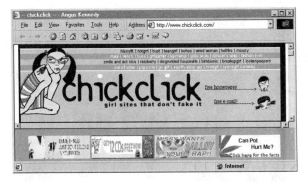

Erack

http://www.erack.com

Selections and exclusives from UK newsstand titles: **Q**, **Select**,
New Woman, **FHM**, **Carworld**, **Maxpower**, **Motorcycle World**,
and **Empire**.

FeedMag

http://www.feedmag.com

Highbrow essays on the technology of culture and vice versa.
Stop by the "loop" to beat it over with the authors and other
media pundits. Not cerebral enough for you? Then try:
http://www.edge.com

Fray

http://www.fray.com

Personal, provocative, and potentially disturbing, Fray melts
haunting graphics over strong prose on criminals, drugs,
work, and hope.

FutureNet

http://www.futurenet.co.uk

Daily news, plus features, from the UK magazine publisher's many titles on computing, gaming, technology, film, and music.

Giant Robot

http://www.giantrobot.com

Selections from the print popzine that scoops into Asian treats like Ultraman, CYF, sumo, **Gamera**, manga, P5, and larger-than-average robotica. More at: http://www.hardboiled.org and http://www.j-pop.com

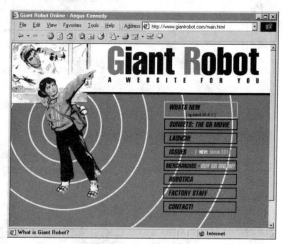

January Magazine

http://www.januarymagazine.com

Dissecting books and authors.

The Onion

http://www.theonion.com

News satire to die for.

Phrack Magazine

http://www.phrack.com

Renowned hackers' quarterly. Never far from controversy.

Salon

http://www.salon.com

Reliably solid features covering modern culture from art to travel with regular columns from renowned US writers such as Camille Paglia, Christopher Hitchens, and James Carville.

Slate

http://www.slate.com

Thoughtful, though dry, news, culture and arts analysis. It's owned by Microsoft, but don't hold that against it.

The Smoking Gun

http://www.thesmokinggun.com

Celebrity shame dug up from police records complete with the photocopied sources.

The Straight Dope

http://www.straightdope.com

Cecil Adams's answers to hard questions. Find out how to renounce your US citizenship, what Kemosabe means, and the difference between a warm smell of colitas and colitis.

Suck

http://www.suck.com

In a smug class all by itself, and arguably the only ezine that ever mattered. Worth reading daily, if not for its cocked eye on all that's wired and painfully modern, then at least for Terry Colon's cartoons.

Swoon

http://www.swoon.com

Dating, mating, and relating. Courtesy of Condé Nast's **Details**, **GQ**, **Glamour**, and **Mademoiselle**.

Underwire

http://underwire.msn.com

Light features from women writers on subjects such as marital politics, table manners, fitness, health, relationships, and car care. You might wonder if you really need to get onto the Net to read this sort of stuff.

Urban Desires
http://www.desires.com

Modern city stories of technology, food, sex, music, art, performance, style, travel, politics, and more.

FASHION

1-800-SURGEON
http://www.surgeon.org

Adjust your imperfection without pills or creams.

Designer City
http://www.designercity.com

London fashion and lifestyle monthly with input from **Cosmo** and **Esquire**.

Elle International
http://www.elle.com

Scraps from the thirty international editions of **Elle**. They barely resemble their glossy paper counterparts but still sport enough swish types in bright duds to make you feel undershopped in any language.

Fashion Net
http://www.fashion.net

More fashion links than you could poke a chapstick at.

Fashionmall.com
http://www.fashionmall.com • http://www.brandsforless.com

Mail order from a swag of US names.

Fashion UK
http://www.widemedia.com/fashionuk/

Another minimal, but fresh, vanity monthly out of London.

Firstview
http://www.firstview.com

Pay to see what's presently trotting the catwalks.

The Lipstick Page
http://www.users.wineasy.se/bjornt/Lip.html

Cosmetic appliances for fun and profit.

Moda Italia

http://www.modaitalia.net

Patch through to the Italian rag traders.

Victoria's Secret

http://www.victoriassecret.com

Order online or request the catalog preferred by nine out of ten teenage boys.

Virtual Makeover

http://www.virtualmakeover.com

Order the demo, scan in your photo, and try on the latest hairdos.

Vogue (UK)

http://www.vogue.co.uk

Celebrity sightings, threadwear news, jobs, catwalk reports, assorted features, and, of course, incessant coverage of the you-know-who's. Still not had enough of them? Then try this for an overdose: http://www.supermodel.com

FILM AND TV

Most TV stations maintain excellent sites with all kinds of extras such as live sports coverage and documentary follow-ups. We won't need to give you their addresses because they'll be flashing them at you at every opportunity. In any case, you'll find them all at: http://www.ultimatetv.com/tv/ If you'd like personalized listings, perhaps delivered by email, try:

> http://www.sofcom.com.au/TV/ (Australia);
> http://www.clicktv.com (Canada);
> http://www.toaster.co.uk (UK); or http://www.gist.com and
> http://www.tvguide.com (USA). Consult **Ultimate TV** or
> your local **Yahoo** for other regions.

Or if you're after a video store, they don't come any bigger than

> Reel.com:http://www.reel.com
> Amazon: http://www.amazon.com and
> Black Star:http://www.blackstar.co.uk

All Movie Guide
http://www.allmovie.com
> Colossal sound and screen directory, complete with reviews and synopses.

Cinemachine
http://www.cinemachine.com
> Movie review search engine. Redirects to the original source.

Dark Horizons
http://www.darkhorizons.com
> Film gossip hub with loads of insides on upcoming releases, plus reviews of the usual suspects.

Drew's Script-O-Rama
http://www.script-o-rama.com
> Hundreds of entire film and TV scripts. Need help writing or selling your own? Try here: http://www.celluloidmonkeys.com

E! Online

http://www.eonline.com

Daily film and TV gossip, news, and reviews.

Empire Magazine

http://www.empireonline.co.uk

News, features, and reviews of every film showing in the UK.

Friends Place

http://www.friendsplace.com

Read through every script of every episode ever. Of course, if you have that much spare time it might make you wish you had some of your own.

God of Actors

http://www.geocities.com/Athens/8907/factor.html

Valuable insight into the John Woo regular who makes Arnie look like Richie Cunningham. Widely regarded as the "coolest man alive".

Greatest Films

http://www.filmsite.org

You're bound to disagree.

Hollywood Reporter

http://www.hollywoodreporter.com

Tinseltown tattle, previews and reviews daily, plus a flick biz directory.

India Talkies

http://www.indiatalkies.com

Take a stroll down Bollywood boulevard.

Internet Movie Database

http://www.imdb.com

You'll be hard pressed to find any work on or off the Net as comprehensive as this exceptional relational database of screen trivia from over 100,000 movies and a million actors.

It's all tied together remarkably well – for example, within two clicks of finding your favorite movie, you can get full filmographies of anyone from the cast or crew, and then see what's in the cooker. Unmissable.

Movies.com

http://www.movies.com

Previews forthcoming Touchstone and Hollywood Pictures. All with short synopses, minute-long sample clips, interviews, stills, and assorted press releases.

Mr Cranky

http://www.mrcranky.com

He mightn't know a thing about films but he sure knows what he doesn't like.

Showbizwire

http://www.showbizwire.com

Top music, theatre, celebrity, film, television, video, and entertainment industry stories aggregated from about fifty major sources as they're released.

The Simpsons Archive

http://www.snpp.com

In barefaced defiance of Fox's "cease and desist" order, fans persist in garnishing the Web with the unofficial sights and sounds of Springfield. Meanwhile, Fox's own at http://www.foxworld.com/simpindx.htm hardly compares.

Screen Network Australia

http://www.sna.net.au

Gateway to Australian film and TV sites. For news, reviews, and interviews, see: http://www.urbancinefile.com.au

Shock Cinema

http://members.aol.com/shockcin/main.html

Picking over celluloid scavenged from Mr Subtlety's dumpster. See also: http://www.bmonster.com and http://www.losman.com

Soap Links

http://members.aol.com/soaplinks/ • http://www.soapdigest.com

Keep up with who's doing what to whom, whom they told, and who shouldn't find out, in the surreal world of soap fiction.

Time For Teletubbies!

http://www.bbc.co.uk/education/teletubbies/tubbies.htm

http://www.pbs.org/teletubbies/

For the official recipe for tubby custard.

Tromaville

http://www.troma.com

Here's your lucky break. Troma, home of class films such as **Toxic Avenger, Chopper Chicks from Zombie Town, Space Freaks from Planet Mutoid, Subhumanoid Meltdown**, and **Fatguy goes Nutzoid**, needs acting outcasts and writers for its Troma Army Bizarre productions.

Ultimate TV

http://www.ultimatetv.com

More on everything televisual than is mentally healthy. Places to vent your gripes, broadcasting addresses, schedules, job vacancies, and links to fan pages of just about every show ever made. By the time you get through this lot, you'll be too plum-tuckered for the neon bucket itself.

Universal Studios

http://www.mca.com

What's in store from the MCA/Universal movie and music stable.

Variety

http://www.variety.com

Screen news fresh off the PR gattling gun.

VCR Repair Instructions

http://www.fixer.com

How to take a VCR apart and then get all the little bits back in so it fits easier into the bin.

Who would you kill?

http://www.whowouldyoukill.com

So which of the Party of Five would you bump off?

FOOD AND DRINK

When following recipes, note where they're from so you don't mix up the measures. For example, an Australian tablespoon is four, not three, teaspoons.

99 ways to open a beer bottle
http://www.inch.com/~brett/

Forgot your bottle opener? No problem: just look for a cop car or fire hydrant.

BarMeister.com
http://www.barmeister.com

Experimental cocktails with companion games to ensure the misfires aren't wasted.

Beershots
http://micro.magnet.fsu.edu/beershots/

Beers of the world put under a microscope. Literally!

Birdseye Recipe Search
http://www.birdseye.com/search.html

Cast your line into the Fish Finger king's own recipe database or trawl through hundreds of other Net collections.

Breworld.com

http://www.breworld.com

None of the usual beer yarns like waking up in a strange room stark naked with a throbbing head and a hazy recollection of pranging your car. Here, beer is treated with the same dewy-eyed respect usually reserved for wine and trains. Want to send your chum a virtual beer? Stumble over to: http://www.pubworld.co.uk

Chile-Heads

http://neptune.netimages.com/~chile/

Dip into chili recipes, chemistry, botanical facts, gardening tips, and general peppering. Find out what's the hottest pepper, what makes it so hot, how your body reacts, and identify that mystery one in your kebab.

Cigar Aficionado

http://www.cigaraficionado.com

Archives, shopping guides, and tasting forums from the US glossy that sets the benchmark in cigar ratings.

Cocktail

http://www.cocktailtime.com

Guzzle your way to a happier home.

Cook's Thesaurus

http://www.northcoast.com/~alden/cookhome.html

Find substitutes for fatty, expensive, or hard-to-find ethnic ingredients.

Crazy Vegetarian

http://www.crazyveg.com

Light-hearted, meatless nutrition raps.

CyberChocy

http://www.caliebe.de/e/cyberchocy.htm

Design your own label. They'll wrap it around a Ritter Sport bar and ship it anywhere worldwide. Can't spare ten dollars? Then send a virtual one instead: http://www.virtualchocolate.com

DineNet

http://menusonline.com

Thousands of US restaurant menus, plus maps to aid fulfillment.

Epicurious

http://www.epicurious.com

Web-only marriage of Condé Nast's **Gourmet**, **Bon Appetit**, and **Traveler** magazines, crammed with recipes, culinary forums, advice on dining out around the world, and ways to stave off hunger with panache.

Fillet

http://www.fillet.com

Weekly tales of food snobbery and quiet drunkenness.

Internet Chef

http://www.ichef.com

Over 30,000 recipes, cooking hints, kitchen talk, and more links than you could jab a fork in.

Kim Chee

http://www.kim-chee.com • http://www.kimchi.or.kr

Learn to love Korean spicy cabbage even if it makes you smell like a rendering plant.

The Kitchen Garden Online

http://www.taunton.com/kg/

For cooks who love to garden, or perhaps vice versa.

Kitchen Link

http://www.kitchenlink.com

Points to more than 10,000 galleries of gluttony.

Moonshine

http://moonshine.co.nz

Get blind (possibly literally) on homemade spirits.

An Ode to Olives

http://www.bayarea.net/~emerald/olive.html

You'll never look at an olive ambivalently again.

Smell the Coffee

http://www.smellthecoffee.com

Develop a nose for the beans and their pleasant effect on your nervous system. Now trace them back to the source: http://www.nationalgeographic.com/coffee/

Restaurant Row

http://www.restaurantrow.com

Key in your dining preferences and find the perfect match
from hundreds of thousands of food barns worldwide.

The Soda Fountain

http://www.sodafountain.com

Hard facts on soft drinks – including the recipe for the
original "real thing".

Spice Guide

http://www.spiceguide.com

Encyclopedia of spices covering their origins, purposes,
recipes, and tips on what goes best with what.

Tasty Insect Recipes

http://www.ent.iastate.edu/Misc/InsectsAsFood.html
http://www.eatbug.com

Dig in to such delights as Bug Blox, Banana Worm Bread,
Rootworm Beetle Dip, and Chocolate Chirpie Chip Cookies
(with crickets).

Teatime

http://www.teatime.com/

Types of tea, tried and tasted, and a turnpike to all that's tea
taken truly. See also: http://www.stashtea.com

Tokyo Food Page

http://www.bento.com/tokyofood.html

Where and what to eat in Tokyo, a sushi decoder, plus a few recipes and tips such as how to detect parasites in your uncooked mullet.

Top Secret Recipes

http://www.topsecretrecipes.com • http://www.copykat.com

At least one commercial recipe, such as KFC coleslaw, revealed each week. Many are surprisingly basic.

The Ultimate Cookbook

http://www.ucook.com

Pinch recipes from hundreds of popular cookbooks. More food porn unplugged at: http://www.cook-books.com

Wine Spectator

http://www.winespectator.com

Before you pick the plonk with the fancy-dress label, run its vital stats against the Spectator's database. Not only will you be assured of quality, but you'll be able to slurp and slur with greater authority at the dinner table.

GAMES

For more, check out "Online Gaming" (p.200).

Blues News

http://www.bluesnews.com

Keep up with what's Quakin'.

Dave's Video Game Classics

http://www.davesvgc.com
http://www.classicgaming.com/vault/

Know someone who grizzles on about old school arcade games such as Pleides, Lunar Rescue, Donkey Kong, and Xevious? Sentence them to ten minutes here.

GameFAQs

http://www.gamefaqs.com

Stuck on a level or just want to know more? Seek help in the FAQs.

Grrl Gamer

http://www.grrlgamer.com

Team up with other game grrls and prepare to kick dweeb boy butt right across their own turf. More reinforcement at: http://www.gamegirlz.com

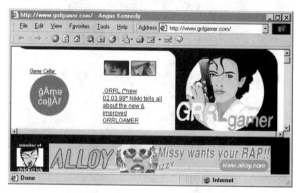

Kasparov vs Deep Blue

http://www.chess.ibm.com

If Kasparov ever takes on Deep Blue again, here's where to watch it live. Apart from that, it chronicles the historical triumph of machine over mortal with links that will tickle any serious chess aficionado. Or if you're up for a game yourself, take your pick from: http://chess.about.com

PC Game Finder

http://www.pcgame.com

Top games search engine that intelligently splits results by reviews, cheats, demos, and required hardware. Indexes most of the leading game lairs.

Playsite

http://www.playsite.com

Play popular table games such as chess, backgammon and go-moku against online opponents. It's all done through Java applets so you won't need any extra software, but it might crash your browser.

PSX Codes

http://www.psxextreme.com

Playstation news, reviews, previews, cheats, and forums.

The Riddler

http://www.riddler.com

Use your Web scavenging, lateral thinking, literary, trivia, and other skills to compete across the Net for prizes.

Video Game Strategies

http://vgstrategies.about.com

Guide to the best PSX, N64, Dreamcast, and other console game sites.

Virtual Vegas

http://www.virtualvegas.com

Showgirls, VRML slot machines, Shockwave blackjack, Java poker, shopping, and a chat-up lounge. VV bucks are virtual, but occasionally the prizes are real.

Webgames

http://happypuppy.com/compgames/webgames/

Pit your wits against the computer or remote opponents.

PC GAMES

For reviews, news, demos, hints, patches, cheats, downloads, and other PC game necessities try:

Adrenaline Vault	http://www.avault.com
Gamecenter	http://www.gamecenter.com
Gamers.com	http://www.gamers.com
Games Domain	http://www.gamesdomain.com
Gamespot	http://www.gamespot.com
Happy Puppy	http://www.happypuppy.com
Macintosh Gamer's Ledge	http://www.macledge.com
Online Gaming Realm	http://www.ogr.com

HEALTH

Achoo
http://www.achoo.com
> Like a Yahoo of health and wellbeing sites. Drill down until you get your medicine. See also: http://www.hon.ch and http://www.patient.co.uk (UK)

Alternative Medicine
http://altmedicine.about.com
> Part of the Net's ongoing research function is the ability to contact people who've road-tested alternative remedies and can report on their efficacy. Start here and work your way to an answer.

Ask Dr Weil
http://www.drweil.com
> **Time** magazine felt Popdoctor Andrew Weil's eagerness to prescribe from a range of bewildering, and often conflicting, alternative therapies earned him front-cover status. Naturally, it had nothing to do with his move from *HotWired* to a vitamin-chain-sponsored corner of Time's pathfinder complex. Here, he answers a medical question each day, and Dr Ruth gives her usual get-fresh tips.

Biorhythm Generator
http://www.facade.com/attraction/biorhythm/
> Generate a cyclical report that can double as a sick note.

Dr Squat

http://www.drsquat.com

Avoid getting sand kicked in your face through deep full squats.

There's more in the Weightlifting FAQ at:
http://www.imp.mtu.edu/~babucher/weights.html

The Drugs Archive

http://www.hyperreal.org/drugs/

Articles, primarily accumulated from the alt.drugs newsgroup, that provide first-hand perspectives on the pleasures and dangers of recreational drugs.

See also: http://www.lycaeum.org and http://www.trashed.co.uk

GYN101

http://www.gyn101.com

Swot up for your next gynecological exam.

But if you're after honors go straight to: http://www.obgyn.net

HealthWorld

http://www.healthy.net

Health megasite aimed at practitioners and patients alike with a healthy balance of the conventional to the alternative.

Medicinal Herb Faq

http://sunsite.unc.edu/herbmed/mediherb.html

If it's in your garden and it doesn't kill you, it can only make you stronger. More leafy cures and love drugs at:
http://www.algy.com/herb/

Medline

http://www.bewell.com/MEDLINE/

For serious medical research go straight to Medline, the US National Library of Medicine's database. It archives, references, and abstracts from some 3500 medical journals and periodicals going back to 1966. You can get to it free from here, along with a raft of other biomedical resources.

Medscape

http://www.medscape.com

Medical forum aimed at health pros and med students but equally useful to anyone concerned with their general well-being.

Mental Health

http://www.mentalhealth.com

Guaranteed you'll come out of this site convinced there's something wrong with you. Worry your way anxiously to: http://www.anxietynetwork.com or http://www.onlinepsych.com

Museum of Questionable Medical Devices

http://www.mtn.org/quack/

Gallery of health-enhancing products where even breaks weren't bundled free.

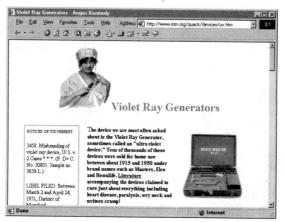

Nutritional Supplements

http://www.nutritionalsupplements.com

First-hand experiences with vitamins, bodybuilding supplements, and other dubious health shop fodder.

Pregnancy Calendar

http://www.pregnancycalendar.com • http://www.parentsoup.com
http://www.parenthoodweb.com

Count down the nine months from conception to pregnancy and get prepared to juggle your life around your new family member. If bub gets sick and you can't get to a doctor try pediatrician Dr Green for advice: http://www.drgreene.com

Online Surgery

http://www.onlinesurgery.com

Human panel beating performed live for the camera by Dr Jake Riviera and associates. No, it's probably not a good idea to enter that competition.

RxList

http://www.rxlist.com

Look up your medication to ensure you're not being poisoned. See also: http://www.virtualdrugstore.com and http://www.pharminfo.com

Phys: In Fitness and in Health

http://www.phys.com

Assess and improve your fitness and diet. Net exclusives plus select features from Condé Nast's **Sports for Women, Mademoiselle, Glamour, Vogue, Allure,** and **Self.**

Quackwatch

http://www.quackwatch.com

Separating the docs from the ducks. Don't buy into any alternative remedies until you've read these pages.

Reuters Health

http://www.reutershealth.com

Medical newswires, reviews, opinion, and reference.

Worldwide Nurse

http://www.wwnurse.com

Springboard to chat groups, research data, professional bodies, jobs, and other nursing resources.

The Virtual Hospital

http://www.vh.org

Patient care and distance learning via online multimedia tools such as illustrated surgical walkthroughs.

The Visible Human Project

http://www.nlm.nih.gov/research/visible/

Whet your appetite by skimming through scans of a thinly filleted serial killer, and then top it off with a fly-through virtual colonoscopy. For higher production values, see the **Virtual Body**: http://www.medtropolis.com/vbody/

Yahooka
http://www.yahooka.com
> Yahoo gone entirely to pot.

Yoga
http://www.timages.com/yoga.htm
> Stretch yourself back into shape with a personalized routine.
> More at: http://www.yogasite.com

HOME AND GARDEN

Dallas Kennedy rose

America's Home Improvement Network
http://www.improvenet.com
> Peruse the latest design ideas and find someone to do the job.
> You can even screen your local builders against public
> records and find the one least likely to quaff all your home
> brew and sell your nude holiday snaps to the **National
> Enquirer**: http://www.nationalenquirer.com

Ask the Master Plumber
http://www.clickit.com/bizwiz/homepage/plumber.htm
> Save a small fortune by unblocking your own toilet.

Australian Real Estate

http://www.showme.net.au • http://propertyweb.com.au

Combines listings from hundreds of Australian brokers.

Feng Shui

http://www.qi-whiz.com

How to recreate the ambience of a Chinese restaurant.

FinanCenter

http://www.financenterinc.com

Figure out your monthly payments or what you can't afford.

Gardening.com

http://www.gardening.com

Includes an illustrated gardening encyclopedia, a problem solver to debug some 700 horticultural ailments, and a guide to hundreds of other groundbreaking sites.

See also: http://gardening.about.com • http://www.gardenguides.com
http://www.vg.com and http://www.talkingplants.com

Gothic Gardening

http://www.gothic.net/~malice/

Grow a little greenhouse of horrors.

Home Tips

http://www.hometips.com

Load your toolbox, roll up your sleeves, and prepare to go in. More advice at: http://www.housenet.net
http://www.doityourself.com and http://www.naturalhandyman.com

Home Scout (US)

http://www.homescout.com

Scan hundreds of US real estate databases at once.

HouseWeb (UK)

http://www.houseweb.co.uk

Rent, buy, or sell property within the UK. See also:
http://www.findaproperty.com and http://www.propertylive.co.uk

International Real Estate Digest

http://www.ired.com

Locate real estate listings, guides, and property-related services worldwide.

Maui Buy the Inch

http://aloha-mall.com/buy-maui/

Stake out a square inch of paradise for a mere $15.99 – about £10.00

Realtor.com (US)

http://www.realtor.com

Lists over a million properties for sale across the US. Run by the National Association of Realtors, the industry's main professional body.

Spring Street

http://www.springstreet.com • http://www.apartments.com

Find an apartment to rent in the US.

This to That

http://www.thistothat.com

So what would you like to glue today?

UpMyStreet

http://www.upmystreet.com

Astounding wealth of house price, health, crime, schools, tax, and other statistics on UK neighborhoods. Mighty useful if you're shifting base.

KIDS (MOSTLY)

It's your choice whether you want to let them at it head-long or bridle their experience through rose-colored filters. But if you need guidance, or pointers towards the most kidtastic chowder, set sail into these realms:

Australian Families Guide http://www.aba.gov.au/family/
American Libraries Assoc. http://www.ala.org/parentspage/greatsites/
Kid's Search Engine http://searchenginewatch.com/facts/kids.html
Surfing the Net with Kids http://www.surfnetkids.com

Adolescent Adulthood
http://www.adolescentadulthood.com
How to flirt, date, kiss, and ultimately dump, so you won't spend the rest of the year being teased at the bus stop.

Animal Information Database
http://www.seaworld.org
Tune in to the Webcams at the right time and you'll catch J.J. the grey whale being fed, or any of thirty-two species of sharks doing the kind of big fish chomping stuff that makes surfers shiver.

Bizarre Things You Can Make In Your Kitchen
http://freeweb.pdq.net/headstrong/
Rainy-day science projects and general mischief such as volcanoes, stink bombs, cosmic ray detectors, fake blood, and hurricane machines.

The Bug Club
http://www.ex.ac.uk/bugclub/
Creepy-crawly fan club with e-pal page, newsletters, and pet care sheets on how to keep your newly bottled tarantulas, cockroaches, and stick insects alive.

Children's Literature Web Guide
http://www.ucalgary.ca/~dkbrown/
Critical roundup of recent kids books, and links to texts.

Club Girl Tech
http://www.girltech.com
Encourages smart girls to get interested in technology without coming across all geeky.

Coloring.com

http://www.coloring.com

Select a picture segment, choose a color, and then shade it in.
You don't need to be Leonardo. Rather create your own
caricature? Then head off to: http://www.magixl.com

Cyberteens

http://www.cyberteens.com

Submit your music, art, or writing to a public gallery. You
might even win a prize.

Disney.com

http://www.disney.com

Guided catalog of Disney's real world movies, books, theme
parks, records, interactive CD-ROMs and such, plus a
squeaky-clean guide to the Net.

Everything Cool

http://www.everythingcool.com

Budding magazine written by under-18s for under-18s.

Fantastic Fractals
http://library.advanced.org/12740/

A fractal is a complex self-similar and chaotic mathematical object that reveals more detail as you get closer. Download the software, follow the instructions, and generate some funky graphics.

Funschool
http://www.funschool.com

Educational games for preschoolers.

Greatest Places
http://www.greatestplaces.org

Which are the world's top spots? See if you agree.

The History Net
http://www.thehistorynet.com

Bites of world history, with an emphasis on the tough guys going in with guns. More at: http://www.historybuff.com

Homework Central
http://www.homeworkcentral.com

Study collections for all grades through to college.

KidPub
http://www.kidpub.org/kidpub/

No drinks served here, just thousands of stories submitted by kids worldwide.

Kids' Space
http://www.kids-space.org

Hideout for kids to swap art, music, and stories with new friends across the world.

Learn2
http://learn2.com

Figure out how to do all sorts of things from fixing a zipper to spinning a basketball. While the interests aren't strictly for kids, there's nothing here that's too hard for a whippersnapper.

The Little Animals Activity Centre
http://www.bbc.co.uk/education/laac/

The second the music starts and the critters start jiggling you'll know you're in for a treat. What's most surprising is

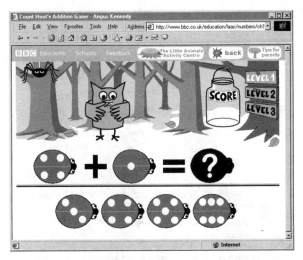

it's seriously educational to boot. Let your youngest heir loose here after breakfast and expect no mercy until morning tea. Quite possibly the cutest site on the Net.

Mr Edible Starchy Tuber Head
http://winnie.acsu.buffalo.edu/potatoe/
Create your own, customized Mr Potato Head.

Name That Candybar
http://www.sci.mus.mn.us/sln/tf/c/crosssection/namethatbar.html
Okay, so how well do you know your chocolate bars?

StarChild
http://starchild.gsfc.nasa.gov
Nasa's educational funhouse for junior astronomers. See also: http://www.earthsky.com

Web66: International School Web Site Directory
http://web66.coled.umn.edu/schools.html
Add your school's Web page if it's not already listed.

White House for Kids

http://www.whitehouse.gov/WH/kids/html/kidshome.html

Follow Socks through the White House to uncover its
previous inhabitants, including the kids and pets. Then,
write to the resident moggy and get the goss on what goes
down in DC after dark.

Yahooligans

http://www.yahooligans.com

Kid-friendly Web directory intuitively organized into subject
groups such as dinosaurs, toys, and homework help. Like big
brother Yahoo, but without the dodgy and heavy stuff.

You Can

http://www.beakman.com

Answers to typical kid questions from the likes of "why poop
is brown" and "why farts smell" to "why your voice sounds
different on a tape recorder" and "why the TV goes crazy
while the mixer is on".

The Yuckiest Site on the Internet

http://www.yucky.com

Fun science with a leaning towards the icky-sticky and the
creepy-crawly. But if you want to get thoroughly engrossed
in the gross, slither right along to: http://www.grossology.org

LEGAL

Advertising Law

http://www.webcom.com/~lewrose/home.html

How far you can push your products has always been at the
iffy end of the law. And on the Internet, where any snake-oil
merchant can set up shop for next to nothing, many business
precedents are yet to be set. Here's help in defining the fine
line between puffery and lies.

Dumb Laws

http://www.dumblaws.com

Legislation with limited appeal.

FindLaw

http://www.findlaw.com

Search the Web for legal info worldwide.

Free Advice
http://www.freeadvice.com

US legal tips in over one hundred topics.

Law.com (US)
http://www.law.com

Legal guides for lawyers, business, students, and the general public. Includes a recruitment agency, lawyer finder, and legalese decoder. See also: http://www.seamless.com and the somewhat less reverent http://www.lectlaw.com

LawGirl
http://www.lawgirl.com

Excellent copyright and entertainment law forums and primers. It's run by one of those cybergrrl types if that means anything to you.

Lawrights
http://www.lawrights.co.uk

Helpful FAQs on various legal issues in England and Wales, plus a free lawyer referral service.

West's US Legal Directory
http://www.wld.com

Accused of grand theft, arson, or murder one? Then whip through this database of over half a million US lawyers who'd rather see you go free than go without their fee.

MONEY

If your bank's on the ball it will offer an online facility to check your balances, pay your bills, transfer funds, and export your transaction records into a bean counting program such as Quicken or MS Money. If that sounds appealing, and your bank isn't already on the case, start looking for a replacement. Favor one you can access via the Internet rather than by dialing direct. That way you can manage your cash through a Web browser whether you're at home, work, or in the cybercafé on top of Pik Kommunisma. For help finding a true online bank, try the

Online Banking Report	http://www.netbanker.com
Qualisteam	http://www.qualisteam.com and
MyBank	http://www.mybank.com

As long as you can resist the urge to daytrade away your inheritance, you'll find the Net will give you greater control over your financial future. You can research firms, identify trends, receive live quotes, join tip lists and stock forums, track your portfolio live, trade shares, and access more news than is fit to read in a lifetime. By all means investigate a subscription service or two – at least for the free trial period – but unless you need pro data feeds or "expert" timing advice you should be able to get by without paying. Start off at

Yahoo Finance	http://quote.yahoo.com

or local counterpart such as

Yahoo Australia	http://quote.yahoo.com.au or
Yahoo UK	http://quote.yahoo.co.uk

Apart from housing the Net's most exhaustive finance directory, Yahoo pillages data from a bunch of the top finance sources and presents it all in a seamless, friendly format. Enter a stock code, for example, and you'll get all the beef from the latest ticker price to a summary of insider trades. In some markets stocks have their own forums, which, let's face it, are there only to spread rumors. In other words, be very skeptical of anything you read or that's sent to you in unsolicited email.

Yahoo is by no means complete nor necessarily the best in every area, so try a few of these as well:

CBS MarketWatch	http://cbs.marketwatch.com
FinancialWeb	http://www.financialweb.com
Investorama	http://www.investorama.com
Microsoft MoneyCentral	http://moneycentral.msn.com
Wall Street City	http://www.wallstreetcity.com
Wall Street Research Net	http://www.wsrn.com

You'll no doubt be after a broker next. As with banking, any broker or fund manager who's not setting up online doesn't deserve your business. In fact, many traders are dumping traditional brokers in favor of the exclusively online houses such as

E*Trade	http://www.etrade.com
Datek	http://www.datek.com
Discover	http://www.discoverbrokerage.com.

Again, services and commissions vary wildly so it pays to shop around. You could start by reading the broker ratings at

Scorecard	http://www.scorecard.com and
Smart Money	http://www.smartmoney.com

If you're outside the US, try your local Yahoo for leads. A word of warning, though: many of these online brokers have experienced outages where they were unable to trade. So if the market plummets, as happened in 1987, it mightn't hurt to play safe and use the phone instead.

BigCharts

http://www.bigcharts.com

Whip up family-sized graphs of US stocks, mutual funds, and market indices. Or if you'd prefer them streaming at you live, proceed to: http://www.livecharts.com

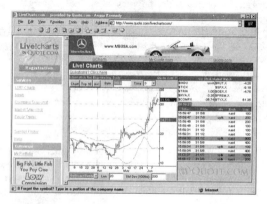

Clearstation

http://www.clearstation.com

Run your stock picks through a succession of grueling obstacle courses to weed out the weaklings or simply copy someone else's portfolio.

Earnings Whispers

http://www.earningswhispers.com

When a stock price falls upon the release of higher than expected earnings, chances are the expectations being "whispered" amongst traders prior to open were higher than those circulated publicly. Here's where to find out what's being said behind your back.

Foreign Exchange Rates

http://quote.yahoo.com • http://quotes.reuters.com

Round the clock rates, conversion calculators, and intraday charts on pretty close to the full set of currencies. To chart further back, see: http://pacific.commerce.ubc.ca/xr/plot.html

DataChimp
http://www.datachimp.com

Plain English primer in the mechanics of financial maths.

Electronic Share Information (UK)
http://www.esi.co.uk

UK share quotes, fundamentals, and online trading. For a brief guide to the best UK financial sites see:
http://cube.icestorm.com/homepage/invest.html

E*Trade
http://www.etrade.com • http:www.etrade.com.au (AUS)
http://www.canada.etrade.com (CAN) • http://www.cpretrade.com (FR)

Discount brokerage that's spreading worldwide faster than Hong Kong 'flu. One of the few places with free real-time quotes.

Financial Times
http://www.ft.com

Business news, commentary, delayed quotes, and closing prices from London. It's free until you hit the archives.

Global Strategist Game
http://www.global-strategist.com

Sprinkle a pretend portfolio around various investments. Whoever ends up with the biggest pie, bags the kitty.

iCreditReport
http://www.icreditreport.com

Dig up any US citizen's credit ratings.

Intermoney
http://www.intermoney.com

Daily briefs on the international money markets.

Investment FAQ
http://www.invest-faq.com • http://www.investyoung.com

Learn the ropes from old hands.

Money Origami
http://www.umva.com/~clay/money/

It's much more fun when you can make something out of it.

Motley Fool
http://www.fool.com

Forums, tips, quotes, and sound advice.

OilWorld
http://oilworld.com

All the gas on petrochemicals.

InvestorWords
http://www.investorwords.com

Can't tell your hedge rate from your asking price? Brush up on your finance-speak here.

RateNet
http://www.rate.net

Tracks and ranks finance rates across over 11,000 US institutions in 175 markets. Also links to thousands of banking sites and investment products. See also, the **Bank Rate Monitor**: http://www.bankrate.com

Shareholder Action Handbook
http://www.bath.ac.uk/Centres/Ethical/Share/

When you buy shares in a public company, you gain certain voting rights. Perhaps you could exercise those rights to the benefit of your community.

Tax & Accounting Sites Directory
http://www.taxsites.com

Links to everything you need to know about doling out your annual pound of flesh.

Wall Street Journal Interactive
http://www.wsj.com

Not only is this online edition equal to the print, its charts and data archives give it an edge. That's why you shouldn't complain that it's not free. After all, if it's your type of paper, you should be able to afford it, bigshot. You'll also find Forbes, Barrons, and Fortune at exactly the addresses you'd expect.

World Bank
http://www.worldbank.org

The World Bank attempts to help developing countries reduce poverty and sustain economic growth. If you're perplexed by how it can give away so much money and still stay afloat, you might come away a little more enlightened.

MUSIC

If you're at all into music you've come to the right place. Whether you want to hear it, read about it, or watch it being performed, you'll be swamped with options. If you're after a specific band, label, or music genre, try:

Ultimate Band List: http://www.ubl.com

Yahoo http://www.yahoo.com/r/mu/

For music news scan

iMusic Newsagent: http://imusic.interserv.com/newsagent/

and follow the links. Before you proceed to the nearest online jukebox, grab all the latest music players.

For PCs that's

RealPlayer http://www.real.com

Media Player http://www.microsoft.com/mediaplayer/

Winamp http://www.winamp.com

For the Mac, get

RealPlayer, Quicktime http://www.quicktime.com and

MacAmp http://www.macamp.com

For more on music players, see p.90 & 427

Addicted to Noise
http://www.addict.com

Monthly news and reviews with a heavy bias towards the rowdy end of the pop rock spectrum.

All Music Guide
http://www.allmusic.com

Massive music database spanning most popular genres, with bios, reviews, ratings, and keyword crosslinks to related sounds, sites, and online ordering. It's well researched, sufficiently critical, and surprisingly comprehensive.

Art of the Mixed Tape
http://www.artofthemix.org

If you have ever killed an afternoon making a mix, spent the evening making a cover, and then mailed a copy off to a friend after having made a copy for yourself, well, this is the site for you. Kind of says it all.

Audio Review

http://www.audioreview.com

Audio equipment reviewed by end users. A fine concept but somewhat flawed by extreme opinions. Still, if you're not satisfied here, you can link on for alternatives.

Canonical List of Weird Band Names

http://home.earthlink.net/~chellec/

Just be thankful your parents weren't so creative. Here's the story behind a few: http://www.heathenworld.com/bandname/

BUYING RECORDS ONLINE

Shopping for music is another area where the Net not only equals, but outshines, its terrestrial counterparts. Apart from the convenience of not having to tramp across town, you can find almost anything on current issue, whether or not it's released locally, and in many cases preview album tracks in **RealAudio**. You might save money, too, depending on where you buy, whether you're hit with tax, and how the freight stacks up. In Australia, for example, you'll be billed by customs if your duty exceeds $50.00, so split your order if it's over US$100.00.

The biggest hitch you'll strike is when stock is put on backorder. Web operators can boast a huge catalog simply because they order everything on the fly, thus putting you at the mercy of their distributors. The trouble is your entire order might be held up by one item. The better shops check their stock levels before confirming your order, and follow its progress until delivery.

As far as where to shop goes, that depends on your taste. In terms of sheer innovation, Tunes.com: http://www.tunes.com stands out by profiling your preferences, recommending selections, linking to reviews, and serving up ample samples. You can't go too far wrong with most of the blockbusters either, such as:

Amazon	http://www.amazon.com
Borders	http://www.borders.com
Boxman (UK)	http://www.boxman.co.uk
Chaos (AUS)	http://www.cmm.com.au
CDNow	http://www.cdnow.com
CD Universe	http://www.cduniverse.com
HMV (UK)	http://www.hmv.co.uk
YALPLAY (UK)	http://www.yalplay.com
Tower Records	http://www.towerrecords.com
Virgin Megastore	http://www.virginmega.com

To compare prices, try:

ACSES	http://www.acses.com
Bottom Dollar	http://www.bottomdollar.com
MySimon	http://www.mysimon.com
Virtual Outlet	http://www.vo.infospace.com

Or, if you're after something more obscure, you'll find no shortage of options under the appropriate Yahoo categories. Like these, for example:

CyberCD
http://www.cybercd.de

Enormous catalog of CDs and vinyl, though not so cheap.

Dusty Grooves
http://www.dustygroove.com

Soul, jazz, Latin, Brazil, and funk on vinyl and CD.

Hard to find records
http://www.hard-to-find.co.uk

Record-finding agency that specializes in house, hip-hop, soul, and disco vinyl.

Record Finder
http://www.recordfinders.com

Stocks deleted vinyl, including over 200,000 45s.

Second Spin
http://www.secondspin.com

Wide range of used CDs and videos.

TimeWarp
http://www.tunes.co.uk/timewarp/
Jazzy grooves, Latin, hip-hop, funk and underground dance.

X-Radio
http://www.x-radio.com
Dub, chill, leftfield, techno, and urban beats.

COOKING YOUR OWN CD

Fancy whipping up your own custom CD? Then try out a DIY compilation shop. Simply run through their catalog, preview what looks good, submit your track listing, and they'll burn it to disk. Expect this to catch on in a big way. For a glimpse of what's to come, see:

Cductive	http://www.cductive.com
Cerberus	http://www.cdj.co.uk
Custom Disc	http://www.customdisc.com
MusicMaker	http://www.musicmaker.com
Razorcuts	http://www.razorcuts.co.uk
Supersonic Boom	http://www.supersonicboom.com

CDDB
http://www.cddb.com
Automatically supplies track listings for the CDs playing in your PC drive.

CD Zapping
http://www.netcomuk.co.uk/~wwl/cdzap.html
Put your flatmate's Verve CD out of its misery.

Classical Music on the Net
http://www.musdoc.com/classical/
Gateway to the timeless. To shop, see:
http://www.classicalinsites.com and http://www.cdmaestro.com

The Dance Music Resource
http://www.juno.co.uk
New and forthcoming dance releases for mail order, UK radio slots, and a stacked link directory. See also: http://www.fly.co.uk

Dancetech

http://www.dancetech.com

One-stop shop for techno toys and recording tips. For more on synths: http://www.synthzone.com and http://www.sonicstate.com

The Daily .Wav

http://www.dailywav.com
http://www.wavcentral.com

Posts at least one new screen theme a day. Fun for assigning to computer events such as new mail. That is, until they drive everyone around you loopy.

Dirty Linen

http://kiwi.futuris.net/linen/

Excerpts from the US folk, roots, and world music magazine. See also Folk Roots: http://www.froots.demon.co.uk

dotmusic

http://www.dotmusic.com

Top source of UK and global music news, weekly charts, and new releases in RealAudio.

Global Electronic Music Market
http://gemm.com

One-point access to over two million new and used records from almost two thousand sources.
See also: http://www.musicfile.com

Harmony Central
http://www.harmonycentral.com

Directory and headspace for musicians of all persuasions.

Independent Underground Music Archive
http://www.iuma.com

Full-length tracks and bios from thousands of unsigned and indie-label underground musicians.

List of Music Mailing Lists
http://www.shadow.net/~mwaas/lomml/

Obsess about your favorite pop tunes with other fans.

Jazz Central Station
http://www.jazzcentralstation.com

Bottomless drawer of beard-stroking delights.
See also: http://www.allaboutjazz.com
and http://www.downbeatjazz.com

Live Concerts
http://www.liveconcerts.com

Major gigs live in RealAudio.

London Techno Events
http://www.sorted.org/london/

What's spinning around London's techno circuit.

Lyrics Server
http://www.lyrics.ch

Search a massive lyrics database by title, artist, or text. Everyone from Aaron Neville to 999.

MIDI Farm
http://www.midifarm.com

Synthesized debasements of pop tunes, TV themes, and film scores. Cheesy listening at its finest.

MP3 Resources

http://www.mp3.com • http://www.mp3meta.com
http://www.goodnoise.com • http://mp3.lycos.com
http://www.mp3spy.com • http://www.amp3.com

Since the average CD track weighs in at around 35 MBs
it's a bit hefty to download. You can reduce it down to
around 3 MBs without sacrificing too much fidelity by
compressing into the MP3 format. Thousands of tracks to
download from these sites, including the odd official
release.

Mr Lucky

http://www.mrlucky.com

Get smooth with advice on rhythm 'n'booze.

MTV

http://www.mtv.com

Ironically, MTV's home on the Web is a bit too much like
hard work. Maybe it's not really fair to complain. After all
the content's there: news, charts, vid clips, interviews,
reviews, and great ladles of its trademark popcultural
blancmange. But you're forced into reading, waiting, and
worst, having to think – surely that's not part of the
grand MTV plan.

Music Festival Finder (US)

http://www.festivalfinder.com

Daily-updated listings of more than 1500 forthcoming
Portaloo playtime across North America. Covers all genres.

MusicVideos.com

http://www.musicvideos.com

Indie music videos on demand via Windows Media Player.
They're impressive, but hardly TV quality.

NME

http://nme.com

Weekly soundclipped record reviews, charts, features, news,
gigs, demos, archives, and live chats from the world's most
influential indie/pop tabloid. For more indie news, features
and over 17,000 album reviews, see

Q Online: http://www.qonline.co.uk And, of course,
there's always the **Rolling Stone**: http://www.rollingstone.com

The Rough Guide to Rock

http://www.roughguides.com/rock/

Probably the world's coolest rock encyclopedia online. And we're not just saying that. Certainly the most democratic, having been developed on the Web with 1100-plus entries using fans as contributors.

Scratch.dk

http://www.scratch.dk

Rated as the number-one hip-hop site by no less an authority than this site itself. More tough talk at http://www.thesource.com and http://www.hiphopsite.com and http://www.rebirthmag.com Gesticulating hands on decks at: http://www.wicked-styles.com and http://www.turntablism.com

Shareware Music Machine

http://www.hitsquad.com/smm/

Tons of shareware music players, editors, and composition tools, for every platform.

Sonic Net

http://www.sonicnet.com

Big-name live cybercasts, streaming audio and video channels, chats, news, and reviews.

Soul Source

http://www.privat.kkf.net/~michael.hughes/

Soul news, reviews, and clips of a distinctly northern aspect. More at: http://www.personal.cet.ac.il/yonin/

Sounds Online

http://www.soundsonline.com

Preview loops and samples, free in RealAudio. Pay to download studio quality. If it's effects you're after, try: http://www.sounddogs.com

SS7x7 Sound System

http://www.ss7x7.com

Mix your own ambient, jazz, and breakbeat tracks instantly in Shockwave.

Taxi

http://www.taxi.com

Online music A&R service. And guess what? You and your plastic kazoo are just what they're looking for.

The Ultimate Band List

http://www.ubl.com

Don't give up if your favorite pop ensemble, music mag, instrument, or record shop isn't stowed in here. While it's probably the most professional effort at an all-encompassing music directory, it's nowhere near complete. Still, if you're after something artist-specific, it's generally ace.

Trouser Press

http://www.trouserpress.com

Entertaining and encyclopedic guide covering alternative rock from the 1970s to the present. More musician and band bios at: http://www.imusic.com

Vietnam Jukebox

http://www.war-stories.com/Oldies/Oldies.htm

Top of the Pops from 1960 through 1975. Only one catch – they're all cheesy midis.

For more music of the live streaming variety, fast forward to the Radio section (p.352.)

NATURE

3D Insects

http://www.ento.vt.edu/~sharov/3d/3dinsect.html

Whiz around a selection of 3D bugs. They're not real insects but at least they don't have pins through their backs.

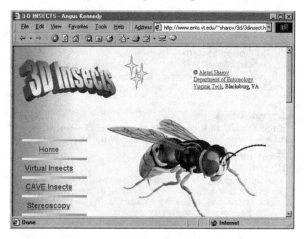

Australian Botanical Gardens

http://www.anbg.gov.au

Guide to Canberra's Botanical Garden and flora down under.

Birding

http://birding.about.com

Birds are such regional critters no one site could hope to cover them all. Use this guide to find one the chirpiest one on your block.

The Complete Hamster site

http://www.hamsters.co.uk • http://www.direct.ca./hamster/

Definitive guides to online hamsters and their inevitable obituaries.

Dog of the Day
http://www.dogoftheday.com

Submit a shot of that drooling retard that adores you unconditionally. Or if it has its own Web page enter it in **Dog Site of the Day**: http://www.st.rim.or.jp/~ito/d/dogmark.html No prize for guessing what's at http://www.catoftheday.com and http://www.petoftheday.com

Environmental Organization Directory
http://www.webdirectory.com

Primary production and green-minded sites sorted by focus.
See also: http://envirolink.org

F@rming Online
http://www.rpl.com.au/farming/

Gateway to predominantly Australian agricultural resources.

Internet Directory for Botany
http://www.botany.net/IDB/

Search engine for serious plantlife research.
See also: http://botany.about.com

Interspecies Telepathic Communication
http://www.cyberark.com/animal/telepath.htm

Relax, you're not hearing voices. It's merely your pets playing mind games.

MooCow
http://www.moocow.com

Living under the influence of cattle as lifestyle accessories.

NetVet
http://netvet.wustl.edu/vet.htm

A certain way to almost anything animalian.

Planet Ark
http://www.planetark.org

Daily environmental news from Reuters.

Sea turtle migration-tracking
http://www.cccturtle.org/satwelc.htm

Adopt a bugged Costa Rican turtle and spy on its passage through the Caribbean and beyond.

NEWS, NEWSPAPERS, AND MAGAZINES

Now that almost every magazine and newspaper in the world from

Ringing World (http://www.luna.co.uk/~ringingw/) to the

Falkland Island News (http://www.sartma.com) is discharging daily content onto the Net, it's beyond this guide to do much more than list a few of the notables and then point you in the right direction for more. The simplest way to find your favorite read would be to look for its address in a recent issue. Failing that try entering its name into Yahoo or one of the search engines. If you don't have a title name and would prefer to browse by subject or region, then try the specialist directories below. Don't stop at one, though, as none is complete.

Newspaper and Magazine Directories

AJR NewsLink	http://ajr.newslink.org/news.html
Editor & Publisher	http://www.mediainfo.com
Metagrid	http://www.metagrid.com
NewsDirectory	http://www.newsdirectory.com
Publist	http://www.publist.com
Ultimate Collection	http://pppp.net/links/news/
UK Media Directory	http://www.mediauk.com/directory/
WebWombat	http://www.webwombat.com.au

Newspapers rarely replicate themselves word for word online, but they often provide enough for you to live without the paper edition. Not bad considering they're generally free online before the paper hits the stands. Apart from whatever proportion of their print they choose to put online, they also tend to delve deeper into their less newsy areas, such as travel, IT, entertainment, and culture. Plus they often bolster this with exclusive content such as breaking news, live sports coverage, online shopping, opinion polls, and discussion groups. In most cases they'll also provide a way to search and retrieve archives, though it might incur a charge. These should get you started:

Australia

The Age	http://www.theage.com.au
The Australian	http://www.news.com.au
Sydney Morning Herald	http://www.smh.com.au

UK

Daily Mail	http://www.dailymail.co.uk
Evening Standard	http://www.thisislondon.co.uk
Express	http://www.express.co.uk
Guardian	http://www.guardian.co.uk
Independent	http://www.independent.co.uk
Mirror	http://www.mirror.co.uk
Telegraph	http://www.telegraph.co.uk
Times	http://www.the-times.co.uk

USA

Boston Globe	http://www.globe.com
Chicago News Network	http://www.chicago-news.com
Christian Science Monitor	http://www.csmonitor.com
Detroit News	http://www.dtnews.com
Houston Chronicle	http://www.chron.com
LA Times	http://www.latimes.com
NY Times	http://www.nytimes.com
The Onion	http://www.theonion.com
Philadelphia Newspapers	http://www.philly.com
San Jose Mercury	http://www.sjmercury.com
Seattle Times	http://www.seattletimes.com
San Francisco Gate	http://www.sfgate.com
USA Today	http://www.usatoday.com
Village Voice	http://www.villagevoice.com
Washington Post	http://www.washingtonpost.com

World

Bangkok Post	http://www.bangkokpost.net
Daily Mail & Guardian	http://www.mg.co.za

El País	http://www.elpais.es
Frankfurter Allgemeine	http://www.faz.de
The Hindu	http://www.hinduonline.com
Irish Times	http://www.irish-times.com
Jerusalem Post	http://www.jpost.com
La Stampa	http://www.lastampa.it
Le Monde	http://www.lemonde.fr
South China Morning Post	http://www.scmp.com
St Petersburg Times	http://www.sptimes.ru
Times of India	http://www.timesofindia.com
Toronto Star	http://www.thestar.com

Like much you do online, reading news can become quite addictive. You'll know you're hooked when you find yourself checking into the newswires throughout the day to monitor moving stories. Try a few of these for a fix:

Breaking News

ABC (AUS)	http://www.abc.net.au/news/
ABC	http://www.abcnews.com
BBC (UK)	http://news.bbc.co.uk
CBS	http://www.cbs.com
CNN	http://www.cnn.com
Fox	http://www.foxnews.com
ITN (UK)	http://www.itn.co.uk
NBC	http://www.msnbc.com
PA Newswire (UK)	http://www.pa.press.net
Reuters	http://www.reuters.com
Sydney Morning Herald (AUS)	http://www.smh.com.au/breaking/
Wired News	http://www.wired.com

Or if you'd like to tap into several sources simultaneously:

News Aggregators

Excite Newstracker	http://nt.excite.com
NewsHub	http://www.newshub.com
NewsNow (UK)	http://www.newsnow.co.uk
TotalNews	http://www.totalnews.com
Yahoo News	http://dailynews.yahoo.com

While most magazines maintain a site, they're typically more of an adjunct to the print than a substitute. Still, they're worth checking out, especially if they archive features and reviews. If you'd rather subscribe to the paper edition try:

http://enews.com • http://mmnewsstand.com
http://www.britishmagazines.com • http://www.acp.com.au

You'll find magazine sites strewn throughout the guide, under "Ezines", or within their relevant subject category.

BBC

http://www.bbc.co.uk

Dig in deep to find BBC TV, radio, World Service, and Education mini-sites of varying quality complete with playlists, schedules, trivia, and assorted fan fodder. Appealing for sure, but the value here is in its blossoming news, weather, and sporting service delivered in text, audio, and video. Although the bulk of its live and archived radio feeds were pulled due to popularity, you'll still stumble across odd exceptions such as Radio 5, the World Service, and Radio One's goofy Digital Update.

Crayon

http://www.crayon.net

Create a custom paper from hundreds of local, national, and international online sources. It grabs the headlines. You click to retrieve the story. Most of the major portals such as MSN, Excite, and Yahoo can do something similar.

Drudge Report

http://www.drudgereport.com

In case you've been in outer space, this is the service that set off the Lewinsky avalanche. Drudge's knack of leaking media moonshine by free email bulletin, before the major press, has brought him widespread notoriety though maybe not respect. Apart from providing forms to subscribe and submit scoops, the top page also serves as a front door to many of the best news beats on the Net.

The Economist

http://www.economist.com

Politics and business commentary, plus a small slab of the magazine free. The lot, when you subscribe.

Infobeat

http://www.infobeat.com

Personalized news, weather, sport, entertainment, snow reports, and reminders delivered to your mailbox free.

Megastories

http://www.megastories.com

Backgrounds and behind-the-scenes reports on many of the world's big flare-ups such as Kosovo and Algeria.

News Index

http://www.newsindex.com

Search current news across a deep list of international online newspapers and news sources.

NGNews

http://www.ngnews.com

Daily eco-news courtesy of the National Geographic.

Pathfinder

http://www.pathfinder.com

Time Warner's attempt at creating an Online Service

experience out of content from its publications such as **Time**, **People**, **Sports Illustrated**, **Life**, **Money**, **Fortune**, **Entertainment Weekly**, and **Vibe** is slated to end with the individual titles taking their own place on the Web. Until then here's how to get to them. Modeled on **Crapfinder**: http://c3f.com/crapfind.html

Ribcast

http://www.ribcast.com

Pay to have all your favorite Russian newspapers dumped onto your desktop using that trendy push technology.

Tabloid.net

http://www.tabloid.net

Sensationalism done sensationally. Acclaimed as some of the best reportage online.

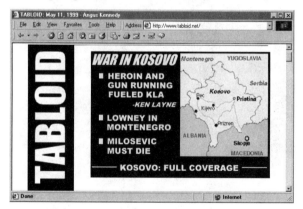

The Top Hundred Stories of the Century

http://www.usatoday.com/2000/general/gen007.htm

Something to argue about over breakfast.

PERSONAL, FRIENDSHIP, AND ADVICE

Adoption.com
http://www.adoption.com
International gateway for placing children.

Alien Implant Removal and Deactivation
http://www.abduct.com/irm.htm
Discover, within a free three-minute phone call, how many times you've been abducted and which implants you're carrying. Then it's just a matter of surgically removing them: http://www.alienscalpel.com and sorting out your mental health. Perhaps the latter is all that's needed.

American Singles
http://www.as.org
Massive free international lonely hearts billboard.

Ask-a-Chick
http://www.ask-a-chick.com
Boys ask girls to set them straight.

Astrology – Atlas and Time Zone Database
http://www.astro.ch/atlas/

Know exactly what was happening upstairs the second of your birth. Or if you prefer your zodiac readings with a touch less pseudoscientific mumbo jumbo, try: http://www.bubble.com/webstars/ or http://astrology.net Now see what old sensible shoes has to say: http://www.skepdic.com/astrolgy.html

Bastard Nation
http://www.bastards.org

Parent search advice, campaigns, and support with a tinge of humor.

Breakup Girl
http://www.breakupgirl.com

How to mend a broken heart and get on with your life. Better still, reject them first:
http://www.xtra.co.nz/content/loveman/reject.html

Cupid's Network
http://www.cupidnet.com

Don't stay home alone playing on your computer. Join a few of these agencies, submit your interests – beer, Quake, footy, and techno, say – and sit back and wait. Before long, you'll be Quakematching by candlelight.

Cyberspace Inmates
http://www.cyberspace-inmates.com

Strike up an email romance with a prison inmate; maybe even one on death row.

Famous Birthdays
http://www.famousbirthdays.com

See who shares your birthday, and estimate how many more to expect.

Genealogy directories
http://www.genhomepage.com • http://www.genealogytoday.com
http://www.familytreemaker.com • http://www.cyndislist.com
http://www.ancestry.com • http://www.familysearch.org

Don't expect to enter your name and produce an instant family tree, but you should be able to fill in a few gaps.

Gulf War Veterans
http://www.gulfweb.org
Lest we forget.

Guy's Rules
http://www.guyrules.com
Learn to conceal your latent femininity.

I Ching
http://www.facade.com/Occult/iching/
If the superior person is not happy with their fortune as told by this ancient Chinese oracle, one can always reload and get another one.

Love Calculator
http://www.cupidnet.com
Enter your respective names to see if you're compatible.

Match.com
http://www.match.com
Browse for a perfect match. All entries come from the Net.

Miss Abigail's Time Warp Advice
http://www.missabigail.com
Solve modern dilemmas with old school logic.

National Center for Missing and Exploited Children
http://www.missingkids.org
Help locate missing children and nail abductors.

Pen Pal Directory
http://www.yahoo.com/Society_and_Culture/Relationships/Pen_Pals/
Exchange email with strangers.

PlanetOut
http://www.planetout.com
Directory to all that's that way inclined. See also:
http://www.qrd.org/qrd/ and http://www.datalounge.com

Rate your risk
http://www.nashville.net/~police/risk/index.htm
See if you're likely to be raped, robbed, stabbed, shot, or beaten to death in the near future.

RSVP
http://www.rsvp.com.au

Seek out a pedigreed Aussie.

Secret Admirer
http://www.secretadmirer.com

Find out whether your most secret crushed one digs you back.

Send a Greetings Card
http://www.cardcentral.net

You can send free multimedia greetings cards from hundreds of sites. Instead of mailing the actual card, they usually send a PIN number, which is used to retrieve the message. This directory lists quite a few, but you'll find dozens more in Yahoo under "Greetings Cards". If bad taste is the object, try: http://www.tackymail.com or http://www.kissogram.com.au or http://www.virtualinsults.com

So There
http://www.sothere.com

A place to post your parting shots.

Steps in Overcoming Urges
http://www.moonmac.com/Mormon_masturbation.html

Having trouble leaving it alone? Here's timely advice from our friends in Salt Lake City.

Toilet Tea Leaves
http://home.golden.net/~treleavn/toilet2.html

Predict your future using the most reliable technique.

Vampire Connection
http://www.cclabs.missouri.edu/~c667539/vwp/connect/

Give blood as an act of love.

See also: http://www.vein-europe.demon.co.uk

Virtual Presents
http://www.virtualpresents.com

Why waste money on real gifts when, after all, isn't it the thought that counts?

Weddings in the Real World
http://www.theknot.comhttp://www.nearlywed.com

Prepare to jump the broom.

POLITICS AND GOVERNMENT

Most government departments, politicians, political aspirants and causes maintain Web sites to spread the word and further their various interests. To find your local rep or candidate, start at their party's home page. These typically lay dormant unless there's a campaign in progress but can still be a good source of contacts to badger. Government departments, on the other hand, tirelessly belch out all sorts of trivia right down to the transcripts of ministerial radio interviews. So if you'd like to know about impending legislation, tax rulings, budget details and so forth, skip the party pages and go straight to the department. If you can't find its address through what we list below, try **Yahoo**: http://dir.yahoo.com/Government/ or better still, jump on the phone. Below is a selection of the most useful starting points in Australia, Britain, and the US:

Australia

John Howard	http://www.pm.gov.au
Democrat Party	http://www.democrats.org.au
Labour Party	http://www.alp.org.au
Liberal Party	http://www.liberal.org.au
National Party	http://www.npa.org.au
Federal Government	http://www.fed.gov.au
State & Local entry point	http://www.nla.gov.au/oz/gov/

UK

Tony Blair	http://www.number-10.gov.uk
Labour Party	http://www.labour.org.uk
Liberal Democrat Party	http://www.libdems.org.uk
Tory Party	http://www.conservative-party.org.uk
CCTA	
Government Information	http://www.open.gov.uk

USA

Bill Clinton	http://www.whitehouse.gov
Democratic Party	http://www.democratic-party.org
Republican National Committee	http://www.rnc.org
House of Reps	http://www.house.gov
Senate	http://www.senate.gov
FedWorld	http://www.fedworld.gov
Gov. Information Exchange	http://www.info.gov
Political Index	http://www.politicalindex.com
Political Resources Online	http://www.politicalresources.com
Thomas (search Congress)	http://thomas.loc.gov

Adopt an MP (UK)

http://www.stand.org.uk

Pester your local member to protect online privacy in the UK.

Amnesty International

http://www.amnesty.org

"If you think virtual reality is interesting, try reality," says Amnesty International, global crusaders for human rights. Discover how you can help in its battles against brutal, militant regimes and injustice.

Antiwar

http://www.antiwar.com

Questions US intervention in foreign affairs, with particular emphasis on the Balkans. If you're after an argument on the latter, try: http://www.serbiancafe.com

The British Monarchy

http://www.royal.gov.uk

Tune into the world's best-loved soap opera.
For more larks starring the royal merrymakers
see: http://www.royalnetwork.com

Noam Chomsky Archive

http://www.worldmedia.com/archive/

The works of Noam Chomsky, MIT Professor of Linguistics
and outspoken critic of US foreign policy. He might change
the way you read the world.

Central Intelligence Agency

http://www.odci.gov/cia/

You're well informed. You watch TV and read the **Weekly
World News** via http://www.weeklyworldnews.com So naturally
you want the beef on political assassinations, arms deals,
Colombian drug trades, spy satellites, phone tapping,
covert operations, government-sponsored alien sex cults,
and the X-files. Well, guess what? Never mind, you won't
go home without a prize: http://www.copvcia.com

Conspiracies

http://www.mt.net/%7Ewatcher/ • http://www.conspire.com

There's no doubt about it. Certain people are up to
something and what's worse they're probably all in it
together. If these exposés of the sixty biggest cover-ups of
all time aren't proof enough, then do your bit and create
one that's more convincing:
http://www.turnleft.com/conspiracy.html

DOE Openness: Human Radiation Experiments

http://tis-nt.eh.doe.gov/ohre/

The improbable annals of Cold War research into nuking
human flesh to see what happens.

FBI FOIA Reading Room

http://www.fbi.gov/foipa/main.htm

FBI documents released as part of the Freedom of
Information Act. Includes a few files on such celebrities as
John Wayne, Elvis, Marilyn, and the British Royals. Check
out who's most wanted now at: http://www.fbi.gov

Foreign Report
http://www.foreignreport.com

Compact subscription newsletter with a track record of predicting international flashpoints well before the dailies.

The Gallup Organization
http://www.gallup.com

Keep up to date with opinion trends and ratings such as the fickle swings of Slick Willy's popularity.

Greenpeace International
http://www.greenpeace.org

Apparently the happy ending starts here.

Hatewatch
http://www.hatewatch.org

Not everyone will agree on the premise: "It's the ignorance of hate groups and their ideologies that allow the spread of these vile and poisonous ideas to continue." In fact, many argue the direct opposite. Whatever the case, there's a bundle of nastiness linked from here, and you'll probably agree that they do look pretty pathetic in the light of day.

Hempseed

http://www.hempseed.com

Score a free POP3 mail account that says you're pro dope for rope.

InfoWar

http://www.infowar.com

Warfare issues from prank hacking to industrial espionage and military propaganda.

Jane's IntelWeb

http://intelweb.janes.com

Brief updates on political disturbances, terrorism, intelligence agencies, and subterfuge worldwide. For a full directory of covert operations, see:

http://www.dreamscape.com/frankvad/covert.html

National Forum on People's Differences

http://www.yforum.com

Toss around touchy topics such as the perennials race, religion, and sexuality, with a sincerity that is normally tabooed by political politeness.

Neofeminism

http://www.neofeminism.com

Help beta test the platform preview of neofeminism. The authors say this release updates and sorts out interoperability problems among feminism, paleofeminism, separatist feminism, postmodern feminism, Marxist feminism, ecofeminism, and radical feminism.

Please report any bugs to the developers.

One World

http://www.oneworld.org

Brings together news from over 350 global justice organizations.

Open Secrets

http://www.opensecrets.org

Track whose money is oiling the wheels in US politics. More keeping 'em honest at:

http://www.commoncause.org

Palestinian National Authority

http://www.pna.net

Official mouthpiece of Palestine on the Net with regular "progress" reports on the settlement process.

Police Officer's Directory

http://www.officer.com http://www.cops.aust.com (AUS)

Top of the pops cop directory with more than 1500 baddy-nabbing bureaus snuggled in with law libraries, wanted listings, investigative tools, hate groups, special ops branches, and off-duty home pages. To see who's in Scotland Yard's bad books see: http://www.met.police.uk

The Progressive Review

http://emporium.turnpike.net/P/ProRev/

Washington dirt dug up from all sides of the fence.

Revolutionary Association of the Women of Afghanistan

http://www.rawa.org

And you think you have problems with men.

Spunk Press

http://www.spunk.org

All the anarchy you'll ever need organized neatly and with reassuring authority.

Trinity Atomic Test Site

http://www.envirolink.org/issues/nuketesting/

See what went on, and what went off, fifty-odd years ago, then file into the archives of high-energy weapon testing, and read who else has been sharpening the tools of world peace.

US Census Bureau

http://www.census.gov

More statistics on the US and its citizens than you'd care to know.

RADIO

Looking for Net radio? Download the latest audio software first (see p.427), then browse the following station directories and broadcast listings.

Station Directories

MIT List	http://wmbr.mit.edu/stations/
Radio directory	http://www.live-radio.net
Shoutcast	http://www.shoutcast.com
Sunset radio	http://sunsetradio.com
Virtual Tuner	http://www.virtualtuner.com

What's On Guides

On Now	http://www.onnow.com
RealGuide	http://realguide.real.com
Windows Media Guide	http://webevents.microsoft.com
Yahoo Events	http://events.yahoo.com

Broadcast.com
http://www.broadcast.com

Real and Windows media broadcasts from over 250 radio and television stations, live sports and music, thousands of CDs on demand, and more in the vaults.

Crystal Radio
http://www.midnightscience.com

Build a simple wireless that needs no battery.

Interface
http://www.pirate-radio.co.uk/interface/

Listen to live London pirate radio wherever you live.

Imagine Radio
http://imagineradio.com

Customize your own live radio station according to your tastes.

Kiss FM
http://www.kissfm.co.uk

Tune into London's Kiss 100 dance station via RealAudio.

NetRadio
http://www.netradio.net

Over 150 channels of streaming audio across a multitude of genres from drum'n'bass to country.

Police Scanner
http://www.policescanner.com

Live police, fire, aviation, and racetrack scanner feeds piped into RealAudio. Eavesdrop on busts in progress.

Phil's Old Radios
http://www.accessone.com/~philn/

If you ever drifted to sleep bathed in the soft glow of a crackling Bakelite wireless, Phil's collection of vacuum-era portables may instantly flood you with childhood memories.

Satco DX Satellite Chart
http://www.satcodx.com

Where to point your dish and what you can expect to receive.

Shortwave Radio Catalog
http://itre.ncsu.edu/radio/

If it's not on the Net, maybe it's crackling over the airwaves.

Spinner
http://www.spinner.com

Choose from over 120 channels in a wide range of genres. While it requires a special player, it's only RealAudio underneath. So although the range is fantastic, the quality is so-so. Try also: http://www.macroradio.net

Triple J
http://www.abc.net.au/triplej/

Listen to the world's coolest national youth network live via RealAudio, or flip through its well-rotated playlist.

Veronica FM Kits
http://www.veronica.co.uk

Build your very own clandestine radio station for less than the price of a PC, and join ranks with:
http://www.0171.com/theradio/pirateradio/pirateradio.html and http://www.frn.net Instructions at: http://www.irational.org/sic/radio/

REFERENCE

Academic Info
http://www.academicinfo.net

Research directory for students and teachers.

Acronym Finder
http://www.acronymfinder.com/

Before you follow IBM, TNT, and HMV in initializing your company's name, ensure it's not something borrowed or stands for something blue.
See also: http://www.ucc.ie/info/net/acronyms/acro.html

Allexperts.com
http://www.allexperts.com

Ask any question and let unpaid experts do the thinking.

Altavista Translations
http://babelfish.altavista.digital.com

Translate text, including Web pages, in seconds. Run it back and forth a few times and you'll end up with something that wouldn't look out of place on a Japanese T-shirt.

alt.culture
http://www.altculture.com

Witty, digital A-Z of 1990s pop culture. Fun to browse, maybe even enlightening, but don't blow your cool by admitting it.

Alternative Dictionary
http://www.notam.uio.no/~hcholm/altlang/

Bucket your foreign chums in their mother tongue.

American ASL Dictionary
http://www.bconnex.net/~randys/
Learn sign language through simple animations.

Anagram Genius
http://www.anagramgenius.com
Recycle used letters.

Aphorisms Galore
http://www.aphorismsgalore.com
Sound clever by repeating someone else's lines.

BabyNamer
http://www.babynamer.com
Why not give your bub a cutesy name like Adolph?
It apparently means "noble hero". Sounds nice.
More suggestions to scar babe for life at:
http://bnf.parentsoup.com/babyname/

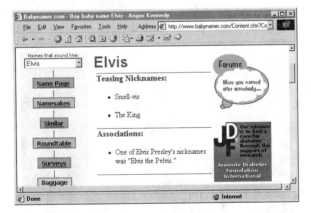

Biography
http://www.biography.com
Recounting more than 20,000 lives.

Britannica Online

http://www.eb.com

Buying this bulky set was never that practical, nor cheap.
And it's not likely you'd ever read it all. So it makes more
sense to leave it on a server where you can get at it as you
need it, and leave it to EB to keep fresh. However, it's only
free for a week. After that you or your masters will have to
fork out.

Calculators Online

http://www.sci.lib.uci.edu/~martindale/RefCalculators.html

Awesome directory of some 6000 online tools to calculate
everything from how much sump oil to put in soap, to the
burden of bringing up brats.

Cliché Finder

http://www.westegg.com/cliche/

Submit a word or phrase to find how not to use it.

Encyclopedia Mythica

http://pantheon.org/mythica/

Hefty album of mythology, folklore and legend.

Evil House of Cheat

http://www.cheathouse.com

Thousands of college essays, termpapers and reports.

Funk and Wagnalls
http://www.funkandwagnalls.com

Free access to the entire encyclopedia set plus Webster's College dictionary. The **Concise Columbia**: http://www.encyclopedia.com and **Encarta**: http://www.encarta.com are also free, but somewhat abridged.

InfoPlease
http://www.infoplease.com

Handy, all-purpose almanac for looking up statistics and trivia across a multitude of topics.

LibrarySpot
http://www.libraryspot.com

Neat selection of the Net's best reference sources.

Macquarie Online
http://www.macnet.mq.edu.au

Tap into the definitive Australian reference set.

Megaconverter
http://www.megaconverter.com

Calculate everything from your height in angstroms, to the pellets of lead per ounce of buckshot needed to bring down an overcharging consultant.

One Look
http://www.onelook.com

Search almost five hundred online dictionaries at once.

Online Dictionaries
http://www.bucknell.edu/~rbeard/diction.html

Links to more than eight hundred dictionaries in 160 different languages.

Princeton Review
http://www.review.com

Crack the SATs.

Rap Dictionary
http://www.rapdict.org

Hip-hop to English. Parental guidance recommended.

Rhyming Dictionary
http://www.link.cs.cmu.edu/dougb/rhyme-doc.html

Get a hoof up in putting together a classy love poem.

Roget's Thesaurus
http://www.thesaurus.com

New format, but useless as ever.

Skeptics Dictionary
http://skepdic.com

Punch holes through popularly accepted superstitions and pseudo-sciences with this terse dinner-party deflator.

Spellweb
http://www.spellweb.com

Compare two words or phrases and see which gets more hits in a search engine. If it demonstrates anything, it's that the Web is strung together with a lot of bad spelling.

Study Web
http://www.studyweb.com

Ideal school research aid with thousands of leads split by topic.

Strunk's Elements of Style
http://www.columbia.edu/acis/bartleby/strunk/

English usage in a nutshell. For more on grammar, see: http://www.edunet.com/english/grammar/

Symbols
http://www.symbols.com

Ever woken up with a strange sign tattooed on your buttocks? Here's where to find what it means without calling Agent Mulder.

US Postal Services
http://www.usps.gov

Look up a Zip code, track express mail, sort out your vehicle registration or just get down and philatelic.

What's in your name?
http://www.kabalarians.com/gkh/your.htm

The Kabalarians claim names can be cooked up to a numerical stew and served back up as a character analysis.

Look yourself up in here and see what a duff choice your folks made. Then blame them for everything that's gone wrong since. Of course, you could always revert to your Pacific island self:
http://www.hisurf.com/cgibin/DM/hawaiian_name.cgi?

What is?
http://whatis.com

Unravel cumbersome computer and Internet jargon without having even more thrown at you.

RELIGION

Anglicans Online!
http://www.anglican.org/online/

Gentle introduction to what Anglicans believe, with links to parishes, groups, and resources worldwide.

Avatar Search
http://www.AvatarSearch.com

Search the occult Internet for spiritual guidance and tips on the lottery.

The Bible Gateway
http://bible.gospelcom.net

Search the Bible as a database.

Catholic Information Network
http://www.cin.org

Scripture, liturgy, early writings, Vatican documents, papal encyclicals, pronouncements, and other Catholic high-jinks.

Celebrity Atheist List
http://www.primenet.com/~lippard/atheistcelebs/

Big names you won't spot in Heaven.

Chick
http://chick.com

Hard-core Christian pornography.

Christian Naturists
http://home.vistapnt.com/markm/

Frolic with other Christian fun-seekers, the way God intended.

Comparative Religion
http://www.academicinfo.net/religindex.html
> Multifaith directory for religious academics.

The Greatest Truth Ever Revealed
http://www.sevenseals.com
> Revelations from survivors of the Waco siege.

The Hindu Universe
http://www.hindunet.org
> Hindu dharma – the philosophy, culture, and customs.

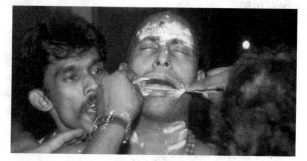

The Holy See
http://www.vatican.va
> Official home of the Pope and his posse.

Internet Satanic Syndicate
http://www.satanism.net
> Enter this address and go straight to hell.

Jesus of the Week
http://www.phoenixnewtimes.com/extra/gilstrap/jesus.html
> The original Mr Nice Guy in 52 coy poses per year. See if you
> can catch him wink at: http://www.winkingjesus.com

Latif.com
http://www.latif.com
> Links to Islamic FAQs, conferences, and social events, Qu'ran
> teachings, Arabic news, and the Cyber Muslim guide.

Maven

http://www.maven.co.il

The Yahoo of Jewish/Israeli links.

Miracles Page

http://www.mcn.org/1/miracles/

Spooky signs that point towards a cosmic conspiracy.

Peyote Way Church of God

http://www.primenet.com/~idic/peyote.html

Unless you're Native American, or live in select southern US states, you stand to be locked up for finding God through the psychedelic cactus. Otherwise, feel free to fry your brain; just don't drive home from church.

Prophecy and Current Events

http://www.aplus-software.com/thglory/

You'll never guess who's coming to dinner. Don't bother cooking, though; he's supposed to be a real whiz with food.

Religious Tolerance.org

http://www.religioustolerance.org

Sign up for a new faith. Certain rules and conditions may apply.

Stories of the Dreaming

http://www.dreamtime.net.au

Selection of enchanting bedtime stories in text, video, and audio that explain creation from an Aboriginal perspective. Don't believe in creation? Go tell it to the jury: http://www. talkorigins.org

Universal Life Church

http://ulc.org/ulc/

You're already a member, just not aware of it yet. Ordain yourself a minister within seconds online and print out the certificate to frame for your bedroom wall.

The Witches' Voice

http://www.witchvox.com

Expresses a burning desire to correct misinformation about witchcraft, a legally recognized religion in the US since 1985.

SCIENCE AND SPACE

Astronomy Picture of the Day
http://antwrp.gsfc.nasa.gov/apod/astropix.html

Enjoy a daily helping of outer space served up by a gourmet astrochef.

Auroras: Paintings in the Sky
http://www.exploratorium.edu/learning_studio/auroras/

If you're ever lucky enough to see the aurora borealis during a solar storm, you'll never take the night sky for granted again. The Exploratorium does a commendable job in explaining a polar phenomenon that very few people understand. Except maybe these champs: http://www.haarp.alaska.edu

The Braintainment Center
http://www.brain.com

Start with a test that says you're not so bright, then prove it by buying loads of self-improvement gear.
Further proof at: http://www.mensa.org or http://www.densa.com or http://www.iqtest.com

Cool Robot of the Week
http://ranier.hq.nasa.gov/telerobotics_page/coolrobots.html

Clever ways to get machines to do our dirty work.

Deep Cold
http://www.deepcold.com

Artistic mockups of chic space racers that never left the hangar.

Documentation and Diagrams of the Atomic Bomb
http://neutrino.nuc.berkeley.edu/neutronics/todd/nuc.bomb.html

Gosh, here's how to make an atomic bomb. Let's hope this doesn't fall into the wrong hands. And here's how much damage it could cause to your neighborhood: http://www.pbs.org/wgbh/pages/amex/bomb/sfeature/mapablast.html

Earth Viewer
http://www.fourmilab.ch/earthview/vplanet.html

View the Earth in space and time. Maps in real time to show the current positioning, lighting, and shadows.

Earthquake Information

http://www.civeng.carleton.ca/cgi-bin/quakes/

Stats and maps of most recent quakes worldwide.

For detail on the latest big one see:
http://www.gps.caltech.edu/~polet/recofd.html

Exoscience

http://exosci.com

Scours the net for the latest astrophysics and astronomy news and particularly that relating to research into the origin, evolution, and distribution of life in the universe.

Inconstant Moon

http://www.inconstantmoon.com

Click on a date and see what's showing on the Moon.

Interactive Frog Dissection

http://curry.edschool.virginia.edu/go/frog/

Pin down a frog, grab your scalpel, and follow the pictures.

History of Mathematics

http://www-groups.dcs.st-andrews.ac.uk/~history/

The life and times of various bright sparks with numbers.

How Stuff Works

http://www.howstuffworks.com

Unravel the mysterious machinations behind all sorts of stuff from Xmas to cruise missiles.

Keirsey Temperment Sorter

http://www.keirsey.com

Classify your personality type. Skeptics at: http://www.dcn. davis.ca.us/go/btcarrol/skeptic/myersb.html insist it's simply a psychological parlor game. You might get closer to the truth here: http://www.learner.org/exhibits/personality/

The Lab

http://www.abc.net.au/science/

Science features and news from the ABC, including fascinating weekly Q&As from Australian pop-science superstar, Dr Karl Kruszelnicki.

MadSciNet: 24-hour Exploding Laboratory

http://www.madsci.org

Collective of more than a hundred scientific smartypantses set up specifically to answer your dumb questions. More geniuses for hire at: http://www.sciam.com/askexpert/ and http://www.sciencenet.org.uk

Mars Home Page

http://mpfwww.jpl.nasa.gov

Get a bit more red dirt live from NASA's space safari before you stake out your first plot at: http://www.marsshop.com For the latest news, see: http://www.marsnews.com

MIT Media Labs

http://www.media.mit.edu

If you've read **Being Digital** or any of Nicholas Negroponte's **Wired** columns, you'll know he has some pretty tall ideas about our electronic future. Here's where he gets them.

Museum of Dirt

http://www.planet.com/dirtweb/dirt.html

Celebrity dirt of an entirely different nature.

NASA

http://www.nasa.gov

Top level of NASA's mighty Web presence. Its projects, databases, policies, missions, and discoveries are strewn across the Net, but you can find them all from here, if you persist.

Netsurfer Science

http://www.netsurf.com/nss/

Subscribe to receive weekly bulletins on science and technology sites.

Net Telescopes

http://www.telescope.org/rti/ • http://inferno.physics.uiowa.edu

Probe deep space by sending requests to remote telescopes.

New Scientist

http://www.newscientist.com

Full features, back issues, daily bulletins, and scientific miscellany from the superlative science weekly.

Nuclear Power Station

http://www.ida.liu.se/~her/npp/demo.html

Play Montgomery Burns and try to curb a meltdown.

PM Zone

http://www.popularmechanics.com

Generous selection of features and home-improvement projects from the magazine that has been showing us "the easy way to do hard things" since the turn of the century.

PopSci

http://www.popsci.com

What's new in cars, computers, home tech, science, and electronics, from **Popular Science**.

Rocketry Online

http://www.rocketryonline.com

Take on NASA at its own game.

Science a GoGo

http://www.scienceagogo.com

Pick of the day's most interesting science news.

Seti@home

http://setiathome.ssl.berkeley.edu

Donate your processing resources to the non-lunatic end of the search for extraterrestrial intelligence by downloading a screensaver that analyzes data from the Arecibo Radio Telescope. Progress reports at http://www.seti.org

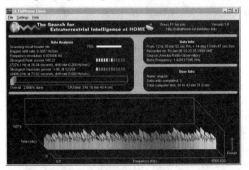

Skeptics Society

http://www.skeptic.com

Don't try to pull a swifty on this crowd.

Solar System Simulator

http://space.jpl.nasa.gov

Shift camp around the solar system until you find the best view.

Space Calendar

http://www.jpl.nasa.gov/calendar/

Guide to upcoming anniversaries, rocket launches, meteor showers, eclipses, asteroid and planet viewings, and happenings in the intergalactic calendar.

Space Telescope Science Institute

http://www.stsci.edu

Intergalactic snapshots fresh off the Hubble telescope.

Volcano World

http://volcano.und.nodak.edu

Monitor the latest eruptions, see photos of every major volcano in the world, and virtually tour a Hawaiian smoky without choking on sulfur fumes.

Web-Elements

http://www.webelements.com

Click on an element in the periodic table and suss it out in depth.

Weird Science and Mad Scientists

http://www.eskimo.com/~billb/weird.html
http://www.student.nada.kth.se/~nv91-asa/mad.html

Free energy, Tesla, anti-gravity, aura, cold fusion, parapsychology, and other strange scientific projects and theories.

Why Files

http://whyfiles.news.wisc.edu

Entertaining reports on the science behind current news.

Yahoo Science

http://www.yahoo.com/science/

All the links you've come to expect plus news of the latest scientific breakthroughs.

SHOPPING

It's safe to say online shopping is finally here. Although it's not exactly a neatly organized experience, it certainly does offer advantages – particularly when you can't find something as cheaply, if at all, in your home town. In some regards, finding a bargain has never been easier. You can visit several stores, in different parts of the world, all at once, simply by opening multiple browser windows. Or you could employ a bargain finder such as **Bottom Dollar** or **Jango** (see p.368, "Bargain Finders"), to find the best deal across several shops within seconds.

Of course, it helps if you know what you're buying, and with whom you're dealing, but these are the risks you always take with mail order. A good sign that a shop is serious is if it uses a secure server. This encrypts your details and makes them almost impossible to intercept as they pass across the Net. But don't get too worried about someone stealing your credit card info surreptitiously – be more concerned about being overcharged, or regularly billed for a subscription you've tried to cancel. If you're tempted to flash your card in the red-light zone, even as identification, expect to be duped. Outside this territory, though, online fraud is exceptionally rare. All the same, do reconcile your statements, keep email records, and consult your bank if you strike problems. If your bank won't help, cancel your card immediately and shift your money.

The concept of shops bundled together into "cybermalls" is as good as dead. Today, most reputable businesses have their own domain name eg, roughguides.com As with any Internet search, the best place to start is with the main directories and search engines. Yahoo, Excite, and Infoseek all stock excellent shopping categories. Naturally, there are also several specialist shopping directories, but they're generally fairly rough, for example:

All Internet Shopping Directory	http://www.all-internet.com
Enterprise City (UK)	http://www.enterprisecity.co.uk
I Want to Shop (UK)	http://www.iwanttoshop.com
Internet Shopper	http://www.internetshopper.com
Shopomatic	http://www.shopomatic.com
Shopping Search	http://www.shoppingsearch.com

Like every section, the following is only meant to get you off the ground. Within two clicks, you could be anywhere. See also our "Books" and "Music" sections for book and CD stores.

Auctions

http://www.ebay.com • http://www.ebay.com/uk/ (UK)
http://www.qxl.co.uk (Europe) • http://www.auctionuniverse.com
http://auctions.yahoo.com • http://www.onsale.com
http://www.sold.com.au (Aust)
http://www.internetauctionlist.com (directory)
http://www.auctioninsider.com (directory)

Here's what's really hot in online shopping. Buyers can instruct a bot to bid intelligently on their behalf and keep them posted on the progress. Once the deal is struck it's up to the buyer and seller to settle proceedings.

Bargain Finders

http://www.roboshopper.com • http://www.mysimon.com
http://www.bottomdollar.com • http://www.pricewatch.com (computing)
http://www.vo.infospace.com • http://www.pricescan.com
http://www.shopper.com (computing) • http://www.addall.com (books)
http://www.bestbookbuys.com (books) • http://www.jango.com

Compare stock and prices across a range of online shops.

Bizrate

http://www.bizrate.com

Rates online vendors through customer surveys.
Check it out before handing over your credit card number.

Catalog Mart

http://catalog.savvy.com • http://www.catalogsite.com

Drive your postie crazy by ordering every catalog in the world.

Classified ads

http://www.loot.com (UK & NY)
http://www.newsclassifieds.com.au (Aust)
http://www.tradingpost.com.au (Aust)
http://www.tokyoclassified.com (Jap)

Just like the paper versions only fresher and easier to search.

Condom Country

http://www.condom.com

The mail-order condoms, sex aids, books, and jokes are pretty
harmless, but the mere mention of the penis size ready
reckoner may prove disquieting to some. You'll find more of
the same by wedging your favorite brand names between www
and com

Conran Shop

http://www.conran.co.uk

Score a flash sofa online without having to suffer the
indignity of sitting in it first.

Consumer Advice

http://www.consumersdigest.com (US)
http://www.consumerreports.org (US)
http://www.choice.com.au (AUS) • http://www.which.net (UK)

Avoid buying a lemon or being scammed.

Coolshopping

http://www.coolshopping.com

Be assured where it's "cool" to shop.

Freeshop

http://www.freeshop.com

Assorted freebies such as magazine trial subscriptions and
samples.

Greengrocer.com

http://www.greengrocer.com.au

Local fruit and vegetable delivery success story run from a
houseboat in Sydney Harbour. If that's a bit far from home
try Sainsbury's: http://www.sainsburys.co.uk or Tesco's: http://www.
tesco.co.uk in the UK; Netgrocer: http://www.netgrocer.com in the
US; or Woolworths: http://www.woolworths.com.au in Australia.

Information Unlimited
http://www.amazing1.com

Dazzling array of serious weird science toys like Tesla coils, electro-hypnotizers, disorientation devices, class 4 laser kits and ultrasonic ray guns.

International Star Registry
http://www.starregistry.co.uk

Raise your flag in outer space.

Interflora
http://www.interflora.com

Punch in your credit card number, apology, and delivery details, and land back in the good books before you get home.

IPrint
http://www.iprint.com

Need some business cards or invitations fast? Design them online for snappy delivery either via email or on the paper of your choice. Naturally, the latter option costs. For quicker delivery in the UK, see: http://www.cardcorp.co.uk

Kellner's Fireworks
http://www.kellfire.com

Mail order light explosives.

Khazana
http://www.khazana.com

Eastern collectibles purchased direct from the artisans and artists, with a "fair trade" policy of payment.

Lakeside Products
http://wholesalecentral.com/Lakeside/

Order the gags you couldn't afford when you needed them most.

Macy's
http://www.macys.com

Order essentials like shirts and stockings online, or email a personal assistant to stock your entire wardrobe.

Mind Gear
http://www.mind-gear.com

Bombarding yourself with light and sound of a certain frequency is meant to bludgeon you into a higher state of consciousness. Here's where to find the gear to realign your noodle.

Mondotronics Robot Store
http://www.robotstore.com

Build machines that do exactly as they're told.

New and Kewl
http://www.new-kewl.com

New and nifty gadgets on sale around the Net. More at http://www.gadgetguru.com

Shopping.com
http://www.shopping.com

Online-only department store that stocks just about everything at pretty reasonable prices.

Sorcerer's Shop
http://www.sorcerers-shop.com

Attract love and fortune with bottled potions rather than charm and skill. If that doesn't work, you might have to resort to Voodoo: http://www.spellmaker.com

Spy Base
http://www.spybase.com

Get to know your neighbors better.

Toy Stores
http://www.etoys.com • http://www.toysrus.com
http://www.faoschwartz.com • http://www.imaginarium.com

It's just like Xmas all year round.

Unclaimed Baggage
http://www.unclaimedbaggage.com

You lose it; they sell it.

Yacht Broker
http://www.yachtbroker.com

Once you've settled on a
clipper it's plain sailing
from then on.

Yahoo Shopping
http://shopping.yahoo.com

Again, don't confuse this
with Yahoo's various
shopping categories, it's merely a single entry point to
search, browse, and compare products and prices on offer
from thousands of Y!Store merchants.

SPORT

Abdominal Training
http://www.dstc.edu.au/TU/staff/timbomb/ab/

Build "abs like ravioli".

Australian Football League
http://www.afl.com.au

Aggregated news, live Netcasts and round highlights from
the official home of aerial ping-pong.

Bullwhip
http://www.bullwhip.org

Get cracking.

Charged
http://www.charged.com

For all that falls under the banner of "extreme sports", from
taking your pushbike offroad to the sort of sheer
recklessness that would get you cut from a will.

CBS Sportsline

http://www.sportsline.com

US sports news, scores, gossip, and fixtures, including live play-by-play baseball action.

Cric Info

http://www.cricket.org

Cricket is some bizarre Zen thing. A test match can span five days in the blazing Faisalabad midsummer sun. Often without result. Yet buffs ponder every ball, awaiting the birth of some new statistic. But the ultimate indulgence is following such a match on the other side of the world, ball by ball, over the Internet, while periodically checking Cricinfo's stat tables during tea breaks. Ommm . . .

ESPN Sportzone

http://espnet.sportszone.com

Live news, statistics, and commentary on major US sports.

Faith Sloan's Bodybuilding Site

http://www.frsa.com/bbpage.shtml

Galleries of the grimacing human form pushed to near-illogical extremes.

Fastball

http://www.fastball.com

Major league baseball scores, news, stats, games, and discussion.

Flyfish.com

http://www.flyshop.com

Trade tips and general exaggeration on aquatic bloodsports.

Goals – Global Online Adventure Learning Site

http://www.goals.com

Follow the progress of adventurous lunatics like Mick Bird, striving to become the first person to row around the world.

Golf.com

http://www.golf.com

Grab the latest news on chipping, driving, and putting tournaments worldwide. Then slip on your checkered strides, cruise into the travel section, and picture yourself in one of 25,000 listed courses belting a ball to your heart's content.

NBA.com

http://www.nba.com

Official home of the NBA with loads of pro basketball news, picks, player profiles, analyses, results, schedules, and highlight videos. See also **Major League Baseball**: http://www.majorleaguebaseball.com.

NFL

http://www.nfl.com

Media schedules, chats, news, player profiles, stats, and streaming highlight videos from the National Football League's past and current seasons.

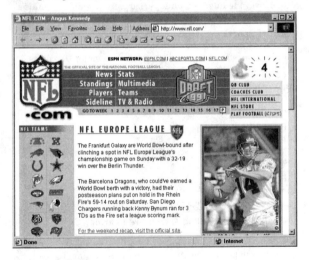

Rugby League

http://www.rleague.com

Read how burly men knock each other down, push each other's faces into the dirt as they're rising, and then meet for a drink together afterwards. Stats, news, and scores posted after every game.

Sailing Index

http://www.sailingindex.com

Neat directory of links to racing authorities, regatta bulletins, commercial suppliers, weather reports, cruising destinations, and sailing clubs.

Scrum.com

http://www.scrum.com

Up-to-date rugby coverage from the Five (Six, next season) Nations to the Super 12. More at: http://www.rugbyheaven.com

SkiCentral

http://www.skicentral.com

Indexes thousands of ski-related sites, such as snow reports, resort cams, snowboard gear, accommodation, and coming events in resorts across the world. If you're into snowboarding, see: http://www.soltv.com http://www.boardtheworld.com.au or http://www.twsnow.com

SkySports (UK)

http://www.skysports.co.uk

Roundup of British and International, sports news and results. See also: **Sport Live**: http://www.sportlive.net and the bookies' favorite, **Sporting Life**: http://www.sporting-life.com

SoccerNet

http://www.soccernet.com

The UK Daily Mail's shrine to football in England and beyond. Not enough news? Try: **Carling**: http://www. fa-carling.com **Nationwide**: http://www.football.nationwide.co.uk **Football365**: http://www.football365.co.uk **When Saturday Comes**: http://www.wsc.co.uk/wsc/ and of course any of the newspaper sites. For game, club, and player stats, see: **Teamtalk**: http:// www.teamtalk.com **Matchfacts**: http://www.matchfacts.co.uk and **Soccerbase**: http:www.soccerbase.com

SportsWeb

http://www.sportsweb.com

Worldwide sports news from Reuters, fresh off the wire.

Stats

http://www.stats.com

Pig in to an overflowing trough of baseball statistics.

Wide World of Sports (AUS)

http://sports.ninemsn.com.au

Australian sports news, results, and live scores.

World Surfing

http://www.goan.com/surflink.html

Regionally sorted links to the sort of dude stuff that real surfers live for. Such as how to forecast waves, where El Niño's at, surfboard shops, Dick Dale riffs, surf reports, and tons of surfcams. And for the only magazine tough guys are allowed to read in public, see: http://www.msp.com.au/tracks/

Wrestling

http://www.wrestling.com • http://www.lordsofpain.net

Vent the frustration of helplessly watching your boofhead heroes being piledriven, suplexed, and moonsplashed, by spilling some hardware juice virtually. If you'd prefer seeing them smack each other in the scone, see: http://www.boxing.com

Yahoo Sports

http://dir.yahoo.com/recreation/sports/

Yahoo's Sports arm is undoubtedly the fattest bag of sports links you'll find. If you can't get to your healthy obsession within a couple of jumps from here, it probably doesn't exist.

TELECOMMUNICATIONS

Campaign for Unmetered Telecommunications
http://www.unmetered.org.uk

Rail against the call charging system that's making the UK an Internet backwater.

Free Fax Services
http://www.tpc.int • http://easyfax.net

Transmit faxes anywhere in the world via the Internet for the price of your connection. In practice, coverage is limited and subject to delays. But give it a shot anyway.

HomeIndia
http://www.homeindia.com

Type in a message. Have it faxed or delivered by post free anywhere within India. Pay to send it worldwide at: http://www.letterpost.com

J-Fax
http://www.jfax.com

Provides a unique phone/fax number in many cities that forwards your incoming faxes and voicemail as email attachments. Plus you can send faxes the same way. Alternatively, EFAX: http://www.efax.com offers similar for free, but you have to make do with a Midwestern US number.

MobileWorld
http://www.mobileworld.org • http://www.unwin.co.uk/phonez.html

Assorted info on mobile phones and cellular networks.

MTN SMS
http://www.mtnsms.com

Send free SMS messages to mobile phones worldwide.

RelayOne (UK)
http://relayone.msn.com

Have your email or attached document printed and delivered by first class Royal Mail.

Reverse Phone Directory
http://www.reversephonedirectory.com

Key in a US phone number to find its owner.

What does your phone number spell?
http://www.phonespell.org

Enter your phone number to see what it spells. The reverse lookup might be useful when choosing a number.

World Time & Dialing Codes
http://www.whitepages.com.au/time.shtml

International dialing info from anywhere to anywhere, including current times and area codes.

TIME

Calendarzone
http://www.calendarzone.com

Calendar links and, believe it or not, calzone recipes.

Daily Drill
http://www.dailydrill.com

Maintain your planner online, if you think it makes a shred of sense. Other variations at: http://www.appoint.net or try http://www.when.com and http://www.planetall.com

The Death Clock
http://www.deathclock.com

Get ready to book your final taxi.

Freeminder

http://www.cvp.com/freemind/ • http://www.candor.com/reminder/

Arrange a timely email reminder.

Everything 2000

http://www.everything2000.com • http://www.mille.org

Celebrations, events, the second coming at: http://www.cynet.com/Jesus/ shopping, computer bugs and all. Use by: 1/1/2000.

International Earth Rotation Service

http://hpiers.obspm.fr

Ever felt like your bed's spinning? The truth is even scarier.

Time and Date

http://www.timeanddate.com

Rig up a custom Java world time clock so you can instantly tell the time in your choice of cities. To keep your PC clock aligned download one of these time synchronizers: http://www.eecis.udel.edu/~ntp/software.html

Virtual VCR Clock

http://www.wvi.com/~odonnell/vcrclock.htm

You'll have to see it to understand.

TRANSPORT

Buying a Car

Before you're sharked into signing on a new or used vehicle, go online and check out a few road tests and price guides. You can complete the entire exercise while you're there, but it mightn't hurt to drive one first. Here's where to start:

Autotrader (UK)	http://www.autotrader.co.uk
AutoWeb	http://www.autoweb.com
CarClub	http://www.carclub.com
CarPrice	http://www.carprice.com
Carseekers (UK)	http://www.carseekers.co.uk
DealerNet	http://www.dealernet.com
Edmunds	http://www.edmunds.com
Exchange & Mart (UK)	http://www.exchangeandmart.co.uk

Kelly Blue Book	http://www.kbb.com
Microsoft CarPoint (AUS)	http://carpoint.ninemsn.com
Microsoft CarPoint	http://carpoint.msn.com

Aircraft Shopper
http://www.aso.com

Troubled by traffic? Rise above it with something from this range of new, used, and charter aircraft.

Air Sickness Bag Virtual Museum
http://www.airsicknessbags.com

Bring up some treasured memories.

All-In-One British Timetables
http://www.ukonline.co.uk

Click on "Travel" to get form access to timetables of leading UK carcass haulers such as BA, Eurostar, British Rail, and National Express coaches plus links to just about everything else that moves across the Isles. Beats waiting on the phone.

Aircraft Accident Database
http://aviation-safety.net/database/ • http://airsafe.com

Way more goes wrong up in the air than you realize. Here's why you should be terrified to fly. If you're still not convinced then see and hear the results of overconfidence behind the joystick at: http://www.univers-cite.qc.ca/tucs/

BAC Testing
http://www.copsonline.com/bac2.htm

Slurring your swearwords, wobbling all over the road, mounting gutters and knocking kids off bikes? Pull over and blow into this site.

FedEx
http://www.fedex.com

Book shipping, track parcels, or compare rates with UPS:
http://www.ups.com and TNT: http://www.tnt.com

Layover
http://www.layover.com

Long, wide loads of essential truckin' stuff, plus special
features such as the diary of a lonely trucker's wife and an
Internet guide for prime movers and shakers.

License Plates of the World
http://danshiki.oit.gatech.edu/~iadt3mk/

Ring in sick, cancel your date, unplug the phone and don't
even think about sleep until you've seen EVERY LICENSE
PLATE IN THE WORLD.

NMRA Directory of Worldwide Rail Sites
http://www.ribbonrail.com/nmra/

Locophilial banquet of railroad maps, databases, mailing
lists, transit details, and hundreds of shunts all over the Net.
For more, including European timetables, see:
http://mercurio.iet.unipi.it/home.html

Professional Pilots Rumor Network
http://www.pprune.com
http://members.aol.com/safeflt/airsafe.htm

First-hand tales of terror in the air.

US Submarines
http:/www.ussubs.com

Scare the fish in your own custom-built U-boat.

Woman Motorist
http://www.womanmotorist.com

Features aimed at the demographic group motor vehicle
insurers prefer.

Yesterday's Tractors
http://www.ytmag.com

Salutes the world's most criminally underrated convertibles.

TRAVEL

Whether you're seeking inspiration, planning an itinerary, shopping for a ticket, or already mobile, the Net pretty much has it all. You can book flights, reserve hotels, research any region, monitor the weather, calculate currency rates, learn the lingo, locate an ATM, scan local newspapers, read traveler's tales, collect your mail from abroad, find a restaurant that suits your fussy tastes, and plenty more. For instance, you can't beat the Net for finding first-hand experiences or traveling companions. Before you set out, join the appropriate newsgroup under the rec.travel hierarchy. As ever, check

Deja.com: http://www.deja.com first.

The **Rough Guides**: http://travel.roughguides.com/journal/ and **Lonely Planet**: http://www.lonelyplanet.com/thorn/ thorn.html also maintains country-specific forums, which aren't so chaotic.

If you're flexible and/or willing to leave soon, you might find a last-minute special. These Net exclusives are normally offered directly from the airline, hotel, and travel operator sites, which you'll find through Airlines.com: http://www.airlines.com or Yahoo. There are also a few Web operators that specialize in late-notice deals on flights, hotels, events, and so forth, such as:

Bargain Holidays (UK)	http://www.bargainholidays.com
Best Fares	http://www.bestfares.com
Lastminute.com (UK)	http://www.lastminute.com
Lastminutetravel.com	http://www.lastminutetravel.com

Then there are the reverse-auction sites such as **Priceline.com**: http:/www.priceline.com and **Travelbids** http://www.travelbids.com where you bid on a destination and wait for a bite. You might strike up a good deal if you bid shrewdly and don't mind the somewhat draconian restrictions. If you're super flexible, you could try Airhitch or a courier:

Airhitch	http://www.airhitch.org
IAATC Air Courier	http://www.courier.org
Air Courier Assoc.	http://www.aircourier.org

Booking a flight through one of the broad online ticketing systems isn't too hard either, but bargains are scarce. For example, unless you're spending someone else's money you'll want to sidestep the full fares offered on these major services:

Biztravel (US)	http://www.biztravel.com
Expedia (AUS)	http://www.expedia.com.au
Expedia (UK)	http://www.expedia.co.uk
Expedia (US)	http://www.expedia.com
ITN (US but ships worldwide)	http://www.itn.com
Preview Travel (US)	http://www.previewtravel.com
Travel.com.au (AUS)	http://www.travel.com.au
Travelocity (Worldwide)	http://www.travelocity.com
Travel Select (Worldwide)	http://www.travelselect.co.uk

Although they list hundreds of airlines and millions of fares, the general consensus is that they're usually better for research, accommodation, and travel tips than cheap fares and customer service. So if you think it's worth the effort, drop in and check which carriers haul your route, offer the best deals, and still have seats available. You can then use their rates as a benchmark. Compare them with the fares on the airline sites and discount specialists such as:

ITravel.com (Worldwide)	http://www.1travel.com
Bargain Holidays (UK)	http://www.bargainholidays.com
Cheap Flights (UK)	http://www.cheapflights.co.uk
Internet Air Fares (US)	http://www.air-fare.com
Lowestfare.com (US)	http://www.lowestfare.com
TravelHub (US)	http://www.travelhub.com

Finally, see if your travel agent can better the price. If the difference is only marginal, favor your agent. Then at least you'll have a human contact if something goes wrong. See how the online bookers rate:

Scorecard http://www.scorecard.com.

A2Btravel.com
http://www.a2btravel.com

One-stop shop for travelling into, around, and out of the UK. Includes: flight booking; up-to-the-minute flight arrival and departure times; hotel finder; car hire comparisons; transport timetables; traffic reports; and loads of travel tips and stories.

Africam
http://www.africam.com

Sneak a peek at wild beasts going about their business.

Airtoons
http://www.airtoons.com

You'll never look at another flight card without smirking.

Occasionally you may choose to throw your hands in the air and wave them like you just don't care.

Air Traveler's Handbook
http://www.cs.cmu.edu/afs/cs/user/
mkant/Public/Travel/airfare.html

FAQ compiled from the **Rec.Travel.Air newsgroup** that's sure to leave you feeling worldlier. More useful Rec.Travel FAQs at:
http://www.travel-library.com

Arab Net
http://www.arab.net

North Africa and the Middle East, their peoples, geography, economy, history, culture, and, of course, camels. See also:

http://www.1001sites.com and http://www.i-cias.com

Art of Travel
http://www.artoftravel.com

How to see the world on $25.00 a day.

ATM Locators

http://www.visa.com/pd/atm/ • http://www.mastercard.com/atm/

Locate a bowser willing to replenish your wallet.

Bed & Breakfast Channel

http://www.bbchannel.com

Special B&B deals worldwide. More at: http://www.innsite.com

CIA World Factbook

http://www.odci.gov/cia/publications/pubs.html

Encyclopedic summary of every country's essential stats and details. Perfect for a school project, if not a military takeover.

Currency Converter

http://quote.yahoo.com/m3?u

Convert between a choice of over 160 live currencies or chart them at: http://pacific.commerce.ubc.ca/xr/xplot.html

Electronic Embassy

http://www.embassy.org

Directory of foreign embassies in DC plus Web links where available. Search Yahoo for representation in other cities.

Epicurious Travel

http://travel.epicurious.com

Tons of tiptop tips from **Traveler** magazine including an indispensable World Events calendar. Now you can plan your holidays around Thaipusam, Bun Bang Fai, and Tomatina.

Erich's Packing Center

http://www.stetson.edu/~efriedma/packing.html

Erich lives for packing geometric shapes into boxes. Why not invite him over next time you're stuffing your rucksack?

Eurotrip

http://www.eurotrip.com • http://www.ricksteves.com

Look out Europe, here you come.

Excite Travel

http://www.city.net

Regionally sorted links to community, geopolitical, health, and tourist info from around the globe. **The Virtual Tourist**: http://www.vtourist.com and **Yahoo Travel**: http://travel.yahoo.com work similarly.

Fielding's Danger Finder

http://www.fieldingtravel.com/df/

Adventure holidays that could last a lifetime.

Find a Grave

http://www.findagrave.com

Trace where celebrities are buried, and in some cases see their graves. It's hard to say whether reuniting the Three Stooges posthumously by juxtaposing their gravestones on a Web page falls within the bounds of good taste, but it certainly stops you in your tracks.

Hotel Discount

http://www.hoteldiscount.com • http://www.hotelnet.co.uk

Book hotels around the world. If you want backpacker rates, try: http://www.hostels.com

How far is it?

http://www.indo.com/distance/

Calculate the distance between any two cities.

Infiltration

http://www.infiltration.org

Confessions of a serial trespasser.

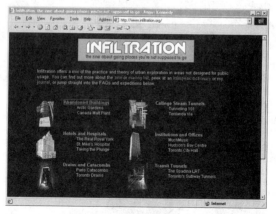

International Home Exchange

http://www.homexchange.com

Swap hideouts with a foreigner until the heat dies down.

International Student Travel Confederation

http://www.istc.org

Getting an international student card and what it's good for.

Journeywoman

http://www.journeywoman.com

Smart ezine for sassy sisters on the road.

Lonely Planet Updates

http://www.lonelyplanet.com

Good for summaries of every country in the Lonely Planet series plus basic info and updates. But of most use for its wealth of first-hand tales posted by backpacking survivors. Find travel partners, advice, and ideas for your next stint away from the keyboard.

Mapquest

http://www.mapquest.com

Generate street maps and driving directions for a host of cities worldwide. A similar experience with business directories and a world atlas, at **MapBlast:** http://www.mapblast.com. The UK is better served by **Multimap:** http://www.multimap.com, which also has an atlas; and **QuickAddress:** http://www.qas.com/html/body_demos.shtml which reconciles UK postcodes and streets. For more maps and geographical resources see: http://geography.about.com

Moon Travel Guides

http://www.moon.com

Read excerpts, and sometimes the full text, of Moon's acclaimed travel books and newsletter.

No Shitting in the Toilet

http://www.noshit.com.au

Comic take on the delights and oddities of low-budget travel.

Paris

http://www.paris.org • http://www.paris-anglo.com/zoom/

Two virtual tours of Paris in the comfort of English – or more challengingly in French.

Roadside America

http://www.roadsideamerica.com

Guide to the strange attractions that loom between squished animals on US highways.

Rough Guides

http://www.roughguides.com

Unique among travel guides, Rough Guides are putting full text of all their books on the web for free. At last check, there were in excess of 10,000 destinations in the database – and counting.

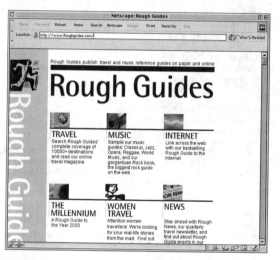

Sidewalk

http://www.sidewalk.com

MSN's useful entertainment and shopping guides to Sydney, Melbourne, and most US metros. **Citysearch**: http://www.citysearch.com covers similar territory within a selection of Australian, Scandinavian, and US cities.

Terraserver
http://www.terraserver.com

Want to see what your house looks like from a Russian spy satellite? Here's your best chance to find out.

Time Out
http://www.timeout.co.uk

Fish through **Time Out**, London's weekly listings guide site, and you'll have no excuse to stay home not just in London, but in 25 of the world's most happening cities.

Tourism Offices Worldwide
http://www.towd.com

Write to the local tourist office. They may send you a brochure.

Traffic and Road Conditions
http://www.accutraffic.com

Live traffic and weather updates across the US.

Travlang
http://www.travlang.com

Add an another language to your repertoire.

Travelmag
http://www.travelmag.co.uk

Several intimate travel reflections monthly.

UK Travel Guide
http://www.uktravel.com

Guide to getting around London and rest of the British Isles. More at: http://www.visitbritain.com

Travel & Health Warnings
http://www.dfat.gov.au (AUS)
http://www.fco.gov.uk (UK)
http://travel.state.gov/travel_warnings.html (US)
http://www.cdc.gov/travel/ (health)

Essential knowledge if you're planning to visit a potential hot-spot or health risk, but not necessarily the last word on safety. Don't ignore these bulletins, but seek a second opinion before postponing your adventure. If you're off on business and you're seriously concerned, you could try a professional advisory such as **Kroll**: http://www.krollassociates.com

WebFlyer

http://www.webflyer.com

Keep tabs on frequent flyer schemes.

World's Largest Subway Map

http://metro.ratp.fr:10001

Estimate the traveling times between city stations
worldwide.

The World Traveler Books & Maps

http://www.travelbookshop.com

Order from a wide range of travel literature. More at:
http://www.gorp.com/atbook.htm

Yahoo's Travel Section

http://www.yahoo.com/Recreation/Travel/

Yahoo's travel section (as distinct from Yahoo Travel) is one
of its best-stacked areas, with links to thousands of travel
and regional sites. Most have one-liners, rather than
reviews, but they'll give you some idea of what to expect.
It's broad, but uncritical.

WEATHER

Intellicast

http://www.intellicast.com

International weather, radar tracking, and half-hourly
satellite feeds in a sleek shell. See also:
http://www.accuweather.com

National Severe Storms Laboratory

http://www.nssl.noaa.gov

If tornadoes, blizzards, and thunderstorms are your idea of
primetime viewing, you'd better read the bit on responsible
storm chasing. It might just temper that Pavlovian frenzy
for the car keys next time a distant rumble snaps you from
your post-prandial stupor.

More at: http://australiansevereweather.simplenet.com

World Climate

http://www.worldclimate.com

Off to Irkutzk next August? Here's what weather to expect.

World Meteorological Organization
http://www.wmo.ch

UN division that monitors global climate. Links to national bureaus worldwide. For the more arcane, try:
http://www.met.rdg.ac.uk/~brugge/

World Weather
http://weather.yahoo.com • http://cnn.com/WEATHER/
http://www.meto.govt.uk (UK) • http://www.bom.gov.au (AUS)

Forecasts, charts, storm warnings, allergy reports, satellite photos, and more for thousands of cities worldwide.

WEIRD

Absurd.org
http//www.absurd.org

Please do not adjust your set.

Aetherius Society
http://www.aetherius.org

When the Cosmic Masters from the Interplanetary Council gave their message to Earth, the late Sir George King, their chosen Primary Terrestrial Mental Channel, would enter a Positive Yogic Samadhic Trance. Sort of like when Ramjet took his protein pills.

Alien Resistance Movement
http://www.armorg.net

Spank hostile saucer jockeys back into outer space.

Anders Main Page
http://www.student.nada.kth.se/~nv91-asa/

Diverse digest swaying toward the occultish side of spirituality, with a fair helping of transhumanism, mad science, discordia, illumination and magik, not to mention onanism.

The Ants are my friends
http://www.enteract.com/~jessicar/lyrics/

Know anyone who always butts in with "I thought you said. . ." and then laughs? It's a pathological disorder called Mondegreenism. The good news is you can legally have them put down. The bad news is they're everywhere: http://www.kissthisguy.com

Bert is Evil
http://www.fractalcow.com/bert/
Sesame Street star exposed in photo shocker.

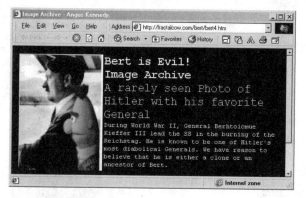

Chocolate Toxicity in Dogs
http://www.netpet.com/articles/choc.tox.html
How to pop off a greedy mutt with household ingredients.

Church of the Subgenius
http://www.subgenius.com
Pipe-puffing Bob's three-fisted surreal preaching. Beyond description.

Clonaid
http://www.clonaid.com
Thanks to the Raelians, we now know all life on earth was created in extraterrestrial laboratories. Here's where you can buy genuine cloned human livestock for the kitchen table. Ready as soon as the lab's finished.

Christian Guide to Small Arms

http://www.frii.com/~gosplow/cgsa.html

Then said he unto them, "But now, he that hath a purse, let him take it, and likewise his scrip: and he that hath no sword, let him sell his garment, and buy one"– Luke 22:36. Ouch, it's not just your right, it's your duty!

CNI Angel Gallery

http://www.cninews.com/CNI_Angels.html

Leading authorities point to evidence that angels may be alien frauds. Backed up at: http://www.mt.net/~watcher/

Circlemakers

http://www.circlemakers.org

Create crop circles to amuse New Agers and the press.

The Darwin Awards

http://www.officialdarwinawards.com • http://www.darwinawards.com

Each year the Darwin Award is presented to the person who drops off the census register in the most spectacular fashion. Here's where to read about the runners-up and er . . . winners.

Derm Cinema

http://www.skinema.com

Adds a whole new meaning to the term "skin flick".

FlyPower

http://www.flypower.com

We have the technology. We can build a bionic blowfly.

Fortean Times

http://www.forteantimes.com

Updates from the print monthly that takes the investigation of strange phenomena more seriously than itself. See also: http://www.parascope.com

Freaks, Geeks, & Weirdness on the Web

http://www.rosemarywest.com/guide/

Points to hundreds of the Net's oddest crowd pleasers.

Gallery of the Absurd

http://www.absurdgallery.com

Strange ways to sell strange stuff.

Great Joy In Great Tribulation

http://www.dccsa.com/greatjoy/

Biblical proof that Prince Chuck is the Antichrist and key dates leading to the end of the world. For more enlightenment, including how to debug the pyramids, see: http://members.aol.com/larrypahl/lpahl.htm

House Vision of the Night

http://home.interpath.net/songbird/houses.html

Evidence that Gore will become the next US president.

I Can Eat Glass Project

http://hcs.harvard.edu/~igp/glass.html

Deter excess foreign suitors and carpet dealers with the only words you know in their language.

Infamous Exploding Whale

http://www.perp.com/whale/

Easy. Take one beached whale carcass, add half a ton of dynamite, turn on the video, and run. In this case not all went as planned.

Klingon Language Institute

http://www.kli.org/klihome.html

Maybe if Capt James T. had taken this course the Enterprise would still be still boldly going.

Mind Control Forum

http://www.mk.net/~mcf/

Horrific tales of being remote controlled by Big Brother's psychotronic devices. Surely, it can be only a matter of time before it's built into Windows.

Mozart's Musikalisches Würfelspeil

http://sunsite.univie.ac.at/Mozart/dice/

Compose a minuet as you play Monopoly.

Mrs Silk's Cross Dressing Magazine

http://www.mrs-silk.com

When you finally step out of the closet, this way you'll do it in style.

News of the Weird

http://www.nine.org/notw/ • http://www.thisistrue.com

Bizarre news delivered to your inbox.

Planetary Activation Organization

http://www.paoweb.com

Prevent inter-dimensional dark forces from dominating our galaxy by ganging up with the Galactic Federation of Light.

Project Destination Moon

http://www.caus.org/destmoon.htm

Help fund the first civilian moon launch, which aims to get to the bottom of the funny business in the Sinus Medii region.

Project Duat

http://www.projectduat.com

First the planet must be engulfed in music that comes from nowhere yet everywhere, then ha-ha! – the world will be his!

Reverse Speech
http://www.reversespeech.com

They say we speak the overt forward and the covert backward. You're not going to believe what Bill Clinton, Tony Blair, and others are hiding. Or maybe you will. You have to watch what you write too: http://www.wildcowpublishing.com/paranormal/reverse.html

Sightings
http://www.sightings.com

Fishy newsbreaks from talk radio truthferret, Jeff Rense. For more real life X-file blather tune into: http://www.artbell.com

Strawberry Poptart Blow Torches
http://www.sci.tamucc.edu/~pmichaud/toast/

Scorch your breakfast guests.

Sulabh International Museum of Toilets
http://www.sulabhtoiletmuseum.org

Follow the evolution of the ablution at the world's leading exhibition of porcelain businessware. No need to take it sitting down: http://www.restrooms.org

Time Travel Devices
http://home.inreach.com/dov/tt.htm

Step back to a time that common sense forgot.

Toilet-train Your Cat
http://www.karawynn.net/mishacat/

How to point pusskins at the porcelain. Literally.

Uncle Chuckie's General Store
http://www.projectduat.com/charles-cosimano/shop.html

Build a simple psionic transmitter out of household refuse to create widespread terror and avenge traffic fines.

The Under Ground Net
http://www.theeunderground.net

News as rolled out by Sollog's prophecies. Stay tuned for a spate of nuclear terrorism live on CNN.

Vomitus Maximus Museum
http://www.vomitus.com

One of the few art galleries that's aptly named.

WearCam

http://www.wearcam.org

Steve Mann has a Netcam fixed to his head. You see what he sees. But that won't stop him having fun.

Why Cats Paint

http://www.netlink.co.nz/~monpa/

Become an aficionado of moggy masterpieces.

World Database of Happiness

http://www.eur.nl/fsw/research/happiness/

Discover where people are happiest and statistically what they mean by that.

ZetaTalk

http://www.zetatalk.com

Nancy's guests today are those elusive aliens that frolic in the autumn mist at the bottom of her garden.

Newsgroups Directory

Whatever you're into – hobbies, sports, politics, music, philosophy, business, or whatever – there's sure to be a Usenet newsgroup devoted to it. In fact, you may be surprised how many others share your interests. Usenet newsgroups provide a forum to meet like-minded people, exchange views, and pose those perplexing questions that have bugged you for years. And the groups are as much yours as anyone's, so once you have the feel of a group, jump in and contribute.

We provide the low-down on reading and posting to newsgroups on p.127. This chapter lists about 700 of the busiest groups. Sounds a lot? Well, it's little more than one percent of the total. Not that anyone knows exactly, as many are only propagated within a local area and new groups are added daily.

We've excluded the newsgroups devoted to "adult interests" – sex, mainly, either talking about it or looking at it. If that's your bag, you won't need our help to browse the alt.sex, the alt.binaries.pictures, or the alt.personals series. If you do browse the murkier areas of sex newsgroups – or the rackets discussed in the pirate software (.warez and .cracks), phone tampering (.2600), or other mischief-making groups – be aware. Just because this stuff is readily available on the Net doesn't make it legal. So don't put anything on your hard drive, or email or post anything you wouldn't like to defend in front of a jury. Also, beware pirate programs bearing surprise gifts . . .

Don't overlook the local hierarchies (aus., uk., etc) for regional topics such as TV, politics, for sale, employment, and sport. For instance, if you want to find out what happened last last week on Buffy in the UK, you might find uk.media.tv.buffy.v.slayer more in tune with your season than alt.tv.buffy.v.slayer

NEWSGROUPS DIRECTORY

For ease of reference, we've broken down newsgroups into the following categories:

Arts, Architecture, and Graphics

ART

alt.artcom	Artistic community
rec.arts.fine	For art's sake
rec.arts.misc	Unclassified arts

ARCHITECTURE

alt.architecture	Building design/construction
alt.architecture.alternative	Non-traditional design

GRAPHICS AND LAYOUT

alt.3d	Three-dimensional imaging
alt.aldus.pagemaker	DTP with PageMaker
alt.ascii-art	Pictures in ASCII characters
alt.binaries.pictures.utilities	Image software
alt.cad	Computer-aided design
comp.cad.autocad	High-end graphic modeling
comp.fonts	Font speak
comp.graphics	Computer-created images
comp.graphics.animation	Creating moving images
comp.graphics.raytracing	Persistence of visionaries
comp.publish.prepress	Desktop publishing
comp.sys.mac.graphics	Macintosh graphic techniques

Authors and Books

REFERENCE

alt.usage.english	English grammar
comp.infosystems.interpedia	The Internet Encyclopedia
comp.internet.library	Electronic libraries

DISCUSSION

For discussion of specific authors of titles, check under the alt.fan and alt.books hierarchies.

Business and Finance

BUSINESS

FINANCE

misc.invest.stocks	Stock market tips
misc.invest.technical	Predicting trends
sci.econ	Economic science
uk.finance	UK stock talk

Buying and Selling

alt.cdworld.marketplace	Trading compact discs
alt.co-ops	Collaborative buying
alt.forsale	Step right up
ba.market.misc	Bay Area trading post
demon.adverts	UK network's classifieds
la.forsale	Los Angeles trading
misc.forsale	Trading series
rec.arts.books.marketplace	Online books trading
rec.arts.sf.marketplace	Science fiction trading
rec.arts.comics.marketplace	Buy and sell comics
rec.audio.marketplace	Low price hi-fi
rec.autos.marketplace	Trade your dream machine
rec.bicycles.marketplace	Buying and selling bikes
rec.music.makers.marketplace	Instrument trading
rec.music.marketplace	Record and CD trading
rec.photo.marketplace	Camera trading
rec.radio.swap	Trading radios
uk.forsale	UK trading post

Comedy and Jokes

alt.adjective.noun.verb.verb.verb	Usenet wordplay
alt.binaries.pictures.tasteless	Spoil your appetite
alt.comedy.british	Best of British chuckles
alt.comedy.slapstick.3-stooges	Pick three
alt.comedy.standup	Comedy industry gossip
alt.devilbunnies	They're cute, but want our planet
alt.fan.monty-python	Cleese and chums

Comics

Computer games

Most popular games have their own groups under the
alt.games or rec.games hierarchies. Also look under the
alt.binaries series for patches, screenshots and software.

Computer technology

For serious discussion about, or help with, any of the
Microsoft products, try the appropriate group under the
microsoft.public series. You'll find the full set under the
free access msnews.microsoft.com server.

MISCELLANEOUS

COMPUTER HARDWARE

alt.cd-rom	Optical storage media
alt.comp.hardware.homebuilt	DIY computing
biz.comp.hardware	Commercial hardware postings
comp.dcom.modems	Data communications hardware
comp.periphs.printers	Paper gobblers
comp.sys.ibm.pc.hardware.misc	PC hardware concerns
comp.sys.laptops	Portable computing
comp.sys.mac.hardware	Macintosh computers
comp.sys.powerpc	RISC processor-driven computers
comp.sys.sgi.misc	Silicon Graphics forum
comp.sys.sun.misc	Sun Microsystems forum

COMPUTER SECURITY

alt.comp.virus	Computer vaccines
alt.security	Keeping hackers out
alt.security.espionage	Cyberspies
alt.security.pgp	Pretty good privacy encryption
comp.society.privacy	Technology and privacy
comp.virus	Virus alerts and solutions
sci.crypt	Data encryption methods

COMPUTER SOFTWARE

alt.comp.shareware	Try before you buy software
biz.comp.software	Commercial software postings
comp.binaries.ibm.pc	PC software postings
comp.binaries.ibm.pc.wanted	Requests for PC programs
comp.databases	Data management
comp.sys.mac.apps	Macintosh software
comp.os.ms-windows.apps.comm	Windows comms software
comp.os.ms-windows.apps.misc	Windows software
comp.sources.sun	Sun workstation software
comp.sources.wanted	Software and fixes
microsoft.public.inetexplorer.ie4	Internet Explorer bugs
microsoft.public.office.misc	Microsoft Office support

NETWORKING AND EMAIL

OPERATING SYSTEMS

Crafts, Gardening, and Hobbies

CRAFTS

GARDENING

HOBBIES

Dance and Theater

Drugs

Education

Employment

Fashion

Food and drink

Health and Medicine

History, Archeology, and Anthropology

rec.org.sca	Renaissance-era period play
sci.anthropology	Studying human evolution
sci.archeology	Can you dig it?
soc.history	Looking backwards

International culture

Almost every culture/ethnic group has a soc.culture and/or an alt.culture group. If yours doesn't, start one!

alt.chinese.text	Chinese character discussion
alt.culture	Cultural forum series
alt.culture.saudi	Arabian might
alt.culture.us.asian-indian	Native American culture
soc.culture	Cultural forum series
soc.culture.african.american	Afro-American affairs
soc.culture.yugoslavia	All ex-Yugoslav factions
uk.misc	All things British

Internet stuff

CYBERSPACE

alt.cybercafes	New café announcements
alt.cyberpunk	High-tech low-life
alt.cyberpunk.tech	Cyberpunk technology
alt.cyberspace	The final frontier
sci.virtual-worlds	Virtual reality

IRC

alt.irc	Internet Relay Chat material
alt.irc.questions	Solving IRC queries

NEWSGROUPS

alt.config	How to start an alt newsgroup
alt.culture.usenet	Finishing school for Usenetsters

SERVICE PROVIDERS

WORLD WIDE WEB

Legal

Movies and TV

Check the alt.tv, rec.arts and alt.fan series for talk on actors and the alt.tv series for individual shows. Check out the regional variants as well. Use your newsreader's groups filter to find them.

rec.arts.movies.reviews	Films reviewed
rec.arts.sf.movies	Science fiction movies
rec.arts.sf.tv.babylon5	Babylon 5 discussion
rec.arts.startrek.current	New Star Trek shows
rec.arts.startrek.fandom	Trek conventions and trinkets
rec.arts.tv	Television talk
rec.arts.tv.soaps	Parallel lives series
rec.arts.tv.uk	UK television talk
rec.video.production	Making home movies

Music

There are hundreds more specialist groups under the alt.music, rec.music and alt.fan hierarchies.

GENERAL

alt.cd-rom.reviews	Read before you buy
rec.music.info	Music resources on the Net
rec.music.misc	Music to any ears
rec.music.reviews	General music criticism
rec.music.video	Budding Beavis and Buttheads

POP

alt.elvis.sighting	Keep looking
alt.exotic-music	Strange moods
alt.gothic	Dying fashion
alt.music.bootlegs	Illicit recordings
alt.music.hardcore	Head banging
alt.music.lyrics	Spreading the words
alt.music.progressive	Almost modern music
alt.rock-n-roll	Counterpart to alt.sex and alt.drugs
alt.rock-n-roll.metal	Heavy, man
alt.rock-n-roll.oldies	The golden years

INDIE AND DANCE

alt.music.alternative .... Indie talk
alt.music.alternative.female .... Indie women
alt.music.canada .... Canadian indie scene
alt.music.independent .... Alternative pop
alt.music.dance .... Water? E? Okay, let's dance
alt.music.hardcore .... Serious punks
alt.music.house ....Repetitive bleats
alt.music.jungle ....Rumble in the bassbin
alt.music.synthpop .... Keyboard capers
alt.music.techno .... Repetitive beats
alt.punk .... The attitude and the music
alt.rave .... Late-night loonies
rec.music.ambient .... Soundscapes
rec.music.industrial .... Metal machine music
uk.music.breakbeat ....Drumming base

WORLD MUSIC AND FOLK

alt.music.jewish .... Klezmer developments
alt.music.world .... Tango to Tuvan throatsinging
rec.music.afro-latin .... African, Latin, and more
rec.music.celtic .... Irish music mostly
rec.music.folk .... Folk/world music/singer-songwriters
rec.music.indian.classical .... Raga sagas
rec.music.reggae .... Rasta nation

COUNTRY

rec.music.country.western .... Both types, C & W

JAZZ

alt.music.acid-jazz..Smooth movements
rec.music.bluenote .... Jazz and the blues

CLASSICAL

rec.music.classical .... Classical music
rec.music.early .... Early music

MUSIC MAKING

alt.guitar .... You axed for it
alt.music.makers.electronic .... Electric friends
rec.music.makers.guitar .... Six string along
rec.music.makers.synth .... Synthesize your mind

HI-FI AND RECORDING

rec.audio.high-end .... Audiophile equipment
rec.audio.opinion .... Hi-fi reviews
rec.audio.pro .... Professional sound recording

MUSIC UTILITIES

alt.binaries.multimedia .... Sound and vision files
alt.binaries.sounds.midi .... Music making files
alt.binaries.sounds.music .... Music files
alt.binaries.sounds.utilities .... Sound programs

Mysticism and Philosophy

alt.astrology .... Soothsaying by starlight
alt.chinese.fengshui .... Mystical interior design
alt.consciousness .... Philosophical discourse
alt.dreams .... Welcome to my nightmare
alt.dreams.castaneda .... Don Juan yarns
alt.hypnosis .... You are getting sleepy
alt.magic.secrets .... Letting the rabbit out of the hat
alt.magick .... Supernatural arts
alt.meditation .... Maintaining concentration
alt.paranet.paranormal .... Psychic phenomena
alt.paranet.skeptic .... Doubters
alt.paranet.ufo .... It came from outer space

Pets

Politics and Media

CURRENT AFFAIRS/POLITICAL ACTION

POLITICAL THEORY

SEXUAL POLITICS

alt.feminism .... Sisters for sisters
alt.politics.homosexuality .... Gay power
soc.feminism .... Gender war zone
soc.men .... Men wanting more
soc.women .... Women wanting more

US PARTY POLITICS

alt.impeach.clinton .... Presidential peeves
alt.politics.democrats .... Democrat party discussion
alt.politics.usa.congress .... US congressional affairs
alt.politics.usa.republican .... Republican party reptiles
alt.president.clinton .... Spotlight on Clinton

MEDIA

alt.fan.noam-chomsky .... Media watchdogs
alt.journalism .... Hack chat
alt.journalism.freelance .... Unemployed lines
alt.news-media .... Don't believe the hype
alt.quotations .... Things people say
aus.media-watch .... Littlemoore than a press punchup
bit.listserv.words-l .... English-language mailing list
biz.clarinet .... ClariNet newsfeed news
biz.clarinet.sample .... ClariNet news samples
uk.media .... UK media issues

Psychological support

To find more support groups, see also "Health and
Medicine" (p.409).

GENERAL PSYCHOLOGY

alt.psychology.nlp .... Neurolinguistic programming
alt.sci.sociology .... Human watching
sci.psychology.misc .... Troubleshooting behavior
sci.psychology.personality .... Why you are you

SUPPORT AND EXPLORATION

Radio and Telecommunications

Religion

Science

GENERAL

ELECTRONICS

ENERGY AND ENVIRONMENT

ENGINEERING

GEOLOGY

Space and Aliens

Sports

Transport

Travel

Software Roundup

Now that Web browsers have become such Internet software lucky dips, it's no longer so important to scout around for programs and accessories, and you certainly needn't pay for some "Internet made easy" kit. All the same, even though you can get by with a minimum of software, there's no reason to limit yourself. The easiest way to stack up on Net software is to install it from the free CDs given away with Internet or PC magazines. But if you want the latest versions as they're released, go direct to the Net itself. Your best bet is to browse the sites that specialize in listing and reviewing software you can download. You'll find a selection of these listed in our Web guide (p.259). This chapter is merely a summary of the most useful downloads to get you started. They're all free – at least for a limited time – though some have superior commercial versions.

Upgrade your browser

Your first concern will be to make sure your system has what it takes to dial up, connect to your Access Provider, and then jettison you onto the Web. Your next operation should be to update your browser to its latest version and, if you like, gradually try the added extras. When you update Internet Explorer, for example, it will interrogate your system to see what you already have and offer you a list of upgrades and accessories. You simply tick the choices, select "Download", and your system will look after the rest. If you accidentally go offline during the process, it's smart enough to recover on your next attempt. The procedure with Netscape works similarly. We've covered this territory amply in earlier chapters (see p.55 and p.146), so let's assume you're online and snuggled up to the Web browser of your dreams.

Downloading, installing, and uninstalling

Downloading a program from the Net should be relatively painless. Just go to its developer's **Web page**, read about it first, decide whether it sounds useful, and if so, fill in any required details, and pick the newest version your system can handle. Some programs come in 16-bit and 32-bit versions. If you're running Windows 95/98, NT, OS/2, or a PowerMac, go for the faster 32-bit versions. These programs will not work with 16-bit operating systems such as Windows 3.x or earlier Macs. Ask your provider if you're unsure.

It's good laboratory technique to download everything onto your Desktop or a **central directory (folder) called, say, "download"**. Once the program's downloaded, copy it to a temporary directory for installation. After it's installed, delete the contents of the temporary directory and either shift the original file into an archive or delete it. (See p.156 for "How to set up your directory structure".)

Most files will **self-extract**, so installation should be as simple as following the prompts. If not, you'll need an archiving program such as **WinZip** or Alladin (Stuffit)

Expander (see p.155) to extract the installation files. Once extracted, read the accompanying text files for installation instructions. It's usually a matter of clicking on a file called "install.exe" or "setup.exe" in Windows, or on an install icon on the Mac. Try it for a few days. If it doesn't serve a purpose, remove it from your hard drive so you don't clog up your system with rubbish. In Windows, that means deleting it from within Add/Remove Programs in the Control Panel. If there's no entry in there, look for an uninstall icon in its Start menu folder. If neither exists, it will be safe to delete the file directly from its folder. Note that some programs will hijack your file associations, so to get file types to open automatically with a previous program you might have to go into that program's settings or re-install it.

If you find yourself regularly frequenting FTP sites, you might like to move on from your Web browser and install a dedicated FTP program such as CuteFTP (http://www.cuteftp.com), WS_FTP (http://www.ipswitch.com) for Windows, and Fetch (http://www.dartmouth.edu/pages/softdev/fetch.html) or Anachie (http://www.stairways.com/anarchie/), for Macs for the PC, or Fetch for Macs (see p.147). These also have the added advantage of being able to resume transfers if something goes wrong along the way. It's also worth downloading Go!Zilla (http://www.gozilla.com) for Windows 95/98 for the same reason. As a bonus, it can also take over your Web and FTP downloads and do all sorts of other marvelous things such as downloading scheduling and file leeching. Try it, you'll never look back.

Sort out your media players

Next sort out your media players, image viewers and plug-ins. Most importantly, grab the latest versions of Shockwave (http://www.macromedia.com/shockwave/) and

RealPlayer (http://www.real.com). And, if you're running Windows, update your copy of Windows Media Player, either through Windows Update or from its home page (http://www.microsoft.com/windows/mediaplayer/). For Macs, fetch the latest release of Quicktime (http://www.quicktime. com). There's also a version for Windows that can come in handy if you ever strike the proprietary QuickTime movie and virtual reality formats. If you're into music you might also like to try an auxiliary MP3 player, such as WinAmp (http://www.winamp.com), MacAmp (http://www. macamp.com), or one of the many listed at MP3.com (http://www.mp3.com).

It also won't do you any harm to install some image viewing software so you can flick through saved pictures, convert them to other formats, and manipulate them if necessary. For Windows 95/98, install ACDSee (http://www.acdsee.com) as a viewer and set it to associate with all image formats. Irfanview (http://stud1. tuwien.ac.at/~e9227474/) can also handle most images and movie files without messing up your system. If you'd like to edit the images, try Paintshop Pro (http://www.jasc.com) which is the next best thing to Adobe's professional, though somewhat overpriced, PhotoShop. For Macs, try Graphic Converter (http://www.lemkesoft.de) and ImageViewer (http://www. imageviewer.com).

Finally, you're sure to encounter the odd portable document file (PDF), especially at government sites. These are like self-contained word-processor documents and can be viewed within your Web browser using Adobe's Acrobat Reader (http://www.adobe.com/prodindex/acrobat/) plug-in. However, because they can contain fonts and images they're often quite bloated compared to their Word or Word Perfect equivalents. It's better to save them to disk first and open them with the main viewer.

Other Internet software

Despite the efforts of Microsoft, AOL, Netscape and Real Networks, there's still plenty of competition left in the boutique end of the Internet software trade. You'll find numerous standout programs mentioned within the relevant sections throughout this book, but of course there are many more, and new strains appear daily. So don't take our word for it. If you become embroiled in Usenet, for instance, investigate several newsreaders and ruthlessly toss them out if they fail to meet your expectations. Check into any of the software guides listed in our Web directory (p.259) and you're sure to leave with a few downloads in progress!

PART THREE

Contexts

A Brief History

Net Language

Glossary

A Brief History
of the Internet

The Internet may be a recent media phenomenon but as a concept it's actually older than most of its users; it was born in the 1960s – a long time before anyone coined the buzzwords "Information SuperHighway". Of course, there's no question that the Net deserves its current level of attention. It really is a quantum leap in global communications, though – right now– it's still more of a prototype than a finished product. While Bill Gates and US Vice-President Al Gore rhapsodize about such household services as video-on-demand, most Netizens would be happy with a system fast enough to view stills-on-demand. Nonetheless, it's getting there.

THE ONLINE BOMB SHELTER

The concept of the Net might not have been hatched in Microsoft's cabinet war rooms, but it did play a role in a previous contest for world domination. It was 1957, at the height of the Cold War. The Soviets had just launched the first Sputnik, thus beating the USA into space. The race was on. In response, the US Department of Defense formed the **Advanced Research Projects Agency (ARPA)** to bump up its technological prowess. Twelve years later, this spawned **ARPAnet** – a project to develop a military research network, or specifically, the world's first decentralized computer network.

In those days, no-one had PCs. The computer world was based on mainframe computers and dumb terminals. These usually involved a gigantic, fragile box in a climate-controlled room, which acted as a hub, with a mass of cables spoking out to keyboard/monitor ensembles. The concept of independent intelligent processors pooling resources through a network was brave new territory that would require the development of new hardware, software, and connectivity methods.

The driving force behind decentralization, ironically, was the bomb-proofing factor. Nuke a mainframe and the system goes down. But bombing a network would, at worst, remove only a few nodes. The remainder could route around it unharmed. Or so the theory went.

WIRING THE WORLD

Over the next decade, **research agencies** and **universities** flocked to join the network. US institutions such as UCLA, MIT, Stanford, and Harvard led the way, and in 1973, the network crossed the Atlantic to include University College London and Norway's Royal Radar Establishment.

The 1970s also saw the introduction of **electronic mail, FTP, Telnet,** and what would become the **Usenet newsgroups**. The early 1980s brought **TCP/IP,** the **Domain Name System, Network News Transfer Protocol,** and the European networks **EUnet** (European UNIX Network), **MiniTel** (the widely adopted French consumer network), and **JANET** (Joint Academic Network), as well as the Japanese **UNIX** Network. **ARPA** evolved to handle the research traffic, while a second network, MILnet, took over the US military intelligence.

An important development took place in 1986, when

the US National Science Foundation established **NSFnet** by linking five university super-computers at a backbone speed of 56 Kbps. This opened the gateway for external universities to tap in to superior processing power and share resources. In the three years between 1984 and 1988, the number of host computers on the **Internet** (as it was now being called) grew from about 1000 to over 60,000. NSFnet, meanwhile, increased its capacity to T1 (1544 Kbps). Over the next few years, more and more countries joined the network, spanning the globe from Australia and New Zealand, to Iceland, Israel, Brazil, India, and Argentina.

It was at this time, too, that **Internet Relay Chat (IRC)** burst onto the scene, providing an alternative to CNN's incessant, but censored, Gulf War coverage. By this stage, the Net had grown far beyond its original charter. Although ARPA had succeeded in creating the basis for decentralized computing, whether it was actually a military success was debatable. It might have been bombproof, but it also opened new doors to espionage. It was never particularly secure, and it is suspected that Soviet agents routinely hacked in to forage for research data. In 1990, ARPAnet folded, and NSFnet took over administering the Net.

COMING IN FROM THE COLD

Global electronic communication was far too useful and versatile to stay confined to academics. Big business was starting to get interested. The Cold War looked like it was over and world economies were regaining confidence after the 1987 stock market savaging. In most places, market trading moved from the pits and blackboards onto computer screens. The financial sector expected fingertip real-time data and that feeling was spreading. The world was ready for a people's network. And since the Net was already in place, funded by taxpayers, there was really no excuse not to open it to the public.

In 1991, the NSF lifted its restrictions on enterprise. During the Net's early years, its "**Acceptable Use Policy**" specifically prohibited using the network for profit. Changing that policy opened the floodgates to commerce with the great general public close behind.

However, before anyone could connect to the Net, someone had to sell them a connection. The **Commercial Internet eXchange (CIX)**, a network of major commercial Access Providers, formed to create a commercial backbone and divert traffic from the NSFnet. Before long, dozens of budding Access Providers began rigging up points of presence in their bedrooms. Meanwhile, NSFnet upgraded its backbone to T3 (44,736 Kbps).

By this time, the Net had established itself as a viable medium for transferring data, but with one major problem. You could pretty much find things only if you knew where to look. That process involved knowing a lot more about computers in general, and the UNIX computing language in particular, than most punters would relish. The next few years saw an explosion in navigation protocols, such as WAIS, Gopher, Veronica, and, most importantly, the now-dominant World Wide Web.

THE GOLD RUSH BEGINS

In 1989, Tim Berners-Lee of **CERN**, the Swiss particle physics institute, proposed the basis of the World Wide Web, initially as a means of sharing physics research. His goal was a seamless network in which data from any source could be accessed in a simple, consistent way with one program, on any type of computer. The Web did this, encompassing all existing infosystems such as FTP, Gopher, and Usenet, without alteration. It was an unqualified success.

As the number of Internet hosts exceeded one million, the **Internet Society** was formed to brainstorm protocols and attempt to co-ordinate and direct the Net's escalating expansion. **Mosaic** – the first graphical **Web browser** – was released, and declared to be the "killer application of the 1990s". It made navigating the Internet as simple as pointing and clicking, and took away the need to know UNIX. The Web's traffic increased by 25-fold in the year up to June 1994, and domain names for **commercial organizations** (.com) began to outnumber those of educational institutions (.edu).

As the Web grew, so too did the global village. The media began to notice, slowly realizing that the Internet was something that went way beyond propeller heads and students. They couldn't miss it, actually, with almost every country in the world connected or in the process. Even the White House was online.

Of course, as word of a captive market got around, entrepreneurial brains went into overdrive. Canter & Seigel, an Arizona law firm, notoriously "**spammed**" Usenet with **advertisements** for the US green card lottery. Although the Net was tentatively open for business, cross-posting advertisements to every newsgroup was decidedly bad form. Such was the ensuing wrath that C&S had no chance of filtering out genuine responses from the server-breaking level of hate mail they received. A precedent was thus established for **how not to do business on the Net**. Pizza Hut, by contrast, showed how to do it subtly by setting up a trial service on the Web. Although it generated wads of positive publicity, it too was doomed by impracticalities. Nevertheless, the ball had begun to roll.

THE HOMESTEADERS

As individuals arrived to stake out Web territory, businesses followed. Most had no idea what to do once they got their brand on the Net. Too many arrived with a bang, only to peter out in a perpetuity of "under construction signs". Soon business cards not only sported email addresses, but Web addresses as well. And rather than send a CV and stiff letter, job aspirants could now send a brief email accompanied with a "see my Web page" for further details.

The Internet moved out of the realm of luxury into an elite necessity, verging toward a commodity. Some early business sites gathered such a following that by 1995 they were able to charge high rates for advertising banners. A few, including Web **portals** such as **InfoSeek** and **Yahoo**, made it to the Stock Exchange boards, while others, like **GNN**, attracted buyers (in their case the Online Service giant, AOL).

But it wasn't all success stories. Copyright lawyers arrived in droves. Well-meaning devotees, cheeky opportunists, and info-terrorists alike felt the iron fists of Lego, McDonald's, MTV, the Louvre, Fox, Sony, the Church of Scientology and others clamp down on their "unofficial Web sites" or newsgroups. It wasn't always a case of corporate right but of might, as small players couldn't foot the expenses to test **new legal boundaries**. The honeymoon was officially over.

POINT OF NO RETURN

By the beginning of 1995, the Net was well and truly within the public realm. It was impossible to escape. The media became bored with extolling its virtues, so it turned to **sensationalism**. The Net reached the status of an Oprah Winfrey issue. New tales of hacking, pornography, bombmaking, terrorist handbooks, and sexual harassment began to tarnish the Internet's iconic position as the great international equalizer. But that didn't stop businesses, schools, banks, government bodies, politicians, and consumers from swarming online, nor the major **Online Services** – such as CompuServe, America Online, and Prodigy, which had been developing in parallel since the late 1980s – from adding Internet access as a sideline to their existing private networks.

As 1995 progressed, Mosaic, the previous year's killer application, lost its footing to a superior browser, **Netscape**. Not such big news, you might imagine, but after a half-year of rigorous beta-testing, Netscape went public with the third largest ever NASDAQ IPO share value – around $2.4bn.

Meantime, Microsoft, which had formerly disregarded the Internet, released **Windows 95**, a PC operating platform incorporating access to the controversial **Microsoft Network**. Although **IBM** had done a similar thing six months earlier with **OS/2 Warp** and its **IBM Global Network**, Microsoft's was an altogether different scheme. It offered full Net access but its real product was its own separate network, which many people feared might supersede the Net, giving Microsoft an unholy reign over information distribution. But that never happened. Within months, Microsoft, smarting from bad press, and finding the Net a larger animal even than itself, about-turned and declared a full commitment to furthering the Internet.

BROWSER WARS

As Microsoft advanced on the horizon, Netscape continued pushing the envelope, driving the Web into new territory with each beta release. New enhancements arrived at such a rate that competitors began to drop out as quickly as they appeared. This was the era of "This page looks best if viewed with Netscape." Of course, it wasn't just Netscape since much of the new activity stemmed from the innovative products of third-party developers such as

MacroMedia (Shockwave), **Progressive Networks (RealAudio)**, **Apple (QuickTime)**, and **Sun (Java)**. The Web began to spring to life with animations, music, 3D worlds, and all sorts of new tricks.

While Netscape's market dominance gave developers the confidence to accept it as the de facto standard, treating it as a kind of Internet operating system into which to "plug" their products, Microsoft, an old hand at taking possession of cleared territory, began to launch a whole series of free Net tools. These included **Internet Explorer**, a browser with enhancements of its own, including **ActiveX**, a Web-centric programming environment more powerful than the much-lauded **Java**, but without the same platform independence, and clearly geared toward advancing Microsoft's software dominance. Not only was Internet Explorer suddenly the only other browser in the race, unlike Netscape, it was genuinely free. And many were not only rating it as the better product, but also crediting Microsoft with a broader vision of the Net's direction.

By mid-1997, every Online Service and almost every major ISP had signed deals with Microsoft to distribute its browser. Even intervention by the US Department of Justice over Microsoft's (logical but monopolistic) bundling of Internet Explorer as an integral part of Windows 98 couldn't impede its progress. Netscape looked bruised. While it continued shipping minor upgrades it no longer led either in market share or innovation. In desperation, it handed over the project of completely reworking the code to the general programming public at Mozilla.org. When AOL bought Netscape in early 1999, little doubt remained. Netscape had given up the fight.

FOUND ON THE INTERNET

Skipping back to late 1995, the backlash against Internet freedom had moved into full flight. The expression "**found**

on the Internet", became the news tag of the minute, depicting the Net as the source of everything evil from bomb recipes to child pornography. While editors and commentators, often with little direct experience of the Net, urged that "children" be protected, the Net's own media and opinion shakers pushed the **freedom of speech** barrow. It became apparent that this uncensored, uncontrollable new media could shake the very foundations of democracy.

At first politicians didn't take much notice. Few could even grasp the concept of what the Net was about, let alone figure out a way to regulate its activities. The first, and easiest, target was **pornography**, resulting in raids on hundreds of **private bulletin boards** worldwide and a few much-publicized convictions for the possession of child porn. BBSs were sitting ducks, being mostly self-contained and run by someone who could take the rap. Net activists, however, feared that the primary objective was to send a ripple of fear through a Net community that believed it was bigger than the law, and to soften the public to the notion that the Internet, as it stood, posed a threat to national wellbeing.

In December 1995, at the request of German authorities, **CompuServe** cut its newsfeed to exclude the bulk of newsgroups carrying sexual material. But the groups cut weren't just pornographers, some were dedicated to gay and abortion issues. This brought to light the difficulty in drawing the lines of obscenity, and the problems with publishing across foreign boundaries. Next came the **US Communications Decency Act**, a proposed legislation to forbid the online publication of "obscene" material. It was poorly conceived, however, and, following opposition from a very broad range of groups (including such mainstream bodies as the American Libraries Association), was overturned, and the decision later upheld in the Supreme Court.

Outside the US, meanwhile, more authorities reacted. In **France**, chiefs of three major Access Providers were temporarily jailed for supplying obscene newsgroups, while in **Australia** police prosecuted several users for downloading child pornography. NSW courts introduced legislation banning obscene material with such loose wording that the Internet itself could be deemed illegal – if the law is ever tested. In **Britain**, in mid-1996, the police tried a "voluntary" approach, identifying newsgroups that carried pornography beyond the pale, and requesting that providers remove them from their feed. Most complied, but there was unease within the Internet industry that this was the wrong approach – the same groups would migrate elsewhere and the root of the problem would remain.

But the debate was, or is, about far more than pornography, despite the huffing and puffing. For **Net fundamentalists**, the issue is about holding ground against any compromises in liberty, and retaining the global village as a political force – potentially capable of bringing down governments and large corporations. Indeed, they argue that these battles over publishing freedom have shown governments to be out of touch with both technology and the social undercurrent, and that in the long run the balance of power will shift toward the people, toward a new democracy.

WIRETAPPING

Another slow-news-day story of the mid-1990s depicted **hackers** gaining control of networks, stealing money, and creating havoc. It made great reading, but the reality was less alarming. Although the US Department of Defense reported hundreds of thousands of network break-ins, they claimed it was more annoying than damaging. While in the commercial world, little went astray except the odd credit card file. (Bear in mind that every time you hand your credit card to a shop assistant they get the same information.) In fact, by and large, for an online population greater than the combined size of New York, Moscow, London, Calcutta, and Tokyo, there were surprisingly few noteworthy crimes. Yet the perception remained that the Net was too unsafe for the exchange of sensitive information such as payment details.

Libertarians raged at the US Government's refusal to lift export bans on crack-proof **encryption algorithms**. But cryptography, the science of message coding, has traditionally been classified as a weapon and thus export of encryption falls under the Arms Control acts.

Encryption requires a secret key to open the contents of a message and often another public key to code the message. These keys can be generated for regular use by individuals or, in the case of Web transactions, simply for one session upon agreement between the server and client. Several governments proposed to employ official escrow authorities to keep a register of all secret keys and surrender them upon warrant – an unpopular proposal, to put it mildly, among a Net community who regard invasion of privacy as an issue equal in importance to censorship, and government monitors as instruments of repression.

However, authorities were so used to being able to tap phones, intercept mail, and install listening devices to aid investigations, that they didn't relish giving up their freedom either. Government officials made a lot of noise about needing to monitor data to protect national security, though their true motives probably involve monitoring internal insurgence and catching tax cheats – stuff they're not really supposed to do but we put up with anyway because if we're law-abiding it's mostly in our best interests.

The implications of such obstinacy go far beyond personal privacy. Business awaits browsers that can talk to commerce servers using totally snooper-proof encryption. Strong encryption technology has already been built into browsers, but it's illegal to export them from the US. If you're downloading Internet Explorer or Netscape from outside the US, you must opt for the weaker version.

THE ENTERTAINMENT ARRIVES

While politicians, big business, bankers, telcos, and online action groups such as **CommerceNet** and the **Electronic Frontier Foundation** fretted the future of privacy and its impact on digital commerce, the online world partied on regardless. If 1996 was the year of the Web, then 1997 was the year the **games** began. Netizens had been swapping chess moves, playing dress-up, and struggling with the odd network game over the Net for years, but it took id Software's **Quake** to lure the gaming masses online. Not to miss out, Online Services and ISPs took steps to prioritize game traffic, while hardcore corporate data moved further back on the shelves.

Music took off, too. **Bands** and **DJs** routinely simulcast, or exclusively played, concerts over the Net while celebrities such as Michael Jackson, Joe Dolce, and Paul McCartney bared their souls in public chat rooms. Web pages came alive with the sound of music, from cheesy synthesized backgrounds to live radio feeds. Many online music stores like **CDNow** reported profits, while **Amazon** became a major force in bookselling.

And then there was the Net as a prime news medium. As **Pathfinder** touched down on Mars, back on Earth millions logged into NASA sites to scour the Martian landscape for traces of life. China marched into Hong Kong, Tiger Woods rewrote golfing history, Australia regained the Ashes, and Mike Tyson fell from grace, all live on the Net. In response to this breaking of news on Web sites and newsgroups, an increasing number of **print newspapers** began delivering online versions before their hard copies hit the stands. In 1997, if you weren't on the Net, you weren't in the media.

THE CASUALTIES

Not everyone had reason to party in 1997. **Cybercafés** – touted as the coolest thing in 1995 – tended to flop as quickly as they appeared, as did many small **Internet Service Providers**, if they weren't swallowed by larger fish. From over thirty **Web browsers** in early 1996, less than a year later, only two real players – Netscape and Microsoft – remained in the game. The also-ran software houses that initially thrived on the Net's avenue for distribution and promotion faded from view as the two browser giants ruthlessly crammed more features into their plug-and-play Web desktops. Microsoft, and scores of other software developers, declared that their future products would be able to update themselves online, either automatically or by clicking in the right place. So much for the software dealer.

Meanwhile, **Web TV** arrived delivering Web pages and email onto home TV screens. It offered a cheap, simple alternative to PCs, but found its way to a smaller niche market than its fanfare predicted.

The whole **Web design industry** was due for a shake-out. Overnight Web cowboys – lacking the programming skills to code, the artistic merit to design, or the spelling standards to edit, yet who'd charged through the teeth for cornering the home-page design scam – were left exposed by the advent of ActiveX, Java, data processing, and print-standard art. New media had come of age. The top Web chimps reworked their résumés and pitched in with online design houses. Major ad agencies formed new media departments, and splashed Web addresses over everything from milk cartons to toothpaste tubes.

Bizarrely though, 1997's best-known Web design team, **Higher Source**, will be remembered not for HTML handiwork, but for publishing their cult's agenda to top themselves in conjunction with the passing of the Hale Bopp comet. This was the Internet as major news story. Within hours of the mass suicide, several sites appeared spoofing both its corporate pages as well as its cult, **Heaven's Gate**. Days later, there were enough to spawn four new Yahoo subdirectories.

Back in the real world of **business and money**, major companies have played surprisingly by the book, observing netiquette – the Net's informal code of conduct. The marriage has been awkward but generally happy. Even the absurd court cases between blockbuster sites such as **Microsoft Sidewalk v. TicketMaster** and **Amazon v. Barnes & Noble** (over the "biggest bookstore in the world" claim) did little to convince Netizens that they were witnessing anything more than carefully orchestrated publicity stunts. Indeed, many felt launching a Web site without some kind of legal suit was a waste of free publicity. It seemed like just a bit of fun. And as big money flowed in, **bandwidths** increased, content improved, ma and pa scuttled aboard, and the online experience richened.

Alas, the same couldn't be said for the new school entrepreneurs. Low advertising costs saw **Usenet newsgroups and email in-trays** choked with crossposted get-rich schemes, network marketing plans, and porno adverts. Further, unprecedented **banks of email** broke servers at AOL, MSN, and scores of smaller providers. Temporarily, Netcom was forced to bar all mail originating from Hotmail, the most popular free Web email service, and consequent safe haven for fly-by-night operators due to the level of spam originating from its domain. At the same time, in July 1997, a mislaid backhoe ripped up a vital US backbone artery darkening large parts of the Net – something many had presumed impossible – and reducing the worldwide network to a crawl. The Net was nuclear-proof maybe, but certainly not invulnerable.

THE WORLD'S BIGGEST PLAYGROUND

By the end of 1997, the Net's population had skyrocketed to well over a hundred million. The media increasingly relied on it for research and, in the process, began to understand it. It could no longer be written off as geek-land when it was thrust this far into mainstream consciousness. Notable among the most recent arrivals were the so-called "grey surfers", predominantly retirees, who in some cases found it the difference between having few interests and few friends, and suddenly finding a reason to live. Indeed, the Net was looking not only useful, but essential, and those without it had good reason to feel left behind.

This new maturity arrived on the back of email, with the Web hot on its heels. As toner sales plummeted, surveys indicated that email had not only overtaken the fax, but possibly even the telephone, as the business communication tool of choice. However, at the same time, it could also lay claim to being the greatest time waster ever introduced into an office with staff spending large chunks of their days reading circulars, forwarding curios, and flirting with their online pals.

Email's speed, and the ease in carbon copying an entire address book, brought new implications to the six degrees of separation. Something with universal appeal, like the infernal dancing baby animation, could be disseminated to millions within a matter of hours, potentially reaching everyone on the Net within days. And, as most journalists were by this stage hooked in, whatever circulated on the Net often found its way into other media formats. Not surprisingly, the fastest-moving chain emails were often hoaxes. One such prank, an address of sensible old-timer advice, supposedly delivered by Kurt Vonnegut to MIT graduates (but actually taken from Mary Schmick's Chicago Tribune column) saturated the Net within a week. "Romeo and Juliet" director, Baz Lurhman, was so taken he put it to music resulting in the cult hit "Sunscreen", which even more incredibly was re-spoofed into a XXXX beer advert. All within six months.

On a more annoying note, almost everyone received virus hoaxes that warned not to open email with certain subject headings. Millions took them seriously, earnestly forwarding them to their entire address books. An email campaign kicked off by Howard Stern propelled "Hank, the ugly drunken dwarf" to the top of People's 100 Most Beautiful People poll as voted on the Net. Meanwhile the Chinese community rallied to push Michelle Kwan into second place. But the biggest coup of all was Matt Drudge's email leaking Bill Clinton's inappropriate affair with Monica Lewinsky, which sent the old world media into the biggest feeding frenzy since the OJ trial. Although it might not have brought down the most powerful man in the world, it showed how in 1998, almost anyone, anywhere could be heard.

THE SHOW MUST GO ON

In May 1998, the blossoming media romance with hackers as urban folk heroes turned sour when a consortium of good-fairy hackers, known as the **L0pht**, assured a US Senate Government Affairs Committee that they, or someone less benevolent, could render the Net entirely unusable within half an hour. It wasn't meant as a threat, but a call to arms against the apathy of those who'd designed, sold, and administered the systems. The Pentagon had already been penetrated (by a talented Israeli hacker), and though most reported attacks amounted to little more than vandalism, with an increasing number of essential services tapped in, the probability of major disaster veered toward looking possible.

Undeterred, Net commerce continued to break into new territories. **Music**, in particular, looked right at home with the arrival of DIY CD compilation shops and several major artists such as Massive Attack, Willie Nelson and the Beach Boys airing their new releases on the Net in MP3, before unleashing them on CD. However, these exclusive previews weren't always intentional. For instance, Swervedriver's beleaguered "99th Dream" found its way onto Net bootleg almost a year before its official release.

By now, celebrity chat appearances hardly raised an eyebrow. Even major powerbrokers like Clinton and Yeltsin had appeared before an online inquisition. To top it off, in April 1998, Koko, a 300-pound gorilla, fronted up to confess to some 20,000 chatsters that she'd rather be playing with Smokey, her pet kitten.

THE RED-LIGHT DISTRICT

Despite the bottomless reserves of free Web space, personal vanity pages and Web diaries took a downturn in 1998. The novelty was passing, a sign perhaps that the Web was growing up. This didn't, however, prevent live Web cameras, better known as **Webcams**, from enjoying a popularity resurgence. But this time around they weren't so much being pointed at lizards, fish, ski slopes or intersections, but at whoever connected them to the Net – a fad which resulted in numerous bizarre excursions in exhibitionism from some very ordinary folk. Leading the fray was the entirely unremarkable Jennifer Ringley, who became a Web household name simply for letting the world see her move about her college room, clothed and, very occasionally, otherwise. She might have only been famous for being famous, but it was fame enough to land her a syndicated newspaper column about showing off and, of course, a tidy packet from the thousands of subscribers who paid real money to access Jennicam.

But this was the tame end of the Net's trade in voyeurism. And these were boom times for pornographers. Research suggested as high as 90 percent of network traffic was consumed by porn images. That's not to suggest that anywhere near 90 percent of users were involved, only that the images consume so much bandwidth. The story in Usenet was even more dire with more than 80 percent of the non-binary traffic hogged by spam and spam cancel messages. Meanwhile, the three top Web search aids, HotBot, Altavista and Yahoo, served click-through banners on suggestive keywords. However you felt about pornography from a moral standpoint, it had definitely become a nuisance.

THE BOTTLENECK

As 1998 progressed, **cable Internet access** became increasingly available, and even affordable in the USA. New subscribers could suddenly jump from download speeds of, at best, 56 Kbps to as high as 10 Mbps. Meanwhile several telcos, such as PacBell and GTE, began rolling out ADSL, another broadband technology capable of megabit access, this time over plain copper telephone wires. However, even at these speeds, users still had to deal with the same old bottleneck. Namely the Internet's backbone which had been struggling to cope with even the low-speed dial-up traffic.

The power to **upgrade the backbone**, or more correctly backbones, lies in the hands of those who own the major cables and thus effectively control the Internet. Over the next few years, the global telecommunication big guns look set to starve the smaller players out of the market. And the emergence of Internet telephony has forced telcos to look further down the track at the broader scenario where whoever controls the Internet not only controls data, but voice traffic as well. They recognize that their core business could be eroded by satellite and cable companies. To survive, telcos need to compete on the same level, provide an alternative, or join forces with their rivals. At the moment all three seem viable options.

There's little doubt their biggest competition will come from the skies. Apart from existing high-speed satellite downlink services from DirecPC, expect to see SkyStation's solar-powered stratospheric airships hovering over large cities and beaming down major megabits before the end of this century. And by 2002, Teledesic, from Gates, Boeing, McCaw, and others, will launch several hundred low-orbiting satellites with the sole purpose of creating an alternative high-speed Internet backbone infrastructure accessible from anywhere on earth with a relatively small dish. So the Information SuperHighway really is on its way. It's merely a matter of when, what it will cost and how you'll pay for it.

But the big question is, will it be for you? The answer is, most likely, yes. But you might not be able to justify spending on broadband unless you're earnestly intent on downloading video and high fidelity audio, and since you can already get that free with TV and radio, the decision is whether you're prepared to pay extra to do your own programming. In this scenario, you might expect the shops to pay for your bandwidth, in the same way they build car parks in the real world. That's yet to be seen. But we will soon become blasé about the Net as a medium and focus on its content. As with magazines, it will be about what's in them, not the paper they're printed on.

Likewise, telcos have given in to Internet telephony. They see it's about the people at the end of the wires, not what they do with them. They just don't know how to work the bills. How this will pan out is anyone's guess, but the boundaries between email, chat, and voice will blur. Presumably this will mean cheaper long-distance phone calls and phone numbers that can move with you. This new mobility will induce many to leave their offices and work from home, and just as likely, while they're on holidays. Just don't be surprised if freedom from the office means never being able to escape work.

THE DUST CLEARS BUT THE FOG REMAINS

As we packed up shop for the millennium, fretting over double-digit date blunders, the Internet settled into a consolidation phase. For the most part, what was hot got hotter while the remainder atrophied. Broadband cable, ADSL, and satellite access forged ahead, particularly in the US and Australia. Meanwhile in the UK, British Telecom stooped to an eleventh-hour exploit on its unpopular metered local call system, weaseling deals with UK ISPs to enable free access by divvying up its phone bill booty. Surprisingly, instead of torching 10 Downing St for allowing the situation to exist in the first place, browbeaten Brits snapped it up, propelling free access pioneer Freeserve to the top of the ISP pops within months. At the time of writing, the situation is thickening with rumors of **budget all-you-can-eat ADSL** on the UK horizon, but the call rate system remains precariously intact.

Interest in online commerce surged with explosive growth in stock trading, auctions, travel booking, and mail order computers. Big-budget empire builders such as AOL, Amazon, Cisco, Disney, Excite, Microsoft, and Real Networks hit overdrive announcing intertwined strategic mergers and continued swallowing and stomping on smaller talent. Most notably AOL, with little more than a dip into petty cash, wolfed down Netscape. Not, as many assumed, for its revolutionary browser but for the sizable userbase still buzzing its browser's default home page. This, however, wasn't the Netscape of the mid 1990s, but a defeated relic that had lost its way, ceased innovating, and appeared unable to ship products. Its legacy had been passed over to Microsoft, which remained in court squabbling over Internet Explorer, Windows 98, and its success in cornering all but some 5 percent of the operating system market share. Apart from whatever voyeuristic pleasure could be gained from king-hitting computing's tallest poppy, the Department of Justice's case grew increasingly meaningless against the broader backdrop. No matter what the outcome, the computer-wielding public had arrived well before their dinner bell and their problem was not lack of choice, but lack of quality. Even Apple's allegedly foolproof iMac fell way short of a sturdy carriage to traverse the Net, play games, and make life generally more pushbutton computerized.

By this stage the Internet was ready to become a public utility, but both the computing and access provision industry remained rooted within a hobbyist mindset. As PC dealers shamelessly crammed their systems with interfering utilities, ISPs continued to supply inadequate bandwidth, unreliable software and irresponsible advice. Yet no alternative existed, and governments appeared incapable of intelligent input. As the 20th century bit the dirt, you didn't have to be a geek to get on the Net, but it sure didn't hurt.

A BRIGHTER TOMORROW

Now that the **people's network** has the globe in an irreversible stranglehold, you might assume the wired revolution is as good as over. Perhaps it is, but for those in the dark, the reality can be less comforting. A passable knowledge of the Internet in 1997 was enough to land you a job. Today, in many fields, it's becoming a prerequisite. It's a case of get online or get left behind. But the most worrisome aspect is not the difficulty in getting online, but the time involved in keeping up to date, and its stress on our physical, mental, and social wellbeing.

Still, like it or not, the Net is the closest thing yet to an all-encompassing snapshot of the human race. Never before have our words and actions been so immediately accountable in front of such a far-reaching audience. If we're scammed, we can instantly warn others. If we believe there's a government cover-up, we can expose it through the Net. If we want to be heard, no matter what it is we have to say, we can tell it to the Net. And, in the same way, if we need to know more, or we need to find numbers, we can turn to it for help.

What's most apparent all up, is that humanity looks in pretty okay shape. That's kind of ironic, because it didn't necessarily look that way before. But we've now been able to see that for every extreme there appears to be many more moderates; for every hate group, a thousand peace-makers; and for every conspiracy theory, if not some sensible explanation, then at least a few attentive ears. We've been able to examine the weirdest and the worst the world has to offer and contrast it against a greater global theme. Now that our boundaries are so much easier to explore, the future of not only the Net, but the planet itself, surely looks brighter.

The problem with such rapid improvement is that our expectations grow to meet it. But the Net, even at age thirty-something, is still only in its infancy. So be patient, enjoy it for what it is today, and complain, but not too much. One day you'll look back and get all nostalgic about the times you logged into the world through old copper telephone wires. It's amazing it works at all.

Net Language

The Internet hasn't always been a public thoroughfare: it used to be a clique inhabited by students and researchers nurtured on a diet of UNIX programming, scientific nomenclature, and in-jokes. Meanwhile, in a parallel world, thousands of low-speed modem jockeys logged into independent bulletin board networks to trade files, post messages, and chat in public forums. These groups were largely responsible for the birth of an exclusively online language consisting of acronyms, emoticons (smileys and such), and tagged text. The popularizing of the Internet brought these two cultures together, along with, more recently, the less digitally versed general public.

Low online speed, poor typing skills, and the need for quick responses were among the pioneers' justifications for keeping things brief. But using Net lingo was also a way of showing you were in the know. These days, it's not so prevalent, though you're sure to encounter Netty terms in **IRC** and, to a lesser extent, in **Usenet and on Mailing Lists**. Since IRC is a snappy medium, with line space at a premium, acronyms and the like can actually be useful – as long as they're understood.

Shorthand: Net acronyms

It doesn't take long in IRC to realize that Net acronyms are peppered with the F-initial. It's your choice whether you add to this situation, but if you don't tell people to "f*** right off" in ordinary speech or letters, then FRO is hardly appropriate on the Net, and nor is adding F as emphasis. However, you may at least want to know what's being said. And, BTW (by the way), the odd bit of Net shorthand may be useful and/or vaguely amusing, even if unlikely to make you ROFL (roll on the floor laughing).

AFAIK	As far as I know
AOLer	AOL member (often not a compliment)
A/S/L	Age/Sex/Location
BOHICA	Bend over here it comes again
BBL	Be back later
BD or BFD	Big deal
BFN	Bye for now
BRB	Be right back
BTW	By the way
CUL8R or L8R	See you later
CYA	See ya
F2F (S2S)	Face to face (skin to skin)
FB	Furrowed brow
FWIW	For what it's worth
GDM8	G'day mate
GRD	Grinning, running, and ducking
GR8	Great
HTH	Hope this helps
IMHO	In my humble opinion
IYSWIM	If you see what I mean
IAE	In any event
IOW	In other words
LOL	Laughing out loud
NRN	No reply necessary
NW or NFW	No way
OIC	Oh I see
OTOH	On the other hand
PBT	Pay back time
RTM or RTFM	Read the manual
SOL	Sooner or later
TTYL	Talk to you later
YL/YM	Young lady/young man
YMMV	Your mileage may vary
|LY| & +LY	Absolutely and positively

Smileys and emoticons

Back in the old days, it was common in Usenet to temper a potentially contentious remark with <grins> tacked on to the end in much the same way that a dog wags its tail to show it's harmless. But that wasn't enough for the Californian E-generation, whose trademark smiley icon became the 1980s peace sign. From the same honed minds that discovered 71077345 inverted spelled Greenpeace's *bête noire*, came the ASCII smiley. This time, instead of turning it upside-down, you had to look at it sideways to see a smiling face. An expression that words, supposedly, fail to convey. Well, at least in such limited space. Inevitably this grew into a whole family of emoticons (emotional icons).

The odd smiley may have its place in diffusing barbs, but whether you employ any of the other emoticons in use is up to your perception of the line between cute and dorky. All the same, don't lose sight of the fact that they're only meant to be fun :-). Anyway, that's up to you, so here goes:

:-)	Smiling	:-L~~	Drooling
:-D	Laughing	:-P	Sticking out tongue
:-o	Shock	(hmm)Ooo.. :-)	Thinking happy thoughts
:-(	Frowning		
:'-(	Crying	(hmm)Ooo.. :-(	Thinking sad thoughts
;-)	Winking		
X=	Fingers crossed	0:-)	Angel
: =)	Little Hitler	}:>	Devil
{}	Hugging	(_)]	Beer
:*	Kissing	:8)	Pig
$-)	Greedy	\o/	Hallelujah
X-)	I see nothing	@}-`—,—`	A rose
:-X	I'll say nothing	8:)3)=	Happy girl

A few others, mostly Japanese anime-derived, work right way up:

@^_^@	blushing	^_^;	sweating
*^_^*	huge dazzling grin	T_T	major tears

If you still want more, try consulting a few unofficial dictionaries on the Web. Use "smiley dictionary" or "emoticon" as a search term at http:/www.hotbot.com

Emphasis

Another common way to express actions or emotions is to add commentary within < **these signs** >.

For example:

<flushed> I've just escaped the clutches of frenzied train-spotters < removes conductor's cap, wipes brow >.

More commonly, and more usefully, Netizens also use **asterisks in email** to *emphasize* words, in place of bolds and italics. You simply *wrap* the appropriate word: Hey everyone look at *me*.

Misspellings and intracaps

Some jokers pointedly overuse **phonetic spellings, puns, or plain misspellings** (kewl, windoze, luzer, etc.) And wannabe crackers like to **intercapitalize**, LlKe tHi5. You can safely assume they're either very young, trying to make an impression, total plonkers, or all of the above.

For more

If you come across an abbreviation or smiley you don't understand, ask its author. Don't worry about appearing stupid as these expressions aren't exactly common knowledge. Alternatively consult one of the many online references such as Netlingo (http://www.netlingo.com) or the Smiley Server (http://www.pop.at/smileys/).

Glossary

A

Access Provider Company that sells Internet connections. Known variously as Internet Access or Service Providers (ISPs).

ActiveX Microsoft concept that allows a program to run inside a Web page. Expected to become a standard.

ADSL Asynchronous Digital Subscriber Line. High-speed copper wire connections at up to 6 Mbps downstream and 640 Kbps up.

Anonymous FTP server A remote computer, with a publicly accessible file archive, that accepts "anonymous" as the log-in name and an email address as the password.

Altavista Web and Usenet search engine at: http://www.altavista.digital.com

AOL America Online. Presently, the world's most populous Online Service.

ASCII American Standard Code for Information Interchange. A text format readable by all computers. Also called "plain text".

Attachment File included with email.

B

Backbone Set of paths that carry longhaul Net traffic.

Bandwidth Size of the data pipeline. If you increase bandwidth, more data can flow at once.

Baud rate Number of times a modem's signal changes per second when transmitting data. Not to be confused with bps.

BBS Bulletin Board System. A computer system accessible by modem. Members can dial in and leave messages, send email, play games, and trade files with other users.

Binary file All non-plain text files are binaries, including programs, word-processor documents, images, sound clips, and compressed files.

Binary newsgroup Usenet group that's specifically meant for posting the above files.

Binhex Method of encoding, commonly used by Macs.

Bookmarks Netscape file used to store addresses.

Boot up To start a computer.

Bounced mail Email returned to sender.

Bps Bits per second. The rate that data is transferred between two modems. A bit is the basic unit of data.

Broadband High-speed Internet access.

Browser Program, such as Netscape or Internet Explorer, that allows you to download and display Web documents.

C

Cache Temporary storage space. Browsers can store copies of the most recently visited Web pages in cache.

Channel Stream of data that's "pushed" onto your computer desktop or browser window. Don't bother.

Client Program that accesses information across a network, such as a Web browser or newsreader.

Crack To break a program's security, integrity, or registration system, or fake a user ID.

Crash When a program or operating system fails to respond or causes other programs to malfunction.

Cyber In IRC, may be short for cybersex, that is the online equivalent of phone sex.

Cyberspace Term coined by science-fiction writer William Gibson, referring to the virtual world that exists within the marriage of computers, telecommunication networks, and digital media.

D

Digital signing Encrypted data appended to a message to identify the sender.

DNS Domain Name System. The system that locates the numerical IP address corresponding to a host name.

Domain Part of the DNS name that specifies details about the host, such as its location and whether it is part of a commercial (.com), government (.gov), or educational (.edu) entity.

Download Retrieve a file from a host computer. Upload means to send one the other way.

Driver Small program that acts like a translator between a device and programs that use that device.

DSL Digital Subscriber Line. Encompasses all forms including ADSL. Sometimes called xDSL.

E

Email Electronic mail carried on the Net.

Email address The unique private Internet address to which your email is sent. Takes the form user@host

Eudora Popular email program for Mac and PC.

F

FAQ Frequently Asked Questions. Document that answers the most commonly asked questions on a particular subject. Every newsgroup has at least one.

File Anything stored on a computer, such as a program, image, or document.

Finger A program that can return stored data on UNIX users or other information such as weather updates. Often disabled for security reasons.

Firewall Network security system used to restrict external and internal traffic.

Flame Abusive attack on someone posting in Usenet.

Frag Network gaming term meaning to destroy or fragment. Came from DOOM.

FTP File Transfer Protocol. Standard method of moving files across the Internet.

G

GIF Graphic Image File format. A compressed graphics format commonly used on the Net.

Gopher Defunct menu-based system for retrieving Internet archives, usually organized by subject.

GUI Graphic User Interface. Method of driving software through the use of windows, icons, menus, buttons, and other graphic devices.

H

Hacker Someone who gets off on breaking through computer security and limitations. A cracker is a criminal hacker.

Header Pre-data part of a packet, containing source and destination addresses, error checking, and other fields. Also the first part of an email or news posting which contains, among other things, the sender's details and time sent.

Home page Either the first page loaded by your browser at start-up, or the main Web document for a particular group, organization, or person.

Host Computer that offers some sort of services to networked users.

HotBot Web search engine at: http://www.hotbot.com

HTML HyperText Markup Language. The language used to create Web documents.

HyperText links The "clickable" links or "hot-spots" that connect pages on the Web to each other.

I

Image map A Web image that contains multiple links. Which link you take depends on where you click.

IMAP Internet Message Access Protocol. Standard email access protocol that's superior to POP3 in that you can selectively retrieve messages or parts thereof as well as manage folders on the server.

Infoseek Web and Usenet search service at: http://www.infoseek.com

Internet A co-operatively run global collection of computer networks with a common addressing scheme.

Internet Explorer Controversial Web browser produced by Microsoft.

Internet Favorites Internet Explorer directory that stores filed URLs.

Internet Shortcut Microsoft's terminology for a URL.

IP Internet Protocol. The most important protocol upon which the Internet is based. Defines how packets of data get from source to destination.

IP address Every computer connected to the Internet has an IP address (written in dotted numerical notation), which corresponds to its domain name. Domain Name Servers convert one to the other.

IRC Internet Relay Chat. Internet system where you can chat in text, or audio, to others in real time, like an online version of CB radio.

ISDN Integrated Services Digital Network. An international standard for digital communications over telephone lines, which allows for the transmission of data at 64 or 128 Kbps.

ISP Internet Service Provider. Company that sells access to the Internet.

J

Java Platform-independent programming language designed by Sun Microsystems. http://www.sun.com

JPG/JPEG Graphic file format preferred by Net users because its high compression reduces file size, and thus the time it takes to transfer.

K

Kill file Newsreader file into which you can enter keywords and email addresses to stop unwanted articles.

L

LAN Local Area Network. Computer network that spans a relatively small area such as an office.

Latency Length of time it takes data to reach its destination.

Leased line A dedicated telecommunications connection between two points.

Link In hypertext, as in a Web page, a link is a reference to another document. When you click on a link in a browser, that document will be retrieved and displayed, played or downloaded depending on its nature.

Linux A freely distributed implementation of the UNIX operating system.

Log on / Log in Connect to a computer network.

Lycos Web search service at: http://www.lycos.com

M

MIDI Musical Instrument Digital Interface. Standard adopted by the electronic music industry for controlling devices such as soundcards and synthesizers. MIDI files contain synthesizer instructions rather than recorded music.

MIME Multipurpose Internet Mail Extensions. Standard for the transfer of binary email attachments.

Mirror Replica FTP or Web site set up to share traffic.

Modem MOdulator/DEModulator. Device that allows a computer to communicate with another over a standard telephone line, by converting the digital data into analog signals and vice versa.

MP3 A compressed music format.

MPEG/MPG A compressed video file format.

Multithreaded Able to process multiple requests at once.

N

Name server Host that translates domain names into IP addresses.

The Net The Internet.

Netscape Popular and influential Web browser – and the company that produces it.

Newbie Newcomer to the Net, discussion, or area.

Newsgroups Usenet message areas, or discussion groups, organized by subject hierarchies.

NNTP Network News Transfer Protocol. Standard for the exchange of Usenet articles across the Internet.

Node Any device connected to a network.

P

Packet A unit of data. In data transfer, information is broken into packets, which then travel independently through the Net. An Internet packet contains the source and destination addresses, an identifier, and the data segment.

Packet loss Failure to transfer units of data between network nodes. A high percentage makes transfer slow or impossible.

Patch Temporary or interim add-on to fix or upgrade software.

Phreaker Person who hacks telephone systems.

Ping A program that sends an echo-like trace to test if a host is available.

Platform Computer operating system, such as Mac OS, Windows, or Linux.

Plug-in Program that fits into another.

POP3 Post Office Protocol. An email protocol that allows you to pick up your mail from anywhere on the Net, even if you're connected through someone else's account.

POPs Points of Presence. An Access Provider's range of local dial-in points.

Portal Web site that specializes in leading you to others.

Post To send a public message to a Usenet newsgroup.

PPP Point to Point Protocol. This allows your computer to join the Internet via a modem. Each time you log in, you're allocated either a temporary or static IP address.

Protocol An agreed way for two network devices to talk to each other.

Proxy server Sits between a client, such as a Web browser, and a real server. They're most often used to improve performance by delivering stored pages like browser cache and to filter out undesirable material.

Push Technique where data appears to be sent by the host rather than requested by the client. Email is a type of push.

R

RealAudio Standard for streaming compressed audio over the Internet. See: http://www.real.com

Robot Program that automates Net tasks such as collating search engine databases or automatically responding in IRC. Also called a Bot.

S

Search engine Database of Web page extracts that can be queried to find reference to something on the Net.

Server Computer that makes services available on a network.

Signature file Personal footer that can be attached automatically to email and Usenet postings.

SLIP Serial Line Internet Protocol. Protocol that allows a computer to join the Internet via a modem and requires that you have a pre-allocated fixed IP address configured in your TCP/IP setup. Has almost completely been replaced by PPP.

SMTP Simple Mail Transfer Protocol. Internet protocol for transporting mail.

Spam Post the same message inappropriately to multiple newsgroups or email addresses.

Streaming Delivered in real time instead of waiting for the whole file to arrive, eg RealAudio.

Stuffit A common Macintosh file compression format and program.

Surf To skip from page to page around the Web by following links.

T

TCP/IP Transmission Control Protocol/Internet Protocol. The protocols that drive the Internet.

Telco Telephone company.

Telnet Internet protocol that allows you to log on to a remote computer and act as a dumb terminal.

Temporary Internet Files Internet Explorer's cache.

Troll Prank newsgroup posting intended to invoke an irate response.

U

UNIX Operating system used by most service providers and universities. So long as you stick to graphic programs, you'll never notice it.

URL Uniform Resource Locator. The addressing system for the World Wide Web.

Usenet User's Network. A collection of networks and computer systems that exchange messages, organized by subject into newsgroups.

UUencode Method of encoding binary files into text so that they can be attached to mail or posted to Usenet. They must be UUdecoded to convert them back. Better mail and news programs do this automatically.

V

Vaporware Rumored or announced, but non-existent, software or hardware. Often used as a competitive marketing ploy.

W

Warez Software, usually pirated.

The Web The World Wide Web or WWW. Graphic and text documents published on the Internet that are interconnected through clickable "hypertext" links. A Web page is a single document. A Web site is a collection of related documents.

Web authoring Designing and publishing Web pages using HTML.

World Wide Web See Web, above.

WYSIWYG What You See Is What You Get. What you type is the way it comes out.

Y

Yahoo The Web's most popular directory at:
http://www.yahoo.com

Z

Zip PC file compression format that creates files with the extension .zip using PKZip or WinZip software. Commonly used to reduce file size for transfer or storage on floppy disks.

Zmodem A file transfer protocol that, among other things, offers the advantage of being able to pick up where you left off after transmission failure.

Still confused . . .

Then try the PC Webopedia (http://www.webopedia.com)
  What is? (http://www.whatis.com)
  and Netlingo (http://www.netlingo.com)

PART FOUR

ISP Directory

Internet Service Providers

The following directory lists some major Internet Service Providers (ISPs) in Britain, North America, Australia, New Zealand, Asia, and beyond. It's by no means complete and inclusion shouldn't be taken as an endorsement. We've selected the larger, established providers with multiple dial-in access points, as these are what most users require. Still, if you access only from home, it's possible you might get a better deal from a smaller, local operator.

Your first priority is to find a provider with **local call access**, preferably without paying a higher tariff for the convenience. If our list doesn't help, ask around locally, or sign up temporarily, get online, and consult one of these **Net directories**:

  http://www.thelist.com (global)
  http://www.netalert.com (global)
  http://www.cynosure.com.au/isp/ (Australia)
  http://www.internet-magazine.com/isp/ (UK)
  http://www.isps.com (USA)

Unfortunately, these lists aren't so comprehensive either. Nor do they offer advice. For something more subjective, read your local **computer/Internet publications**; in the UK, for example, *Internet* magazine (http://www.internet-magazine.com) runs monthly performance charts. If you're still having problems, once online, try posting to the newsgroup: alt.internet.services

What to ask your provider

Choosing an Access Provider is an important decision. You want a reliable, fast connection; good customer support; and a company who'll stay in the game, so you won't need to change account or (worse) email address. The best approach is to **ask around, read magazine reviews, and see what others recommend**. If someone swears by a provider, and they seem to know what they're talking about, give it a go. That's about the best research you can do.

So if you know someone who's hooked up, ask them: Is it fast and reliable? Does it ever get so slow you feel like giving up? Is it ever difficult collecting or sending mail? Do you often strike a busy tone when dialing in? Are the support staff helpful? Have you ever been overcharged?

If you're not in that boat, and have to do your own research, look for answers to the following questions – maybe by calling a few of the Freecall numbers listed in the sections following and asking for their information packs and access software. It might seem laborious but it's not as painful as being stuck with poor access. First up, find out how much it's going to sting your pocket:

Do you offer a free trial period?

If so, give them a go. The only thing you have to lose is your email address if you decide not to proceed.

If not, what is your start-up cost?

Avoid paying a start-up fee if possible.

What will it cost me?

Most providers offer a choice of billing plans based upon your usage requirements. This normally takes the form of a monthly fee, and then an hourly rate once you've exceeded a certain number of free hours. That's unless you sign up for unlimited access, in which case you'll simply pay a set monthly fee. You'll have to do your sums to work out what's best for you.

Free providers

Internet access provision is a costly business to run so it might surprise you that some firms can give it away. The only way they can afford to do this is by earning the revenue from someone else. In the UK, where free Internet access is almost becoming the norm, it's quite simple - they strike up a deal with your telco and take a cut of your phone bill. This situation can exist only because the UK has metered local calls, so the longer you stay online, the more you pay. They might also charge you a premium to call their support lines. Where local phone calls are untimed or free such as in the US, the only way to turn a profit is to charge, or take commissions from, advertisers.

Expect to see more permutations of free access offers over time, especially in Britain. For instance, electrical retailer Tempo (http://www.tempo.co.uk) offers completely free access (including telephone calls) if you switch to Localtel's telephone service. You'll find these sorts of deals generate wads of publicity so keep an eye on your local paper for details. Remember, if you're paying to be online it's not entirely free so don't put up with bad service.

Can I access for the price of a local call?

If you have to pay long-distance rates, it will cost you more. Many providers maintain a toll-free national number; however, it might incur a surcharge. Get a local number if possible and ask if it has multiple points of presence (POPs). Don't forget: phone charges aren't included in your Internet bill!

Are there any premium charges?

Premium charges are one of the main drawbacks with the Online Service giants such as CompuServe, which provide quality commercial databases as well as Internet access. But having to pay extra to use certain services is not necessarily a bad thing, as you don't want to have to subsidize something you don't use.

Will I be charged extra if I go over a download limit?

This mainly applies to cable and satellite operators who charge a base rate per month, up to a limited number of megabytes. Once you go over the limit, you're billed extra per megabyte. Avoid this kind of plan if possible.

Is it cheaper to access at certain times?

In an effort to restrict traffic during peak times, providers may offer periods with reduced or no online charges. Think about when you're most likely to use your connection. Try during the cheap period. If you can't connect, it's slow, or you'd rarely use it at that hour, then it's no bargain.

How long have you been in business, who owns the company, and how many subscribers do you have?

First up, you need to know with whom you're dealing. Big operators may offer certain advantages such as national and even global dial-up points, security, guaranteed access, stability, and close proximity to the high-speed backbone. However, they can be slow to upgrade because of high overheads and may have dim support staff. Small, younger providers can be more flexible, have newer equipment, more in-tune staff, cheaper rates, and faster access, but conversely may lack the capital to make future critical upgrades. There aren't any rules; it's a new industry and all a bit of a long-term gamble.

What is your maximum user to modem ratio?

The lower this ratio, the less chance you'll strike a busy tone when you call. As a yardstick, anything over 10:1 should start sounding warning bells that they're under-equipped.

Which backbones do you connect to, and at what speed?

Backbones are the high-speed longhaul connections that carry Internet traffic between ISPs and around the globe. A good ISP should tell you which backbone it uses and how big its connections are – or even provide a map of its backbone links around the world. Be suspicious of any ISP that can't answer this question. Better ISPs connect to more than one ISP – a practice called multi-homing. This means they're not bound to one route and can thus choose the fastest connection per request.

For more about backbones including the current state of traffic, see: http://www.cybergeography.org and http://www.mids.org/weather/

What are your support hours?

It's not essential to have 24-hour support, but it's a bonus to know someone will be there when you can't get a line on the weekend or at 11pm.

Do you supply a start-up disk and if so, what's on it?

If you have Windows 98, an iMac, or a Mac running OS 8.5 or later, you already have all the Internet software you need to get started. If not, most providers can supply you with a free, or cheap, installation disk. Bear in mind there's nothing they'll give you that you won't be able to get for free off the Net once you're online, so don't value it too highly.

Can you supply me with a sheet of clear setup instructions for my system?

If you're running one of the above systems you already have the software, you need only the configuration settings and a little guidance filling them out. Unless you're running an older system, avoid any provider that insists you have to install their special connection software. Assure them that as soon as you get online you intend to download the latest version of either Internet Explorer or Netscape Communicator. If they have a problem with that, take a hike.

Can you support my modem type and speed?

Modems like talking to their own kind. When modems aren't happy with each other, they connect at a slower rate. It's not much use if your 56K X2 modem can only connect at 33.6 Kbps. Ask what connection speeds they support. If it's incompatible, or lower than your modem's top speed, look elsewhere.

Do you, or will you soon, offer high-speed access such as ISDN, DSL, multilink modem, or cable?

If the answer's yes, find out the cost all up, including the hardware, wiring, rental, and call charges. If it's affordable, ask for installation contacts. In some parts of the US, for example, ISDN installation is only about $20.00, and thereafter costs the same as a telephone.

Do you carry the newsgroups in Usenet? If not, how many do you carry and which ones do you cut?

Usenet has more than 60,000 groups and it's still growing. That's 95 percent more than you'll ever want to look at in your lifetime. Most providers carry only a portion, but it's still usually over 15,000. The first ones to be axed are often foreign language, country specific, provider specific, and the adult (**alt.sex** and **alt.binaries**) series. If you particularly want certain groups, your provider can usually add them, but it may have a policy against certain material.

How many email addresses will I get, and what will they end in?

Prefer a provider that throws in more than one address as part of the deal. Then you can keep separate addresses for different types of mail, and dish out an address or two to family and friends. You always have the option to choose the first part of your email address. You might like to use your first name or nickname. This will then be attached to the provider's host name. Check if your name's available and what the host name would be. You don't want a name that could reflect badly on your business plans. For instance, if you register with the UK Service Provider Demon, your email address will end with demon.co.uk – perhaps not the ideal choice for a priest (though one vicar who used the first edition of this book reckons it's a conversation point).

If you want your own domain name, a provider should be able to register your choice for you. For instance, if John Hooper trains ducks to use computers, he could register "duckschool.com" and give himself the email address **john@duckschool.com**. Then it would be easy to remember his address, just by thinking about who he is and what he does.

How much does it cost for personal Web page storage?

Most Access Providers include a few megabytes of storage free so you can publish your own Web page. In general, if you go over that megabyte limit there'll be an excess charge.

Do you have or offer national or global roaming and how is it charged?

If you travel a lot it's handy to know you can still get connected, though if it comes at a high price it may not be worth it. See "On the Road" (p.237) for more details.

Apart from Internet access, what else do you offer?

While your first priority should be to get fast reliable Internet access, see what else you can get with the deal, either as part of the bundle or as an added extra.

INTERNATIONAL ISPs

Most Access Providers operate in only one country (or the US and Canada). For truly international access, if you plan to use the Net on your travels (see "On The Road" – p.227), consider one of the following. Most charge extra outside your local area.

Provider	Web address	Points of Presence
AOL	http://www.aol.com	Worldwide
CompuServe	http://www.compuserve.com	Worldwide

EUNet Traveller	http://traveller.eu.net	Worldwide
IBM Global Net	http://www.ibm.net	Worldwide
Microsoft Network	http://www.msn.com	UK, US, Japan
Netcom	http://www.netcom.com	North America, UK

BRITAIN

Provider	Telephone number	Web Address
BT Internet	0800 800 001	http://www.btinternet.com
BT ClickFree*	0800 731 7887	http://www.btclickfree.com
Cable & Wireless	0500 200 980	http://www.cwcom.co.uk
Cable Internet	0500 541 542	http://www.cableinet.co.uk
CIX	0845 355 5050	http://www.cix.net.uk
Demon Internet	0181 371 1234	http://www.demon.net
Direct Connection	0800 072 0000	http://www.dircon.net
Easynet	0541 594 321	http://www.easynet.co.uk
Freeserve*	0990 500049	http://www.freeserve.com
Free-Online*	0870 7060504	http://www.free-online.net
Netcom	01344 395 600	http://www.netcomuk.net.uk
Netkonect	0171 345 7777	http://www.netkonect.net
NTL Internet	0800 607 608	http://www.ntli.com
TescoNet*	0845 605 0200	http://www.tesco.net
UUNet (Pipex Dial)	0500 474 739	http://www.uk.uu.net
Virgin Net*	0500 558 844	http://www.virgin.net

* Free ISP – you pay only for telephone charges and support.

EUROPE

Provider Web address	Telephone number Points of Presence
TeleNordia http://www.algo.net	08 587 587 00 Sweden
Madrid Online http://www.mol.es	918 518 275 Spain
Centrum http://www.centrum.is	575 1000 Iceland
Deutsches Provider Network http://www.dpn.de	0203 309 3101 Germany
Easynet http://www.easynet.fr	01 44 54 53 30 France, UK
Eunet Traveller http://traveller.eu.net	+32 16 39 80 80 (Belgium) Europe and beyond
Wanadoo http://www.wanadoo.fr	0 801 105 105 France
GlasNet http://www.glasnet.ru	095 785 1100 Russia
Hellas Online http://www.hol.gr	0965 37777 Greece
Internet Finland http://www.icon.fi	09 4780 8470 Finland
Ireland Online http://www.iol.ie	01 604 6800 Ireland
Itnet http://www.it.net	010 650 3781 Italy

| LvNet | 777 7777 |
| http://www.lvnet.lv | Latvia |

| NetMedia | 1800 300 301 |
| http://www.netmedia.co.il | Israel |

| Pingnet | 01 439 1313 |
| http://www.pingnet.ch | Switzerland, Liechtenstein |

| Scandinavia Online | 22 58 38 00 |
| http://www.sol.no | Norway |

| T Online | 0800 330 1000 |
| http://www.t-online.de | Germany |

| Telepac | 1 800 200 079 |
| http://www.telepac.pt | Portugal |

| XS4all | 020 3987654 |
| http://www.xs4all.nl | Netherlands |

NORTH AMERICA

Provider Web address	Telephone number Points of Presence
@Home (cable access) http://www.home.com	See Web page USA, Canada, Netherlands, Australia
AT&T WorldNet http://www.att.net	1 800 967 5363 USA
Bell Atlantic http://www.bellatlantic.net	1 800 422 3555 USA
Concentric Networks http://www.concentric.net	1 800 939 4262 USA, Canada
EarthLink Network http://www.earthlink.com	1 800 395 8425 USA, Canada

Flashcom (DSL specialists)	1 877 FLASHCOM	
http://www.flashcom.com	USA	
GTE Internet	1 800 927 3000	
http://www.gte.net	USA	
IBM Internet Connection	1 800 722 1425	
http://www.ibm.net	USA, Canada	
iStar	1 888 GO ISTAR	
http://www.istar.ca	Canada	
MCI Internet	1 800 444 3333	
http://www.mci.com	USA	
MindSpring (Netcom & Sprynet)	1 888 MSPRING	
http://www.mindspring.com	USA	
Netcom Canada	1 888 655 7671	
http://www.netcom.ca	Canada	
NetZero (free provider)	1 818 879 7250	
http://www.netzero.com	USA	
PSINet	1 800 395 1056	
http://www.psi.com	USA, Canada	
Prodigy	1 800 213 0992	
http://www.prodigy.com	USA	
Sympatico	800 773 2121	
http://www.sympatico.ca	Canada	

AUSTRALIA

Provider	Telephone number	Web address
AAPT	1300 651 414	http://www.smartchat.net.au
Connect	1800 818 262	http://www.connect.com.au

EISA	1300 300 928	http://www.eisa.net.au
IBM Global Network	1300 307 005	http://www.ibm.net
Internet Primus	1300 303 081	http://www.primus.com.au
Mira Networking	1300 360 080	http://www.mira.net
One.Net	1300 303 312	http://www.one.net.au
Optus Internet	1300 301 325	http://www.optusnet.com.au
Ozemail	132 884	http://www.ozemail.com.au
SatNet (satellite access)	136 292	http://www.satnet.com.au
Telstra Big Pond	1800 804 282	http://www.bigpond.com.au

NEW ZEALAND

Provider	Telephone number	Web address
Clear Net	0508 888 800	http://www.clear.net.nz
Telecom XTRA	0800 22 55 98	http://www.xtra.co.nz
Voyager	0800 869 243	http://www.voyager.co.nz

ASIA

Provider Web address	Telephone number Points of Presence
Brain Net http://www.brain.net.pk	111 222 777 Pakistan
Global Online http://home.gol.com	03 5334 1720 Japan, USA, Canada
Internet Thailand http://www.inet.co.th	642 7065 6 Thailand

| Jaring | 03 966 5000 |
| http://www.jaring.my | Malaysia |

| Mackay | 02 2696 3999 |
| http://www.mky.com | Taiwan |

| MagicNet | 1 312 063 |
| http://www.magaicnet.mn | Mongolia |

| Pacific Surf | 1 800 872 1455 |
| http://www.pacific.net.sg | Singapore |

| Pinter | 3190 0162 |
| http://www.pacific.net.id | Indonesia |

| VSNL | 22 432 0220 |
| http://www.vsnl.net.in | India |

REST OF THE WORLD

Provider Web address	Telephone number Points of Presence
Africa Online (Prodigy)	781 395 5500 (US)
http://www.africaonline.com	(233 21) 226802 (Ghana)
	(254 2) 243775 (Kenya)
	(255 51) 116088 (Tanzania)
	(263 4) 702 202 (Zimbabwe)
	(225) 21 90 00 (Ivory Coast)
Impsat	01 318 8333
http://www.impsat.com.ar	Argentina, Latin America
Cybernet	21 553 5577
http://www.cybernet.com.br	Brazil
DataNet	5 118 4673
http://www.data.net.mx	Mexico

Egypt Online 202 395 4111
http://www.egyptonline.com .... Egypt

Global Internet Access 0860 11 39 38
http://www.global.co.za .... South Africa

Itinet .... 305 577 9750 (Miami FL)
http://www.itinet.net .... Argentina, Chile, El Salvador,
Guatemala, Honduras, Nicaragua, Panama, Puerto Rico,
Dominican Republic, Venezuela, Paraguay, Spain and Florida

INDEX

51 things to do with this book

You're on the Net, so where now? Has it all been worth the effort? Here, in no particular order, are 51 ways to idle away your online time. Just key in the Web address or go to the page in this book for instructions.

1. Look yourself up on the Web
http://www.hotbot.com

2. Re-ignite an old flame
See p.176

3. Deactivate an alien implant
See p.342

4. Get fresh with the US President
http://www.whitehouse.gov

5. Go undercover
See p.117 & p.188

6. Dig up dirt on a movie star
http://www.imdb.com

7. Flirt with a stranger
See p.186

8. Land a cushy job
See p.284

9. Cast a voodoo spell
http://www.vudutuu.com

10. Join a kooky cult
See p.359 and p.391

11. Kick butt
See p.200

12. Tune in to foreign radio
See p.352

13. Work from the Bahamas
See p.227

14. Rekindle your childhood interests
See p.127 and p.160

15. Make your first billion
See p.320

16. Get fanatical about football
See p.372

17. Move to Mars
http://www.marsshop.com

18. Confirm you're mad
http://www.mentalhealth.com

19. Plot an exotic adventure
See p.382

20. Cast no doubt on your ancestry
See p.342

21. Become a whiz with nuclear arms
See p.362

22. Cheat your way through college
See p.354

23. Stock up on frilly bras
See p.294

39. Show off your baby snaps
See p.110 and 208

40. Consult a mad scientist
http://www.madsci.org

41. Become a minister of the Universal Life Church
See p.361

42. Indulge in hypochondria
http://www.diagnosticdoc.com

43. Learn how to be cool
http://www.geocities.com/SunsetStrip/4160/big.html

44. Torment a teen idol
http://www.sonicnet.com

45. Start an argument
See p.122 and 127

46. Attend a live gig
http://www.liveconcerts.com

47. Master your own music compilation CD
See p.325

48. Disappear with the Foreign Legion
http://www.specialoperations.com

49. Surround yourself in bargains
See p.367

50. Email a smoochy tune
See p.111

51. Admit you now have a problem
http://www.internetaddiction.com

Got a favorite site or activity on the Net?
Then let us know by email at: angus@easynet.co.uk

Acknowledgements

Writing any book takes a fair amount of patience, not just from the writer but also from those whose lives become involuntarily entwined in it. This book has been no exception. I'd like to thank my friends and family who've understood this and stuck by me through the madness that has coincided with researching and writing each edition.

I am especially indebted to those who contributed text: Michael Shapiro, author of "Internet Travel 101: How to Plan Trips and Save Money Online", put in the hard yards against the online ticket touts; David Pitchford stamped his authority in HTML; Gerry Browne marked his scent in Online Gaming; Richard Baguley, of Internet Magazine, joined in the missing dots in ISPs; and Paul Bennett helped me round down a gazillion Web sites to the nearest couple of thousand. I would also like to thank the hundreds of you who sent me URLs, news clippings, and feedback on the fourth edition.

Finally, I'd like to praise my editor Mark Ellingham and all at the Rough Guides and Penguin, particularly Liz Statham, Shaun Snow, Andy Hilliard, Henry Iles, Vanessa Dowell, Kate Hands, Geronimo Madrid, Susanne Hillen, Julia Bovis, Katie Pringle, Richard Trillo, Simon Carloss, Niki Smith, Jean Marie Kelly, and Johanna de Wever-Grant, for doing such a remarkable job of polishing up this book and putting it in more hands than I'd ever imagined.

Angus Kennedy
angus@easynet.co.uk